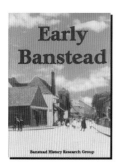

EARLY BANSTEAD
An introduction to the s
historic times to the 192

CU00704439

(1998) Quarto 27pp. Illustrated.
Price: £4.00   ISBN: 0-9512741-5-5

MEMORIES OF BANSTEAD
WARTIME DISTRICT
A compilation of individual recollections of life in
the Banstead district under attack from the air in
World War II.

(2002) A4 88 pp. Illustrated.
Price: £7.50   ISBN: 0-9512741-6-3

A HISTORY OF POOR LAW AND CHARITY
RELIEF IN BANSTEAD
How from the 17th to the 20th centuries the poor
and sick in Banstead received a measure of help
from charitable gifts and Poor Law provision.

(2004) A4 36pp. Illustrated.
Price: £5.00   ISBN: 0-9512741-8-X

Banstead History Research Group (BHRG)
The Banstead History Research Group is a non-profit organisation whose
objects are to research the history of the district and to make known the
results of that research by means of exhibitions, talks and publications.

The group welcomes information from any source. New members are
always welcome. For enquriries on membership of the Group please contact
the Secretary whose address is on the Group's website:
www.bansteadhistory.com.

Frontispiece: *Looking west down Banstead High
Street with the Woolpack on the left. c.1920s.*   April 2005

Banstead History Research Group

Publications

www.bansteadhistory.com

The History of

BANSTEAD Volume II

How a Village
Grew and Changed

BANSTEAD HISTORY RESEARCH GROUP

2005

Banstead is a village not far from Epsom on the North Downs in the County of Surrey. It is an old village which has a history going back to Anglo-Saxon days.

Volume I of the History of Banstead starts with what is known about the occupation of the Romans and Anglo Saxons in the district. It then proceeds to describe century by century the major events, people and conditions in Banstead up till 1840 set against the general historical background of the times.

Volume II of the History of Banstead is a revised and updated version of "Banstead - A History" published by the BHRG in 1993. After a brief summary of the village's earlier history it deals in detail with the story of Banstead from 1841 to the present day.

Both Volume I and Volume II are self contained, illustrated and indexed. Together they tell the fscinating story of the village throughout the period of its known existence.

Second Edition, completely revised, April 2005
First Edition November 1993

Copyright © 2005 Banstead History Research Group.
All Rights Reserved.

No reproduction permitted by any means without the express permission in writing of the Publishers:
Banstead History Research Group

ISBN 0-9512741-9-8

Front Cover: The High Street Banstead looking east. The Woolpack Inn is on the right with the Smithy further down on the left. (1900).

Published by the Banstead History Research Group
For details of other publications published by the group visit
www.bansteadhistory.com

Printed by the Print Solutions Partnership
55, Sandy Lane South, Wallington, Surrey SM6 9RQ UK

Preface

This is a revised and updated version of the book "Banstead - A History" first published in 1993. By way of a tribute to people who took part in preparing that book but are no longer with us, the original preface is here repeated.

A hundred and fifty years ago, Banstead was still a small village centred round the Village well and stretching from that end of the High Street only as far as All Saints Church. Apart from that, the neighbourhood consisted mostly of open fields, downland and woods, with a few large residences with their grounds and parkland - notably Nork House -and scattered farmhouses and cottages.

The village grew slowly until the Inter-War period of the 1920s and 1930s, when it expanded rapidly. The old Nork Estate came to house a large new community, and housing also spread in other directions. The process of growth continued after the Second World War.

The only substantial history of Banstead in book form remains "The History of Banstead in Surrey" by H.C.M. Lambert, (later Sir Henry Lambert), published in 1912, with a supplementary volume in 1931. In his first volume Henry Lambert included descriptions of the village as it was in the early 19th century; but he did not deal in any detail with its later growth, and even in 1931 modern Banstead had only begun to emerge.

This book is intended to show how the village and community of Banstead, including Nork and the areas from Tattenham Corner to Preston Lane, have grown into their modern form. Part I is in chronological order, starting with a brief account of the early history of the area. It goes on to describe the village and community in the 1840s, and then, step by step, their change and growth over the years up till recent times. Part II deals with a selection of subjects without limitations of time. So accounts of prominent families in the district, such as the Buckles and Lamberts, stretch from the 16th to the 20th centuries, and notable individuals recorded include Hubert de Burgh, a powerful figure in the 13th century, and Lord Tedder, Deputy Supreme Commander of the Allied Forces in Europe in the Second World War.

The book is the product of the Banstead History Research Group. In 1987 the Group published "Banstead, Then and Now", which contained pictures of parts of Banstead as they were in the past and corresponding views in modern times, with information in the form of captions.

Illustrations in the present book are all different from those in the earlier book, and the two books should be regarded as complementary.

Many members of the Group have assisted in creating this book. The Committee which had special responsibility for it consisted of John Sweetman, who contributed the major part of the text, ably assisted by Ted Purver and Mark Cory; Doreen Johnson, who was concerned particularly with the illustrations; and John Hind with the maps and with the financial and business aspects. Two people outside the Group contributed parts of the text: the chapter on buses was extracted from a note by John Clifford, and much of the chapter on the postal services was provided by Leslie Bond.

The Group wishes to thank all those - whether official bodies, companies, firms, societies or individuals - who have so willingly and helpfully provided the Group with information or with access to information in their possession. Without their co-operation the project could not have succeeded.

Special thanks are due to Cathy Aubin, who deciphered all the written first draft of the book and converted it into typed form.

Finally, it is almost inevitable that in a book such as this mistakes will be found to have been made. For any such the Group apologises, and will welcome comments from readers, together with any additional information which they can contribute.

It has to be added that the present edition owes much to the efforts of a number of people, to Geoffrey Robinson, Mark Cory and Lewis Wood for their contributions and amendments, to Ralph Maciejewski for his technical wizardry and my daughter Cathy Aubin for her endless patience in deciphering and typing my scribbles deserve special mention.

John Sweetman
Banstead,
April 2005

Contents

Chapter 6

Chapter 7

Chapter 8

Chapter 9

Chapter 10

Chapter 11

Chapter 12

Chapter 13

Chapter 14

Chapter 15

Illustrations

Acknowledgements

We wish to acknowledge the following individuals and institutions who have kindly given us permission to reproduce material in their possession.

Surrey History Service.
For permission to reproduce the drawing of All Saints church which appears in the Views of all the Churches and Chapels of Ease in the County of Surrey by Charles Thomas Craklow.

London Borough of Lambeth, Archives Department
The illustration of Burgh House from their copy of the History of Surrey by Manning and Bray.

Chapter 1

The Village and Manor of Banstead prior to 1841

Nobody knows when community life started in what is now the district of Banstead. There is some evidence of people living there in the period of the Roman occupation of England - from the first century B.C. to about 400 A.D. Stane Street, one of the great military roads constructed by the Romans, from Londinium (London) to Noviomagnus (Chichester), passed through Ewell, within a mile or two of the downland hills of the district. The diarist, John Evelyn, recorded on the 27th of September 1658 that he had heard of medals, apparently Roman, dug up near what was then known as Great Burgh.[1] From this he assumed that there had been "a Roman city" there. This assumption seems to have nothing to support it; but there have been other reports of findings of Roman coins in the Banstead area, and there was a Roman villa at Walton-on-the-Hill. It is possible that some prosperous Roman may have fancied a residence on the Banstead Downs; but we may never know.

Henry Lambert,[2] who had made a detailed study of mediaeval documents, could find no conclusive evidence of the existence of a village or community in Banstead before late Anglo-Saxon times. One can say, from the discoveries of antiquarians in recent years, that such a community did exist in the seventh or eighth centuries A.D.[3] There is also the documentary evidence

---

1 The entry read: "Riding over these Downes, and discoursing with the shepherds, I found that on digging about the bottom neere Sir Christopher Buckle's, neere Banstead, divers medalls have been found, both copper and silver, with foundations of houses, urns etc... Here, indeede, anciently stood a City of the Romans: see Antonine's Itinerary." The house would have been Burgh House, later renamed Great Burgh, near what is now the junction of Reigate Road and Great Tattenhams.

2 A History of Banstead, Vol. 1, p.9.

3 Excavation, Fir Tree Road. Surrey Antiquarian Collection, Vol. 76, p.l0l, (1985). Another excavation has revealed a burial ground, thought to be of the 7th Century, in the Headley Drive area.

Figure 1. The Old Forge Banstead c.1938

of a charter from King Edgar in A.D. 967, which makes it clear that by that date the monastery of Chertsey held lands in "Benstede". The name is now commonly believed to derive from a combination of the Anglo-Saxon 'bean' (a bean) and 'stede' (a place).

The Domesday survey of 'Benestede' in 1086 is the first positive record of a community at Banstead. There was by that time a well-established community which had been under the proprietorship of a man called Alnod (or Aethelnoth) of Canterbury, who, during the reign of Edward the Confessor, had been an important Kentish theign.

In 1086 'Benestede' was a Manor held under the feudal system by Richard of Tonbridge as sub-tenant of Odo, who was Bishop of Bayeux and half-brother of William the Conqueror.

The population included twenty-eight 'villeins', fifteen 'cottars' and seven 'slaves'. There was a church, farming land, woodland and a mill (probably a watermill some distance away at Beddington). Other property belonging to the Manor included a house in London for the Lord of the

Manor, and another house in Southwark. The value of the Manor as a whole was assessed at eight pounds. Unfortunately it was enough for the taxation purposes of the Domesday survey to record no more than this somewhat scant information.[4]

It would be outside the scope of this volume to trace the history of Banstead from the time of the Domesday survey to the nineteenth century in anything beyond a brief outline. (Volume I deals with the early history in detail).

In general terms, the Manor of Banstead, which included sub-manors known as Great Burgh, Little Burgh, South Tadworth, North Tadworth, Perrotts and Preston, comprised much the same area as the ecclesiastical parish of Banstead, as it then was and as it remained until comparatively recent times.[5] At that time, the Parish was important not only for church purposes, but also for local administration generally. The present boundaries of the Borough of Reigate and Banstead in this district still largely reflect these old manorial and parish boundaries, in spite of many modern exclusions and alterations.

Ownership of land was the basis of the feudal manor. The ultimate ownership of land lay with the king, from whom estates, which often included a large number of manors, were held directly by powerful men as 'tenants-in-chief.' In 1086 Odo was tenant-in-chief of estates that included the Manor of Banstead, and Richard of Tonbridge was Lord of the Manor as Odo's sub-tenant. Richard in turn had 'tenants' who held land within the Manor under a wide variety of conditions.

The most fortunate of these tenants held land 'in free socage'. They owed only very limited services to the Lord, sometimes only a duty of military service, if so required. (This was later to develop into 'freehold'). Other tenants were under obligation to work and provide services for the Lord in return for their occupation of land on which to live, to grow crops and to keep animals. Their obligations were specified in the records of the manorial court. On the lowest rung of the social ladder were the serfs, originally known as 'slaves', with little or no land or freedom.

4   In translation, the entry reads:Richard holds Banstead from the Bishop. Alnoth held it from King Edward. Then it answered for 29 hides, now 9.5 hides. Land for 16 ploughs. In lordship 2 ploughs: 28 villagers and 15 cottagers with 15 ploughs. A church: 7 slaves. A mill at 20 shillings, woodland at 20 pigs. In Southwark one house at 40 pence belongs to this manor. In London one Lord's dwelling, which was Alnoth's belongs to this manor. Now Adam son of Hubert holds it from the Bishop. Value of the whole manor before 1066, 10 pounds, later 100 shillings, now £8. Geoffrey holds 5 hides of the land of this manor from Richard; Ralph 2 hides, Ulsi 2 hides, total value 6 pounds and 10 shillings. (References to pounds, shillings and pence are to a pre-decimal currency. Their real value in modern terms would be much greater).

5   The Manor later included property in the Weald, e.g. at Leigh and Horley.

Figure 2. All Saints Church 1823 *(Views of Surrey Churches - C.T.Cracklow)*
Copyright of Surrey History Service

In Banstead, the Lord held as 'demesne lands' most of the land south of the High Street as far as Park Downs, some fields west of Holly Lane, and the 'Freedown' or 'Hundred Acres' (on part of which the Downview and Highdown Prisons now stand). The demesne lands were farmed for the Lord, usually through a steward or bailiff, with labour provided compulsorily by the tenants and by the serfs.

The Lord also held as his own particular property the Banstead Woods, a large part of which was enclosed as a Royal Deer Park until late in the fifteenth century.

From the tenants' point of view, an essential part of the Manor in the Middle Ages was 'the Commonfield'. This was an open area of cultivable land, over which the tenants shared rights. In Banstead it included the area between the High Street and the Banstead Downs, as well as adjoining land to the west as far as what was then Potters Lane (just short of what is now Green Curve) and some adjoining land to the east of Sutton Lane. The Commonfield seems to have been divided into an East Field and a West Field. Within these fields tenants were allotted 'shots'. These were plots of an acre or more which they could cultivate according to rules laid down by the custom of the Manor. After the harvest, the whole area was open for the grazing of hogs or sheep.

Finally, there were in the Manor untenanted 'wastelands', rough heath or downland over which the tenants had certain rights, including most importantly the right to graze a number of sheep. The Lord owned these areas, which became known as 'Commons', but he was restricted from doing anything which would effectively deprive the tenants of their rights. The Commons of Banstead included Banstead Downs, Park Downs, Burgh Heath and Banstead Heath.

The Manor was far from being simply a matter of ownership and management of land. The Lord of the Manor was responsible for administration of most of the affairs of the area within the limits of the Manor. As well as practical matters connected with land and property, these included legal disputes and minor offences against the law. A steward or bailiff would usually deal with practical matters on his behalf, and would also act as chairman of the Manor court. The court dealt with land and property disputes as well as with the punishment of offences against the established customs of the Manor.

There was a Manor House in Banstead. It seems clear that this stood east of the older part of the churchyard, in modern terms within the angle of Avenue Road and Court Road. Henry Lambert was able to work out some idea of the building from items in the manorial records. In brief, it would have been a rambling timber building with tiled roofs, and with a great barn and stables nearby.[6] In its time, it would have been the centre of administration of the Manor; but at some time before 1680 it was demolished, and the centre shifted to Court Farm (or Court House), a building on the site of what is now St. Anne's R.C. School.

Among the Lords of the Manor of Banstead were a number of important persons. Outstanding among them was Hubert de Burgh, Earl of Kent, a powerful figure during the reigns of King John and King Henry III. He held

---

6   For details, see Lambert's 'History' Vol. 1, pp. 15,49 & 127, and his "Lectures" pp.18-21, listed in Appendix C.

Figure 3. Burgh House (later known as Great Burgh) rear view. (*History of Surrey by Manning and Bray*) *Reproduced by permission of London Borough of Lambeth, Archives Department.*

the lordship from 1217 to 1243.[7] In 1273 the Manor was acquired from Hubert's son, Sir John de Burgh, by King Edward I; and after that, it was held directly by the Crown until 1370. From that date until 1464, it was either 'leased' or 'granted' to various persons. Then the Crown resumed direct control of the Manor until 1536. During each period of the Crown's direct holding of the Manor, it was normally 'granted' or 'settled' on successive queens, the last of whom was Catherine of Aragon. She continued to hold it even after her divorce from Henry VIII. Then a great landowning family, the Carews of Beddington, held the Manor from 1536 until 1762, apart from an unfortunate interval of fifteen years after 1539, when Sir Nicholas Carew fell foul of his childhood friend, Henry VIII, and was executed for alleged treason.

Banstead was thus for a very long time associated with royalty or people of high rank. It seems unlikely that any of the Lords of the Manor in those days normally resided in Banstead, though Hubert de Burgh spent his last four years there. On the other hand, it is known that the Plantagenet kings, Edward I, II and III, paid visits to the Manor House, probably when they were engaged in the popular royal sport of hunting. The Manor in fact served a double purpose for royalty, yielding a useful income as well as providing a convenient hunting ground.

By the fourteenth century, the feudal system had begun to break up, and the process was accelerated by the effect of a series of plagues. Known as the Black Death, these plagues killed off great numbers of the rural population. Henry Lambert deduced, from the large number of holdings left vacant in 1354, that the Black Death had struck the Banstead area severely in the period since 1325.[8] This put the surviving tenants in a much stronger position and no doubt contributed to the replacement of 'villeinage' tenures, under which the villagers had to work extensively for the Lord. Many of these had existed in 1325. By 1364 they had largely been changed into tenancies under which most of the obligations to the Lord had been replaced by specified money payments. Serfdom was also fading away, though it did not disappear until some time in the fifteenth century.

By the end of that century, 'villeinage' was practically extinct, and had been replaced by 'copyhold tenure' at a money rent with greatly increased security. The position of the copyhold tenant depended upon entry of his tenancy on the Court Roll of the Manor, and any sort of dealing with or succession to the tenancy had also to be entered on the Roll. This was security at a certain price, because such entries involved paying fees to the court and

---

7   A brief account of Hubert de Burgh's life and career appears in Chapter 13
8   Henry Lambert, A History of Banstead, Vol. 2, p.15.

probably also to lawyers. Copyhold tenure persisted long after most other features of the feudal system had vanished. It was still to be found in Banstead in the middle of the nineteenth century, and was not legally abolished until 1926.

Banstead in the Middle Ages was a small hamlet, and not a place of strategic importance. Clustered almost entirely east of All Saints church, it housed the farmers of some fairly indifferent land and, more importantly, the owners and shepherds of the flocks of sheep, which were the main produce and source of wealth. The major events of past centuries do not seem to have involved the villagers to any great degree. There is no record of Banstead men following Wat Tyler in 1381. Some of the villagers were involved to some extent in Jack Cade's revolt in 1450, but received pardons. In 1588 the so-called Tumble Beacon, whose site can still be seen in a garden in The Drive, must have been ready to signal the arrival of the Spanish Armada, but it was not needed.

In the seventeenth century, the Civil War briefly threatened to spread actively into the district. There was a plot for Royalists to assemble under cover of one of the race meetings which had become customary on the Downs, but it attained little success. The Commonwealth period involved some interference with the church, including the appointment of a new incumbent, but there was no fighting or drama. The Great Plague of London in 1665 may not have directly affected Banstead. John Aubrey,[9] did record that he saw on a wooden post in the road, in the parish of Banstead, an inscription, 'Here lyeth the body of a poor man who dyed in the Sickness Yeare 1665'. This inscription was evidently remarkable enough to be specially recorded, and the fear of the plague enough for him to be buried outside the village itself.

By this time, Banstead had become known to Londoners for three reasons. One was the foot or horse races on what were referred to as Banstead Downs. Samuel Pepys, in his Diary entry for 30th July 1663, mentioned the talk about 'the great foot-race run this day on Banstead Downs'. In 1724, Daniel Defoe gave a graphic account of racing on Banstead Downs. They were 'covered with coaches and ladies, an innumerable company of horsemen, as well gentlemen as citizens... the racers flying over the course as if they touched not and felt not'.[10] These races were on the open downs, anywhere between Carshalton and Epsom, but at least the name of Banstead was becoming familiar.

---

9   Natural History and Antiquities of Surrey.
10 Tour of the Whole Island of Great Britain, 1724.

Besides foot and horse racing, Banstead was becoming well-known to Londoners for its health-giving air and the excellence of its mutton. John Aubrey in 1673 said that Banstead was 'famous for its wholesome air, and formerly much prescribed by the London physicians to their patients as the ultimum refugium'. He went on to add that it was also 'famous for its small sweet mutton'.

Already there were a few London merchants, including the Lambert family, who had their businesses and town houses in London, but who lived mostly in Banstead. In "Town and Country Mouse", published in 1685, Matthew Prior expressed this new custom in verse:

> *"So merchant has his house in town*
> *And country seat near Banstead Down,*
> *From one he dates his foreign letters,*
> *Sends out his goods and duns his debtors;*
> *In t'other, at his hours of leisure,*
> *He smokes his pipes and takes his pleasure".*

As the eighteenth century progressed, more London merchants and gentry began to find it both pleasant and feasible to have a country residence on the Surrey hills. One of these men, Rowland Frye, in 1762 bought the Manor of Banstead from the Carew family. By then, most of the feudal aspects of the Manor would have vanished. The Court did, however, continue to be the place of record for copyholds; the demesne lands and the Banstead Woods still passed with the lordship; and so did ownership of the Commons, subject to the rights of the villagers or 'commoners'. The Commonfield appears to have been split up by 1680 into plots of land over which individuals claimed to be copyhold tenants. As a residence for the Lords of the Manor, a house had been built by that time on the edge of the Banstead Woods, in part of what is now known as Park Farm. This house was on occasion referred to as Banstead Park House, Park Wood House or Banstead House. Lordship of the Manor remained with family successors of Rowland Frye until 1853.

By the time that Rowland Frye bought the Lordship of the Manor in 1762, the Lambert family had long since acquired, either as freehold or copyhold, a great deal of the land in the vicinity of the village. They also held the Sub-manor of Perrotts, which roughly corresponded to what is now Perrotts Farm.

On the other side of the Sutton to Reigate road, the Buckle family had, since the early seventeenth century held the Sub-manors of Great Burgh, North Tadworth, Little Burgh and Preston. In effect, their estate, based on the house at Great Burgh mentioned by John Evelyn, included almost all the land on that side of the road westwards to Epsom Downs and southwards to what is now Shelvers Way, except for the Burgh Heath Common.

At about 1731, Christopher Buckle began to plough up an area of land at the northern end of the Great Burgh estate which had since 1647 been let out as a sheepwalk and rabbit warren. There was a legal dispute as to his title to the land, but this seems to have petered out; and in 1740 he built a large house on the land, to be known as Nork House, for his eldest son (also Christopher). The rest of the land was laid out as a park.

It appears that the northern boundary of the park was planted with fir trees, and so the road which ran along the boundary acquired its name.[11]

So although Rowland Frye became Lord of the Manor he was in practice the owner of only one of the large estates in the Manor.

Rowland Frye and other people thinking of having a country residence in Banstead, were no doubt encouraged to do so by the improvement of the roads from London. These started with a turnpike or toll road from Southwark to Sutton, authorised by an Act of Parliament in 1718. The Sutton to Reigate extension was authorised under an Act of 1755. Further Acts were passed in 1755 to authorise new roads from Ewell to the Reigate Road at Burgh Heath, and from Tadworth to the bottom of Pebble Hill. These roads would make travel to and around the district much easier.

By the end of the eighteenth century, extra trade and employment for the villagers must have been provided by the arrival of additional people with families occupying large or fairly large houses in the area. Yet the community was still essentially rural, living and trading within the immediate vicinity. Most of the men and some of the women were employed on the farms. Domestic service in the large houses would offer alternative employment for some. Changes in a small village like Banstead would be slow, as would be the growth in population. In 1801 this stood at 717. Thirty years later, it had risen to 991. Although this was no longer the hamlet of the Middle Ages, Banstead was still only a moderately-sized village.

---

11 Henry Lambert, A History of Banstead Vol. 2 pp 78-80

Chapter 2

Early Victorian Banstead

Until the 1840s, only limited information is available about landholdings around Banstead, about its population or their occupations. From 1840 onwards, a clearer picture can be drawn.

The official census of population taken in 1841 was the first to include details of every household, its inhabitants and their occupations. Four years earlier, in 1837, State registration of births, deaths and marriages had been set up. In 1842, a map of the Parish was prepared and published for the purpose of assessing and levying the Poor Rate, with an index dealing with each property. In 1843, a Tithe Apportionment Map was completed. This was on a similar basis to the Poor Law Map.

At this time public administration was reorganised and reforms introduced through the determined efforts of a small number of influential individuals. The rapid development of railways also revolutionised communication between towns across the country.[1] With this improvement in communications, central government could increasingly direct and control even remote locations, largely through statutory bodies created on a common pattern. As London inexorably spread, Banstead could not fail in time to be affected.

The Banstead villager of the 1840s would, however, probably have been little aware of these developments, because Banstead would not have been outwardly much affected. The High Street in 1841 would have looked much the same as in 1831, nor would it be much different in 1851.

---

1 'Radicals, Reforms and Railways' by Richard Tames. Published by Batsford, 1986, in 'Living through History' series.

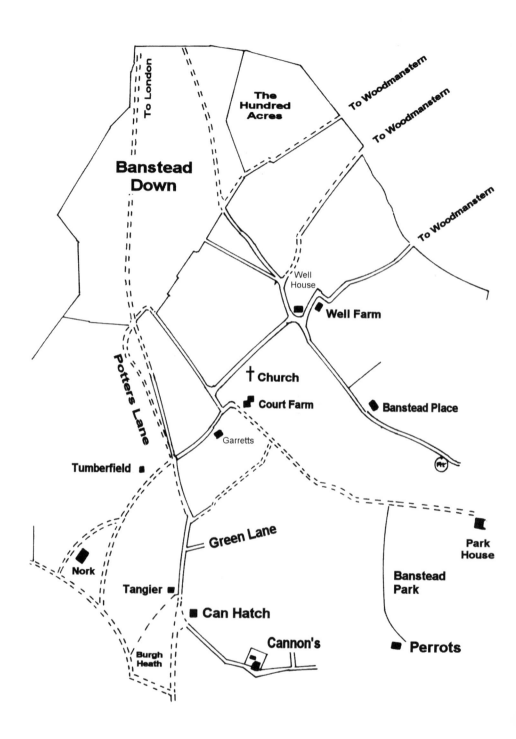

Figure 4. The Parish of Banstead - 1841

Banstead in 1841 was still a small village clustered at or near the eastern end of what was then, and remains today, the High Street. In what is now Park Road (then more often called Banstead Street) was the village well, which, with other wells serving individual houses or groups of houses, was the chief source of water supply. There was a pond on a property at the corner of the two roads. Apart from this cluster of houses, shops and cottages, there was the Vicarage, just west of the entrance to All Saints Church. Some larger residences, as well as farmhouses and cottages, were spread more widely through the neighbourhood.

The village High Street was only the width of a small country lane with no house on either side west of the church and vicarage, except for a farmhouse on the northern side (Winkworth or Wingfords Farm). Adjoining the street were two large ponds, one halfway along the northern side, and another at the western end of the High Street, at its junction with the southern part of Bolters Lane.

Along most of the northern side of the High Street was open land, falling away to the Banstead Downs, with the houses of Belmont and Sutton in view in the distance. A large house, belonging to a branch of the Lambert family and known as Buff House, stood on this side of the High Street towards its eastern end. Near the eastern end stood a smithy, a few shops and other buildings. There were also a few buildings in Salisbury Court, a cul-de-sac which is now part of Salisbury Road. Another Lambert residence, Well House, stood at the eastern end of the High Street; and there were a few shops, cottages and other premises, including the old Woolpack Inn, on the southern side of the High Street near this end.

A little further away, along Woodmansterne Lane, Well Farm stood on the southern side, and Longcroft on the northern side. A little way down Park Road (or Banstead Street) were two large houses: Yewlands on the east, opposite Rooks Nest (now part of Castle House) on the west. Continuing down, on the east side was a house known as Apsley Cottage (now Apsley House), and Banstead Place. On the west side was a new building called Jireh (later Wilmot) Cottage, Park Cottage, and an eighteenth-century building called Woodmans Cottage. Within a parish of over 5,500 acres, this built-up area was very small.

It is interesting to note some of the principal landowners in the parish at this time. The private properties of the vicar, the Reverend W.L. Buckle, included Warren Farm, Great Burgh, North Tadworth Farm, and Preston and Canons Farms. Then there was Lady Arden, widow of Lord Arden, who had bought the Nork Park estate from the Buckles. Another of the Arden family,

Figure 5. Nork House c.1828. - *Etching by Prosser*

Lord Egmont, was the owner of Reads Rest, a house and farm off Canons Lane. Mrs. Spencer, Lord of the Manor and last of the Frye dynasty, was living at Banstead Park House (adjoining the Banstead Woods), and she owned the woods, the demesne lands and the Commons. Banstead Place was owned by John Motteux.

The oldest established of the large landowners in the district were still the Lambert family, along with the Buckles. Daniel Lambert owned Perrotts Farm and Well House, as his ancestors had for centuries. John Lambert owned Well Farm; and William Lambert had land in the area of Sutton Lane.

Robert Shallcross, a member of a notable farming family in the Banstead area, owned Green Lane Farm. Other members of this family owned a certain amount of land and farmed other land on the larger estates as tenants.

There were in all about thirty owners of properties of considerable size, which included most of the land in the parish.

The large landowners at this time were not necessarily resident in the area. Land was the most secure and widely recognised form of invested wealth. It was common practice for wealthy people to own and let out properties, residences as well as land, and to enjoy an income from them as absentee landlords. It is known that some members of leading families did live in their houses in Banstead and take a major part in local affairs. The Buckle family, who for many years held the right of presentment to the incumbency of All Saints, Banstead, held the post of vicar through three generations, from 1823 to 1906. The Lamberts of Well House and Perrotts were regularly resident. Others had town houses and used their Banstead residences, if at all, as places to resort to for the summer days, for country pastimes such as riding, hunting and shooting, and for the social life of the "county class".

The actual farming was mostly in the hands of local residents such as the Shallcross (or Shallcrass) family. Other local farmers were Thomas Harrison, who was tenant of much of the Buckle estate, and William Steer, who farmed much of the demesne lands of Mrs. Spencer. A farming family who owned their land were the Morrisses, who held Mint Farm at this time and indeed until modern times.

It may be said that at this time Banstead, an agricultural community, comprised three main layers: the country gentlemen or rich merchants who owned large estates; the tenant or yeoman farmers who actually farmed the lands, often parts of two or more estates; and the labourers, who were mostly employed by the farmers and sometimes lived in the farmhouse. There were also some reasonably prosperous residents, such as lawyers, corn merchants and colonial brokers, and "fundholders" living on invested income. In the 1840s, however, this was a small group.

The two main employments open to villagers were either working on the farms, or serving other needs of the landed gentry, the merchants and the larger farmers. These needs and the requirements of the villagers themselves afforded employment to a certain number of tradesmen in the village. There were small shops, such as a grocer, butcher, baker, tailor, carpenter and shoemaker. There was a blacksmith and a couple of bricklayers, who were or would probably become small builders. Further afield were a wheelwright, a timber merchant and a couple of dressmakers and laundresses. At the windmill, then on the Hundred Acres (later the site of Banstead Hospital and now of Downview and Highdown Prisons) were both a miller and a baker. There was no post office in the full sense in the village. Mail was received at the grocer's shop of John Cooper, who was also a bricklayer. (Mail arrived every day at twelve noon and was dispatched at 4.30 p.m.). The census of 1851 records that out of a total of some 310 men living in this part of the

Figure 6. Well House and the Well - *R.A. Michell*

parish, about ninety were agricultural labourers; while out of some two hundred women, some sixty were domestic servants.

For most of the 1840s, Banstead was wholly dependent on horse transport for communication with the outside world. Other places had a river or canal or even a railway at hand. Banstead had none of these. A railway from London reached Croydon and beyond just before 1840, but that would have been a fair distance to travel. The same applied to the branch line from West Croydon to Sutton, opened in 1847.

A glance at the plan on page 12 will show that the basic pattern of roads in 1841 has survived to the present day. Of course, the roads have been widened and realigned again and again, and the surfaces have been improved out of all knowledge. Some roads have been renamed, and a new network added. But the present High Street is simply a modern version of the old High Street. From its eastern end, access is still had to Park Road, Woodmansterne Lane, Croydon Lane and Sutton Lane. From its western end, Bolters Lane still leads northwards to the Brighton Road and Fir Tree Road, and southwards to Holly Lane and Garratts Lane.

The Brighton Road, as constructed in 1755, was still a turnpike (or toll) road in 1841. In 1826 or thereabouts, its line had been altered at the point where it left Banstead Downs, to take it in a straight line on to the top of Garratts Lane. Until then it had followed the line of the old road known as Potters Lane. This can still be traced just beyond the gardens of houses on the eastern side of Green Curve.

Winkworth Road, Avenue Road and Court Road did not exist in 1841. A road or track which at that time led to Cheam no longer exists, except as a neglected footpath. Yet the essential links remain, although the mode of conveyance is very different today. No doubt many of the better-off inhabitants in the 1840s had their own coaches, chaises, traps and so on. Others could make arrangements to hire, borrow or get a lift on some kind of vehicle. Or they could go on horseback. Failing that, they would walk much further than would be thought acceptable today.

As for public transport, two services to London were available. A coach (described by 1845 as 'an omnibus') left the Woolpack Inn every morning, except Sunday, at 9.15, returning at six o'clock in the evening. Each Tuesday and Friday, there were two regular carriers to take goods, and probably a few passengers, to the 'Catherine Wheel' at Borough and the 'Cross Keys' in Gracechurch Street. These returned the same day, presumably at a much slower rate than the coach. It is probable that there were many other informal arrangements of which records do not survive.

Banstead was in the 1840s to an extent affected by new laws as to registration of births, deaths and marriages; by a new regime of Poor Law under Boards of Guardians; by a system of grants to schools by the Board of Education; and by regulation of Church affairs by the recently formed Ecclesiastical Commissioners. But it would be wrong to give the impression that life in the village had at this time become highly regulated.

The main instrument of local government at county level was still the Quarter Sessions, Justices of the Peace from all over the County meeting quarterly. Below this was the Parish Vestry, composed of the vicar and churchwardens and elected representatives of the inhabitants. The Vestry was concerned with church and charitable affairs as much as with local administration. It had formerly been responsible for administering the Poor Law, including a Parish Workhouse at Tadworth; but in 1837 a Board of Guardians had been set up at Epsom to cover the district, and the Parish Workhouse had been sold. The Vestry, however, remained responsible for setting and collecting a Poor Rate in the parish.[2]

---

2 For details see "A history of Poor Law and Charity Relief in Banstead" BHRG, 2004

The Metropolitan Police had been set up in London in 1829, but county forces were not even permitted until 1839, and an Act in 1842 reinforced the duty of parishes to appoint their own constables. The Banstead Vestry did so as late as 1847. (His name was William Bence, a butcher by trade.)

The Vestry was responsible for highways in the parish other than toll roads; and a Highway Rate was levied as well as the Poor Rate. A local man would be appointed annually as Assistant Overseer of the poor, and other local men would be appointed as Surveyors of Highways.

Apart from this, there was little local government activity in the modern sense; but the Vestry did have a wide range of concerns, of which one example may suffice. In February 1844 the Vestry approved the grant of £30 as emigration expenses to send two children, William Bennett, (aged ten), and Elizabeth Bennett, (aged eleven), to join their father in Australia. He was working as a shepherd in Dunmore, Morpeth, New South Wales, and his employer, Mr. Lang, had appealed to the Vestry to send them out to join him. They embarked for Sydney on the first of June 1844.

Education in Banstead in the 1840s seems to have been truly elementary. A school for girls was run by the daughter of Peter Aubertin, the owner of Yewlands, with the help of a young Miss Mary Morris. It appears that by 1846 there was a school on the northern side of the High Street, with twenty boys and thirty girls on the roll, and a Sunday school with twenty-eight boys and twenty-two girls. At Burgh Heath a small Church of England school had been set up in 1839.

As to recreation or entertainment at this time, not much is known. It is significant that there was a field called Townfield. This ran south from the High Street, and included what are now the cricket ground (The Green) and the Lady Neville recreation ground. It is known that cricket was being played on the Green by 1850, and it is reasonable to assume that the villagers had been allowed to use the field for recreation, at least occasionally, before that. They also had access to the Downs and Commons, officially for grazing sheep and other practical purposes, or over public rights of way. Unofficial access probably included uses connected with the cooking pot.

Village life would have centred largely round the old Woolpack Inn, which was the place where parish business was transacted for the "Town end" of the parish, whilst the Tangier public house, on the Brighton Road near Burgh Heath, was used for "the Burgh or Tadworth end". Another public house or alehouse was the Black Boy, on the Brighton Road, near the junction with Garratts Lane. There does not seem to have been any other recognised meeting place or hall for use by the villagers at this time.

One aspect of the small village community at this time deserves mention for its contrast with modern circumstances. That is the large size of families and households, both rich and poor. For instance, in 1841 the household of the vicar included his wife, seven children and five house servants. At Canons Farm, Thomas Harrison and his wife lived with eight children, five servants and one labourer. At Reads Rest, the farmer was widow Ann Muggeridge, aged sixty, with three children, two servants and three agricultural labourers. And at Wingfords Farm, the household of Thomas Simmonds, an agricultural labourer aged fifty, comprised his wife, five children and three farm labourers.

Chapter 3

Banstead in the 1850s and 1860s

The story of a village is in reality a continuous one, with changes occurring gradually and sometimes almost imperceptibly, whilst in the main things go on much as before. It was said earlier that the village in 1841 would not have differed in major respects from the village in 1831 or 1851. But, by the late 1860s, there were to be some major changes; and perhaps the change with the most far-reaching consequences would be the availability of rail travel.

Development of the railway system in the immediate vicinity of Banstead was not so rapid as in some other districts. The Downs were a formidable obstacle, and the district was almost entirely given over to agriculture and use for sporting activities. Moreover, it was sparsely populated. The line from London to Croydon and beyond, opened in 1839, had been extended by means of a branch line to Sutton and Epsom in 1847. This enabled Banstead people who could afford it to get to a railway station and so on to the spreading network of railways; but it was not until 1859 that a direct line from London to Epsom via Raynes Park was open, as well as another line via Wimbledon.

It was a further six years before a railway line actually reached Banstead, and even then it was an inconvenient distance from the village. This was the Sutton to Epsom Downs line. It was designed to serve the demand for access to the Epsom Downs Racecourse rather than to take the limited amount of traffic to and from the intermediate stations of Belmont (at first called California) and Banstead.[1]

While the story of Epsom Racecourse is only of marginal importance in the story of Banstead,[2] the new railway line did have implications for the

---

1 The line was opened on Derby Day 1865, when no less than 70,000 people passed through Epsom Downs Station.
2 The story is well told in "Epsom Racecourse" by David Hunn, published by Davis Poynter.

Figure 7. Epsom Downs Station, Derby Day, 1907

development of the village. In the 1850s and on into the 1860s, England enjoyed a remarkable period of expansion and prosperity. Rail travel had become commonplace, and the railway companies had made the most of the situation by providing cheap excursions to the coast and country, as well as special services to districts around the big cities. Improved transport often brings building development in its wake. It was only to be expected that in places like Banstead thoughts would increasingly turn to housing and building development.

Although there were changes affecting the pattern of land owning and the life of the village, there was not much building development in the neighbourhood of Banstead in the 1850s. One positive change in the village, however, was that for the first time ordinary people did have a fully established school to which to send their children.[3]

3   The whole story is told in "Village School, Banstead, and Henry Knibbs, Victorian Schoolmaster", by Irene O'Shea. BHRG, 1981.

It was founded as a Church of England School in 1852. Donations and annual subscriptions provided much of the funds, whilst parents paid "school pence", graduated roughly according to their means. At first the pupils met in a schoolroom north of the High Street, opposite the Woolpack Inn; but in 1857 it was decided to build a new school, including a master's house. This was completed and opened in 1858 on a site donated for the purpose by Mr. John Lambert of Garratts Hall. The site was south of the High Street and immediately to the west of what was shortly to become Avenue Road. Although the building and the site itself were later extended, this continued as the village school, subsequently the "First School", until 1990.

Another innovation in 1852 was a Metropolitan Police Station, in a building adjoining the north side of the High Street, between the street and Buff House. By 1862 this was occupied by a detachment of two Police Sergeants and twelve Police Constables. They clearly had an impact on the village, both on and off duty, as some of them lived with their families in Banstead, and others were in lodgings there.

Mention of John Lambert of Garratts Hall leads to consideration of changes in ownership of the larger estates, which had in the early 1840s been dominated by the Buckles, the Arden family, various branches of the Lambert family, and by Mrs. Spencer as Lord of the Manor.

The Buckles had sold the Nork Park estate to the then Lord Arden in 1812. In 1846 they sold Great Burgh House and its estate to the sixth Earl of Egmont, son and heir of Lord and Lady Arden. The widowed Lady Arden continued to occupy Nork House until her death in 1851, after which the Earl of Egmont became beneficial owner of both the Nork Park and the Great Burgh estates.

Green Lane Farm on the eastern side of the Brighton Road was added to the combined estate in 1857. It now included most of the land in the parish west of the Brighton Road, from the junction with Fir Tree Road to a point beyond Burgh Heath (near what is now Shelvers Way), as well as Green Lane Farm, Canons Farm and Reads Rest Farm on the east side of the Brighton Road.

The Buckle family were no longer major landowners in the parish. The Earl of Egmont's estate was now the largest. Lordship of the Manor, however, still carried with it a considerable amount of demesne land, including Court Farm, Banstead Park House and Banstead Wood and, in addition, ownership of the four Commons.

Figure 8. Park Farm, adjacent to Banstead Park House, viewed from the woods.

Mrs. Spencer, the Lord of the Manor, died in the early 1850s, pre-deceased by her only son. In 1853 her daughters sold the Lordship of the Manor, as well as the lands that went with it, to Thomas Alcock of Kingswood. The Lordship remained in his hands until his death in 1866. Although by that time he had sold most of the demesne lands, the Commons had remained his property.

Faced in 1864 with keeping the Commons in some sort of order, but lacking the ample income from copyholders and others which earlier Lords of the Manor had enjoyed, Alcock applied for statutory inclosure of the

Commons to the exclusion of Commoners. The Inclosure Commissioners, however, rejected Alcock's application. This prompted him to join the newly formed Commons Society, which wanted all Metropolitan Commons to be open and statutorily regulated. After his death in 1866, his executors made a fresh application to the Commissioners. This was again rejected, but the threat to the Commoners' rights was evidently still very much alive.

The other main landowners in the 1840s had been the Lamberts, who had figured largely in the history of Banstead since early in the 16th century. The Well House branch continued in the 1850s and 1860s to own that house and Perrotts Farm. In 1857 this property passed from one Daniel Lambert to his son of the same name. On the son's death the following year, 1858, the property passed to his brother, Benjamin.

The Buff House estate, comprising part of the old Commonfield north of the High Street and five acres of land on the south side of the High Street, including the old Woolpack Inn, remained much as before, in the hands of Henry Thomas Lambert.

The rising star of this landowning family, however, was John Lambert, son of the John Lambert who had owned Well Farm in 1841. Although the younger John Lambert appears not to have inherited Well Farm on his father's death in 1850, he later bought it from the Reverend William Lambert, one of the Woodmansterne branch of the family. In 1854 John Lambert bought the Townfield and other land from Thomas Alcock. By inheritance and purchase John proceeded to increase his estate in Banstead, until in the end he outstripped all other owners in the parish except the Earl of Egmont.

In 1857 John Lambert bought Garratts Hall, a sizeable house lying south of Garratts Lane. This included Little Garratts, which survives today, and some twenty-three acres of land bounded roughly by what are now Shrubland Road, the public footpath from Pound Road to Holly Lane, and Holly Lane itself. Lodges at the end of drives which led to the house still stand at the corners of Holly Lane and Shrubland Road. John Lambert must have taken great pleasure in this purchase, as Garratts Hall had belonged to his family for two centuries before it was sold in 1734; and he enlarged and improved the house considerably.

Amongst his other purchases were, in 1859, Board Field, in which Court Road was later constructed; Longcroft, in 1860, with fourteen acres of land; the 163 acres of Well Farm, also in 1860; part of the old Commonfield; and Banstead Place, with 284 acres of land. He also had a town house in Kensington. In 1866 he is recorded[4] as owner of 665 acres in Banstead, and

4   The details appear in an Award of Compensation for loss of commoners' rights from the
    construction of the Sutton-Epsom Downs railway line - National Archives, Ref. MAF/2/189

Figure 9. Garratts Hall, South Front, c.1920

this included much of the land formerly owned by Thomas Alcock. At this time, most of the old Commonfield appears to have been almost equally divided between John and the Buff House Lamberts; it was being farmed under lease as Winkworth Farm.

Banstead Park, which included the House and Wood, had for some years been held under lease by Horatio Kemble, a Colonial Broker who also had sporting rights over Perrotts Farm. Thomas Alcock, who had acquired this and other land together with Lordship of the Manor, sold the freehold to Thomas Henry Maudslay, a member of a celebrated family of Marine Engineers. After occupying and improving the house, he did not live long to enjoy it, since he died in 1864.

Alcock also sold land in the area bounded, in modern terms, by the Brighton Road, Northacre, The Orchard, Bolters Lane, and that part of

Winkworth Road which connects Bolters Lane with Banstead Cross-roads. This area was first the subject of building development in 1854, when Alcock sold to Mrs. Sarah Martin a strip of land some three hundred to three hundred and fifty feet wide, running from Bolters Lane to the Brighton Road. She had two substantial houses built on this strip, lying back in ample grounds, each with a separate drive and lodge, and with a common drive leading to Bolters Lane. The house whose land fronted on Bolters Lane was at first called Wingfield Lodge (later Bentley Lodge); the other house, with land fronting on the Brighton Road, was called Walton Lodge. Later, the owners of each of these properties bought additional land to the south.

A Mr. John Cookes owned Bentley Lodge, which was to remain in his family for many years. Walton Lodge was bought by a Mr. Mullins in 1859; and passed to Mr. R.T. Nevins in 1867. The two properties now form in general the area of The Horseshoe and the buildings and land immediately adjacent.

The next bout of sales of land in this particular area had obvious connections with the project for the Sutton to Epsom Downs railway, with its proposed station for Banstead. Two men closely involved were Charles Garrett, the contractor for the construction of the line, and Captain Lanrook Flower, the original engineer for the line. By 1864 they had bought land and had houses built for themselves in the area north of Walton Lodge. Captain Flower had also bought extra land adjoining his premises for building purposes.[5]

Garrett's house, called Banstead House, was near the north end of the area, with a frontage to the Brighton Road. Flower's house, called The Larches, and also with a frontage to the Brighton Road, adjoined Walton Lodge. Not long after the erection of these houses, two other houses were built on the vacant ground: Basing House, which adjoined Banstead House on the south; and south of that again, a large house known as Banstead Hall. Both of these fronted on to the Brighton Road, so that the western side of the area was then fully developed from near the Banstead Cross-roads to what is now Northacre. The eastern side of the area, from Bentley Lodge northwards, remained open land.

There were a few other new buildings in or near the village in this period. The railway station was accompanied by a house for the Stationmaster. A farmhouse, named The Lodge, was built on the eastern side of the Brighton Road, just north of a field formerly used as the Village Pound. A new public

5   This information is given in an account by John Morgan quoted in the Nork Quarterly, October 1978.

Figure 10. Wilmot
(formerly Jireh)
Cottage,
Park Road, c.1904

house, the Victoria Inn, was built at the western end of the High Street. In Park Road, a row of cottages was built next to Apsley Cottage (now Apsley House).

The village still retained, however, its rural aspect. The High Street was still narrow, and for much of its length it was bounded, on the north by open fields, and on the south by gardens.

Village life no doubt centred round All Saints Church; but we know of one Free Church in Banstead in the 1850s. This was a congregation of the Calvinistic Independent church who in 1851 were recorded as occupying two rooms in a villa in Park Road then known as Jireh Cottage. These rooms were fitted out for worship on Sunday evenings. There was space for a congregation of thirty five. Jasper Shallcross was named as the Manager. We do not know the later history of this congregation. The villa was, by the 1860s occupied by the Reverend Edward Buckle, then Curate of All Saints; and its name became, and remains today, Wilmot Cottage.

As in the 1840s, the community was still mostly agricultural. Land ownership was concentrated in even fewer hands than before. The Earl of Egmont to the west of Brighton Road, and the Lamberts to the east, were by far the largest landowners. The farmers themselves continued to own fairly small holdings. In 1866 Maria Shallcross, widow of Robert Shallcross, owned fourteen acres, which included Great Diceland, Little Diceland and Horsecroft, in addition to the Black Boy beerhouse. The farmers occupied much larger areas as tenants; and certain farms were under the control of bailiffs or stewards, employed by the landowners.

Many of the villagers were still employed either on the farms or in domestic service. The total population of the parish rose from 1168 in 1841 to 1461 in 1861, and to 1668 in 1871: a steady rather than spectacular increase. There were in 1871 only a few more shops and tradesmen in the village: two more grocers, one of whom ran the Post Office; a plumber; a linen draper; a baker; and, perhaps a sign of the times, a house and estate agent, who was also agent for an insurance company.

In 1871, out of a total of some three hundred men in this part of the parish, about eighty-five were agricultural labourers. Of a little over two hundred and fifty women, sixty-five were in domestic service. There were also just over twenty men in domestic service, and some thirty were employed as gardeners. Compared with 1851, this seems to be an indication of a slight fall in employment on farming work, and a slight increase in domestic service.

Transport to and from the village for longer distances was increasingly a matter of getting to a railway station. The horsedrawn coach, or "omnibus", which had run from the Woolpack to London, was by 1855 running only to Sutton station, leaving every morning at nine o'clock and returning at six in the evening. The carrier, William Griffin, continued to provide a service to London on Tuesdays and Fridays, returning the same day. The last mention of this service in Kelly[6] is in 1867. Presumably the business could not long survive the arrival of the railway in Banstead.

Pressure from the railways may also have been one of the causes of the freeing of the Brighton Road from toll charges in 1859. By the end of the 1860s, it was quite possible for people of reasonable means to live in Banstead and travel to work in London. The make-up of the population seems to confirm that a small number of residents of professional or merchant status were beginning to "commute" to London.

---

6   Kelly's (Post Office) Directories are most valuable sources of information during this period.

In 1871 the only large landowner without some other occupation seems to have been the Earl of Egmont, who had been a Rear-Admiral in the Navy. There were about fifteen professional or business people of some standing and prosperity, judging by the fact that between them they employed more than forty domestic servants. A local builder, William Taylor, was living at Buff House, and was the employer of thirteen men and two boys. There were also a few residents recorded as fundholders or annuitants, probably mostly retired people.

Local administration had hardly changed since the 1840s. The Vestry continued to be the authority responsible at the Parish level for highways, poor rate, county rate and a few other matters. Policing, however, had been entirely handed over to the Metropolitan Police. Quarter sessions remained the higher level of local government, responsible for the County.

Education for the village children was no doubt greatly improved by the use of the new school premises and the zeal of the school master, Henry Knibbs, who had arrived in December 1862, and was to keep a strict eye on pupils and non-attenders. The school was also overseen by the Vicar, and was annually inspected by Inspectors from the Board of Education.

Henry Knibbs soon began to figure largely in village life. One of his enthusiasms was for cricket. In the summer after his arrival, he formed a school cricket club, of present and past pupils, who played matches against other schools. He was also interested in village cricket on the Green.

Cricket on the Green evidently continued and flourished in this period, though Banstead Cricket Club had not yet been formally constituted. A proper "square" of pitches was laid, and the line of lime trees on the northern side of the ground was planted in 1857, at the expense of Sir George Glyn, a banker and Member of Parliament then living at Banstead Place. The ground was apparently used under informal arrangements with the landowner, who from 1854 was John Lambert.

Little is known as to other organised recreation or entertainment in the village at this time. When not needed for other purposes, the school may have been available, as it was later. There does not appear to have been a village hall. We know that the children had time off for Shroving, May Garlands, the Oddfellows' fete and other special occasions which must have involved parents and other adults. There was great excitement on Derby Day, when there was a great rush of traffic through the village. Harvest was a busy time for everyone, including the children; and if the harvest was late, the beginning of the school's Autumn term might have to be postponed. Life in the village was not always dull or uneventful.

Chapter 4

Banstead from 1870 -1895

The Village School

The year 1870 was notable for the Elementary Education Act, which for the first time provided compulsory elementary education for all children. This would be in schools run either by new statutory bodies (normally a District Board) or by existing voluntary bodies such as the Church of England or the Free Churches, which had up to then supplied most of the schools for children whose parents could not pay for private schooling. The Village School in Banstead was a Church of England School erected with the aid of a Government grant, and was already subject to scrutiny annually by inspectors from the Board of Education.

Following the passing of the 1870 Act, the School Managers had to decide whether they could continue to meet the requirements of the Education Department for the school premises, as well as the schooling provided there. They reluctantly decided that they could not. The school was accordingly handed over in 1874 to a statutory board, called the School Board for the United District of Banstead and Kingswood. This soon provided funds for repairs, refurbishing and enlargement.

An express reservation was made in favour of the Vicar and Churchwardens of Banstead, who were in effect representative of the villagers as well as the church. They were to have full use of the school premises on Sundays and whenever these were not required for schooling. So the school premises were used not only for "Sunday schools" run by the Church, but also for general Village purposes, such as winter evening programmes of "entertainments".

Figure 11. Village School Staff 1898
Backrow: (L) Henry Knibbs (Headmaster) (R) Mr. Blackford
Seated: (2nd from L) Clara Balchin (R) Mrs Norrington

Henry Knibbs and his wife remained at the school, he as Headmaster and she as a teacher, after 1874, and the Vicar continued to take an active interest, so that there was no great change in the running of it.

New Institutions

This period was one in which several large institutions came to Banstead. In 1870 there were no large public or educational institutions in the village or its neighbourhood. By 1877, the population of the parish had been almost doubled by what was then called the London County Lunatic Asylum. This was situated on the downlands which, up till then, had been the site of a windmill, miller's houses and farmlands known as The Hundred Acres.

Though its early regime was grim by modern standards, it was a great improvement on the existing madhouses in London, and was one of the first of its kind. The open spaces of nearby Surrey seemed to the Metropolitan authorities of the time ideal for such institutions. A number of these were built in the neighbourhood, notably near Epsom as well as two at Coulsdon. The Banstead Asylum was designed to be, as far as possible, self-contained and self-sufficient. It had its own heating and water supply systems; its own laundry and other services; a farm to supply it with vegetables and milk, and its own chapel.

All the same, it inevitably made some impact on life in Banstead. There were a few staff houses on the southern edge of the site, in Freedown Lane. Some staff lived in the village. Others had connections there. This provided employment for some of the village tradesmen, as well as for some of the men in the village.

One of the village residents who benefited financially from the arrival of the Asylum was the village schoolmaster, Henry Knibbs. He had become part-time Assistant Overseer of the Poor. His duty of collecting Poor Rate for the Parish entitled him to a percentage of the receipts. He successfully asserted that the enormous increase of rateable value, arising from the coming of the Asylum, did not affect his right to the fixed percentage. It is not known, however, how long this arrangement lasted after 1877.

Another important new social institution was created in the parish in 1880. This was called The Kensington and Chelsea District School. It was a pioneering project to remove and rehabilitate children who were subject to the Poor Law, and who had up to that time been left with adults in workhouses in Kensington and Chelsea. The School provided accommodation and schooling for them in smaller groups under "house-parents" in a self-contained "village".

Figure 12. Banstead Asylum, 1986

The "village" originally comprised about 140 acres, one hundred of which were used for farmland. The School buildings were erected on a site of forty acres, on a long strip of land between Fir Tree Road and a stretch of the Epsom Downs branch of the London, Brighton and South Coast Railway. They included twenty-four houses for children and staff, medical rooms, workshops, a chapel, and a gymnasium. The School lasted under changing names and forms until 1974, when it was known as Beechholme. Today the site is occupied by the housing estate known as High Beeches.[1]

Banstead also in these years became the home of a private school for children with well-off parents. It stood on the eastern side of the Brighton Road, near what is now Dunnymans Road, where today stand blocks of flats and houses. The school was known as Banstead Hall, after the name of its

1   For details see "Beechholme" BHRG, 1998

main building, which had been built around 1870. In 1889 it was leased to Mr. E. J. Maitland for use as a preparatory school for boys under fifteen years of age. In 1891 Maitland bought the freehold; and as time went on, he bought more land for playing fields in the same area, between the Brighton Road and Bolters Lane, both east and north of the Hall.

Soon after the end of the period dealt with in this chapter, other upper-class preparatory schools would come to Banstead.

The arrival of such large groups of people, with no previous connection with Banstead or the surrounding countryside, could not fail to affect the character of the neighbourhood. Banstead could no longer be considered a quiet, sequestered rural community, largely free from outside influence.

Changes in ownership of property coincided with this development. In the early 1860s, almost all the land west of the Brighton Road formed part of the estate of the Earl of Egmont. Most of the land east of that road belonged either to one of the branches of the Lambert family, or to Thomas Alcock as Lord of the Manor.

The Fight for the Commons

The death of Thomas Alcock in 1866 had been an event of great local importance. It had put in increased jeopardy all the open Commons around Banstead. Alcock's Executors applied to the Inclosure Commissioners to authorise their inclosure. When their application to inclose the Commons was rejected, they sold the Lordship of the Manor, but not what was left of the demesne lands, to Sir John Hartopp. His interest was undisguised. He wanted to inclose most of the Commons, particularly Banstead Downs, and build over them. He was prepared to go to great lengths to succeed in this, realising what an immensely profitable proposition it would be. He and his solicitors conceived the idea of accomplishing this by buying out the rights over the Commons held by residents in the old Manor.

At an expense estimated at over £18,000, he completed a number of such transactions. They included a bargain with John Lambert, who acquired the ownership of Park Downs, subject to the Commoners' rights. Even the then Earl of Egmont was disposed to agree. In 1876 Hartopp launched an application for inclosure, and went so far as to build a row of houses in what is today Downs Road, Belmont. This aroused the fury of local residents and of the Commons Preservation Society. Together they opposed the application, and in 1877 they started proceedings in the Courts to restrain Hartopp from inclosing the Commons.

It is impossible here to follow all the twists and turns of the subsequent proceedings. A brief summary is contained in Appendix A.

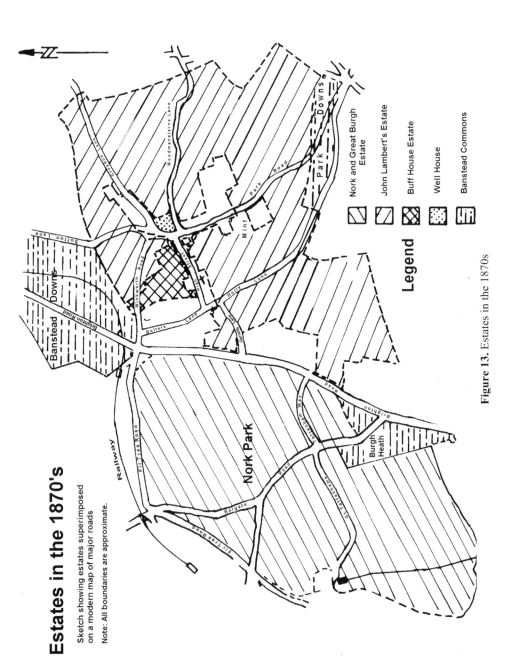

Figure 13. Estates in the 1870s

Incredibly, it was not until April 1889 that the action started in 1877 was finally decided in favour of the Commoners and the inclosure avoided, at heavy cost to all involved.[2] Even then, the matter was not put to rest. The Commoners made application to the Board of Agriculture for a scheme to regulate the Commons under the Metropolitan Commons Act, and the issue was contested in Parliament. However, in 1893 an Act of Parliament provided for statutory regulation of the Commons, and this remains in force to this day. So the Commons have remained open and public access has been maintained.

Other Properties

Whilst all this was going on, there were a number of other developments affecting ownership of property in the district.

Two events of great consequence were the death of John Lambert of Garratts Hall in 1878, and the death of his son and heir, John Wilmot Lambert, childless, in 1884. Their respective wives, and the three daughters of John Lambert, survived both, and indeed lived on for a number of years. As a result, John Lambert's Trustees did not sell off the residuary estate until 1919.

The process of disposal of his extensive estates did, however, start soon after his death in 1878. Three years later, in 1881, Garratts Hall with its grounds and fields were sold to his cousin, Frederick Lambert. A series of sales followed. Banstead Place and Apsley House were sold in 1891. A number of pieces of land were sold for building purposes to William Taylor. These included the site of Parkside in Park Road; sites in Avenue Road; and the land north of The Green which is now the Lady Neville Recreation Ground. The extensive collection of properties that had been acquired by John Lambert was to continue to dwindle gradually over the years.

Another major property transaction was the acquisition of the Banstead Park House and Estate by the Honourable F.H. Baring, which took place about 1881.

This was another occasion when a threat to the countryside was averted. The company which had owned the Woods for some years put them up for auction with two alternative proposals for development. One was for a large house to be built in the heart of the woods. The other was for roads to be constructed through the woods and an estate of houses to be built adjoining those roads. This was a fully surveyed and detailed project. Fortunately, Mr. Baring came along and the woods survived.

---

2   A fuller account is contained in Chapter XI of a book called Commons, Forests and Footpaths, by Lord Eversley, first chairman of the Commons Preservation Society, published by Cassell and Company, 1910.

Figure 14. The Garden Front, Banstead Wood *(from an old engraving c.1890)*

In the heart of the Banstead Woods he had built for him a fine large house, designed by the well-known architect, Norman Shaw. The old house near the road was relegated to use by the bailiff of the estate.[3] In 1893 Baring's property, which amounted to some 486 acres, was sold to a sugar and brewing magnate, Charles Henry Garton, who later added to the estate.

West of the Brighton Road, the Earl of Egmont's Estate came up for sale in 1890. This comprised Nork House and Park, Tumble Farm, Little Burgh, Warren Farm and North Tadworth Farm, amounting in all to about 1320 acres. It was bought by Frederick Edward Colman, sometime Chairman and Managing Director of the Colman's Mustard Company. Another part of the estate, east of the Brighton Road, including Canons Farm, Reads Rest Farm and Great Oatlands, was bought by H.Cosmo Bonsor, M.P., who in 1885 had bought the Kingswood Warren Estate. So the old Great Burgh Estate was finally broken up.

By 1895 the old families of landowners had in this way largely gone, and most of their land had passed into new hands, though the Lamberts of Buff

3   The old house was demolished in the 1950s, when the Council formed its Park Farm depot.

House and of Well House had retained their properties. Apart from the building of a small number of houses and the arrival of the Institutions, there had however not been any corresponding change in the actual use of land in the district.

One relic of the feudal days vanished in 1886, when the Manorial Court of Perrotts was held for the last time. Mr. Bonsor, the only remaining copyhold tenant, had acquired the freehold of the property, and the Court had become completely obsolete.

Railway Projects

Mr. Bonsor, who later became Sir Cosmo Bonsor, Baronet, lived in Kingswood Warren. He was in the brewing business as well as being a Member of Parliament for the Wimbledon constituency, the Lord of the Manor of Banstead, director of the South East Railway company and a Governor of the Bank of England. He was well acquainted with Allen Sarle, Secretary and General Manager of the London, Brighton and South Coast Railway. Sarle, who was knighted in 1896, lived in Banstead, at first in Bentley Lodge and later at Greenhayes, a house on the eastern edge of Bolters Lane. Bonsor secured Sarle's support for a project, which he and others had thought up, for a railway to serve Walton-on-the-Hill, Tadworth and Kingswood. This was to run from a junction with the Epsom Downs branch of the London, Brighton and South Coast Railway, near Drift Bridge, and to pass through Tattenham Corner. With this in view, Bonsor and two others had bought Corner Farm and another two hundred acres of land at Tadworth as a speculation.[4]

A Bill was introduced in Parliament to authorise this railway. This was passed in June 1892, in spite of strenuous opposition by Mr. F. E. Colman, through whose Nork Estate it would run. But Colman had made the proposal less attractive by selling a strip of land to the Epsom Race Course to create a "Straight Mile" from the Grandstand to what is now Chapel Way. As this would have necessitated a tunnel under it for the railway, that railway project was never put into effect.

Bonsor then switched his attention to an alternative project: this was for a line from Purley along the Chipstead Valley to Tadworth and Tattenham Corner. This was planned in conjunction with the rival South Eastern Railway, of which Bonsor soon became, first a Director and then Deputy Chairman. This project was to succeed where the other had failed, and was to prove a vital element in future development of the district.

4   Details are given in an article by Alan A. Jackson in The Railway Magazine, June 1975.

In the meantime, the Epsom Downs line continued to serve race-goers in particular and more generally, Londoners seeking excursions in the open air. In addition, the railway yards at Belmont and Banstead provided a goods service; and temporary sidings served large-scale developments such as the Banstead Asylum and Beechholme.

New Buildings

Building in this period consisted mostly of sizeable houses. One of these was built in Park Road by William Taylor, on a piece of land bought from John Lambert's Trustees in 1891, apparently as a speculative venture. It was to become another institution, The Boys' Surgical Home; then Edith Edwards House; and it is now part of Parkside Nursing Home.

Two new large houses with grounds on the eastern side of Bolters Lane were called Greenhayes and Castleton. Greenhayes was demolished in the 1930s. Castleton became a Nursing Home, and survived till some twenty years later. A large house was built on the western side of Bolters Lane and is now embodied in the Priory School. Another new residence was Heath House in Sutton Lane. This is now part of Greenacre School. In Avenue Road five houses were built. These were additional to the two already existing next to the Village School.

These were all substantial properties. Some smaller houses were also built in the village or nearby. Eight more houses were added in Salisbury Court (the southern end of what is now Salisbury Road.) There were some additions to Mint Cottages, and new cottages on the north side of Pound Road.

The development of the Shrubland Road/Brighton Road area began with the construction of a length of Shrubland Road with five houses fronting on it; and a length of Diceland Road led off it. By 1891 there were twenty-three households in Diceland Road, with a total of 107 persons in those households. This was a significant development. It was an estate of small houses, at some distance from the existing village; and it formed practically a separate community, with its own shops and tradesmen, and the former beer house, "The Black Boy", which in the 1870s became the Wheatsheaf Inn.

Population and Employment

The main category of jobs available for men throughout the period from 1871 to 1891 remained that of agricultural labourer; and for women, that of domestic servant. Though the population increased considerably, there seems to have been no equivalent increase in the number of agricultural workers; but the number of women in domestic service did show a large increase. This was one indication that the village and its surrounding area were beginning to house a larger number of middle-class people. Their households would include at least two or three servants, and sometimes as many as seven or eight. Most of these would be women, though men would be needed as coachmen, grooms and, above all, gardeners.

One farm which had for some years been a large employer was North Tadworth Farm, built at some time before 1861, with a Jam Factory adjoining it. It was run by William Hodson, who grew raspberries and strawberries for the purpose in the adjoining fields, in the vicinity of what is now Marbles Way. Mr. Hodson had imported staff for the factory from Cambridge. Jam from the factory was taken by horse-and-cart to London for sale in the big shops there. The journey took about three hours. Having completed his deliveries, the driver would stay the night in London. The factory continued to operate until about 1910. Mr. Hodson was not just a jam maker. The 1861 Census stated that at that time he was farming about 815 acres, and employing twenty men and six boys, a farm bailiff, a groom and two servants.

There were two other tenant farmers occupying large areas of land. At Well Farm, Mr. R. H. Freeman was in 1881 farming 630 acres and employing twenty-four men and twelve women, including eight women farm labourers. At Canons Farm, Mr. A. J. Brown was then farming 437 acres and employing twelve labourers and three boys. A smaller farmer was Thomas Gilbert, licensee of the Victoria Inn, who had 120 acres.

The increase in the population of the Civil Parish of Banstead in this period is shown by the figures in the Censuses taken in 1871, 1881 and 1891. The figures are for the whole Parish, including Burgh Heath and Tadworth, but excluding the inmates of the Asylum. The population was shown as 1,668 in 1871, 1,995 in 1881, and 2,395 in 1891. The number of inhabited houses in the Parish rose similarly: 312 in 1871, 365 in 1881, and 438 in 1891.[5]

As there was no great increase in the number of jobs as agricultural labourers, it was fortunate for the men of the village that there was a greater diversity of jobs available by 1891. There were more carpenters, house painters and bricklayers. Three men were designated in the census return as plumbers, two as railway porters and two as postmen. There was a chimney sweep, a tailor, and a hairdresser's assistant. Four men were commercial clerks; and seven were railway clerks, perhaps owing something to the influence of Sir Allen Sarle. There were more shops, and a firm of coal merchants at the station. At a slightly different level, there were five

5   For some reason, no details are entered in the 1891 Census return for the residents of Canons Farm, Reads Rest, Can Hatch and Perrotts Farm. Census figures are never totally reliable; but the discrepancies are not of much significance in the present context.

publicans, five farm bailiffs, five gamekeepers, a railway station-master, and six men rated as blacksmiths. Two men were recognised as building contractors. The Metropolitan Police force was represented by an Inspector, three sergeants and eleven constables.

For women, on the other hand, there were not a great many jobs available apart from domestic service. Sixteen were recorded as being laundresses, and eight as dress-makers. One or two worked with their husbands in their shops - tailoring and drapery. There were six women school teachers, and four nurses. At the other end of the scale, six women were still working as farm labourers. In all, rather less than a third of the females of fourteen years of age or more were in paid employment, and of these at least three out of four were in domestic service.

Amongst the more prosperous people in the Banstead village area, the variety of businesses and professions in 1891 is evident, as is the fact that many of them would have to travel to London or further to work. Sir Allen Sarle, who was General Manager of the London, Brighton and South Coast Railway, was a regular "commuter" on the railway. Others may have travelled less regularly. They included five wine merchants. (Banstead had long been the home of wine importers.) Professional people included a solicitor, a doctor in general practice, a civil engineer, an electrical engineer, an insurance underwriter, an architect, a banker, and a company secretary who was stated also to be a Professor of Music. There was a shipowner, and manufacturers of such useful items as varnish, dog biscuits, linen and mustard. In 1871 the number of residents in this sort of prosperous category had been about fifteen. By 1891 there were at least twice as many. The pattern of jobs available in the village was inevitably affected.

The Mail

One of the needs of the changing community would be a better mail service. The staff of the grocer/sub-postmaster in Banstead in 1881 included a Post Office telegraphist, two letter carriers and a telegraph messenger. By 1895, Mrs. Betsy Ann Tonge had succeeded her husband as grocer/postmistress; and there was another sub-post office at Burgh Heath. Letters arrived at the offices by horse messenger three times each weekday, to be dispatched four times each day. On Sunday there was one arrival and one dispatch.[6]

Delivery of the mail sometimes carried certain hazards. On New Year's Day 1881, a letter carrier, Joseph Harbour, was charged before the Epsom Justices with being drunk in charge of letters at "North Hill, Banstead"

---

6   Further details of postal services to the village are contained in Chapter 16.

(probably what we know as Nork today). The offence took place at 3.00 pm on Christmas Day. The Epsom Postmaster said that Harbour had started work at 4.30 am.; had had nothing to eat; and had been given home-made wine at two places. The magistrates, however, were unsympathetic. Harbour was fined one pound and ordered to pay nine shillings costs.

Transport

Transport to and from the village still depended heavily on access to the railways. The only new users of the roads would have been cyclists. Throughout the country these road-users had swollen in numbers as the bicycle developed from the unwieldy penny-farthings of the 1870s into machines with pneumatic tyres in the 1880s. Apart from these cycles, traffic on the roads continued to consist almost entirely of horses and horse-drawn vehicles. Motor cars would not make their appearance until the 1890s. If any at all appeared in Banstead, they would have ranked as peculiar rarities, officially restricted during this period to a maximum speed limit of four miles an hour, and subject to a requirement that a man with a red flag should walk in front.

Local Government

Although a root-and-branch reform of local administration was made towards the end of this period, the new machinery of local government needed time to settle down. The reforms saw the abolition of the civil administration functions of County Quarter Sessions. These were transferred to elected County Councils set up under the Local Government Act of 1888. The local government functions of the Parish Vestry were also abolished in 1894, and the Vestry was left only with its duties in connection with the Church.[7]

The first Surrey Council elections were held in January 1889. The councillors were largely of the classes which had dominated local affairs for generations. They included nineteen described as "gentlemen", seven lawyers, six brewers and wine merchants, and five retired army or navy officers. After much argument, the county headquarters were located at Kingston-upon-Thames, and the County Hall was built there in 1893.

From 1894, Urban and Rural District Councils were created to take over sanitary and other matters from existing bodies which had dealt only with particular aspects. An exception was the Poor Law, which continued to be dealt with by the Boards of Guardians. Elected Parish Councils were formed

---

7   This and other aspects of local government are dealt with in Surrey through the Century, 1889-1989, by David Robinson, published by the Surrey County Council in 1989.

at the beginning of 1895, and there was provision for Parish Meetings at which the parishioners in general could comment on local issues.

Under the new structure, Banstead became part of the area of the Epsom Rural District Council, with representatives elected to that body. The Epsom Board of Guardians continued to levy the Poor Law Rate and to administer the Poor Law, with a Medical Officer at Banstead. At the first meeting of the Banstead Parish Council, Allen Sarle was elected Chairman, with Henry Knibbs as Clerk of the Council.

The village school continued to provide elementary education under the strict eyes of Mr. and Mrs. Knibbs. The County Council had at that time no power to provide elementary education; but it was given power by the Technical Instruction Acts of 1889 and 1891 to promote "technical and manual instruction". This included the teaching of children over elementary school-leaving age, as well as adults, in technical, scientific, artistic and domestic subjects.

The County Council Educational Committee provided scholarships to existing secondary schools for children of 12 to 14 over a period of three years. The Committee also made "science grants" to some of these schools. They cooperated with local bodies to found new schools. Among these new schools was the Sutton County Secondary School. Other measures included the provision of gardens for teaching practical horticulture in schools. By 1894 one such garden, described as a "Fruit School", had been set up at Banstead.

The Banstead Cricket Club

Cricket on the Green continued to flourish. The status of the Banstead Cricket Club was formalised and established, though its tenure of the ground remained precarious. A preliminary meeting had taken place on 21 April 1874, when seven members were present: the Honourable P.C. Glyn, son of Lord Wolverton, of Banstead Place; Tom Gilbert, licensee of the Victoria public house; Frederick Lambert; J. Moore, a carpenter; E. Oakshott, a carter; Allen Sarle, now General Manager of the London, Brighton and South Coast Railway; and John Robertson, a wine shipper. The original membership of the club reflected a fair mixture of class and occupation.

With the club thus established, a second meeting was held the same day to appoint Tom Gilbert captain, with responsibility for the mowing and rolling of the pitch. Keys were to be held by him and Henry Knibbs.

During the following week, on 29 April 1874, a Committee meeting was held to consider seventy applications for membership. These included the

Earl of Egmont; Frederick, John, F.A.H., D.H., and E.W. Lambert; Lewis Shallcross; James Tonge; and Police Sergeant Waters. The club clearly enjoyed enthusiastic and influential support.

The main threat to its future lay in its tenure of the ground. Even after 1874, this was simply by permission of the owner, John Lambert of Garratts Hall, at a nominal rent. It was thought that he had promised to leave the ground to the Parish when he died; but he made no such gift in his Will. In 1889 the Trustees of his Estate gave the club notice to quit the ground. The Club's position was secured only by a generous gesture of the Honourable F.H.Baring. He bought the ground and conveyed it to the Vestry under a Trust Deed establishing a Board of Managers of six Trustees.

The Minutes of the Cricket Club over the rest of this period show what a close interest was taken in it by a number of the most prominent residents. For several years Mr. (later Sir) Allen Sarle took the Chair at meetings; whilst the Earl of Egmont was President until 1889, when the Honourable F.H. Baring took over. Later, Mr. Wigram (of Longcroft) acted as Chairman. Certain families had long associations with the club: the Maynard Taylors of Heath House; the Bennetts; the Knibbs; and others.

In 1887, the club asked permission to hold Jubilee Celebrations for the Queen. On a more mundane level, in October 1893, there was discussion over a bill from Mr. Hipwell of ten guineas "for brakes to out matches". This was evidently the normal transport arrangement for "away" games. A horsebrake was a large wagonette with a box seat in front for two passengers and the coachman; with two seats behind, facing inwards, taking five or six men on each side.

The rural aspect of the village, still prevailing in 1894, is illustrated by a complaint to the Club Committee. A number of gentlemen of the Surrey Farmers Staghounds had ridden over the Cricket Ground in pursuit of the hounds, materially damaging the pitch. The action approved was to write a letter asking for an assurance that there would be no repetition of the incident. Such a reaction might strike us as refreshingly mild today!

Entertainments

The village school continued to serve as a venue for various events. A programme of Winter Evening Entertainments at the school for the winter of 1874/5 shows that six events were arranged between November and March. They ranged from a "Chemical Lecture" with experiments and another on "The Philosophy of Heat and Cold" to an Entertainment by "The Royal Black Diamonds of Louisiana" and a Literary and Musical Entertainment by

Messrs. G. Grossmith and Son. A season ticket cost seven shillings and sixpence, whilst seats for one evening cost half a crown, or one shilling and sixpence for back seats. The events were run by a Committee of leading names in the village, with Henry Knibbs as Honorary Secretary.

There was still no public hall in the village and no doubt this meant that the public houses continued to be common meeting places. How far football and other pastimes of the period, such as cycling, were favoured by the villagers of Banstead is a matter for conjecture.

For the richer members of the community, there would have been plenty of scope for riding, shooting and hunting. There were house parties for friends and relations, and grand occasions from time to time. One such was a fancy-dress ball, given by Mrs. Frederick Lambert at Garratts Hall around 1890. It was held on Twelfth Night, and was reported to have been a great success in spite of the weather, which prevented the arrival of some guests, owing to the bad state of the roads.

As it was, over one hundred and fifty guests did arrive. The band of the Middlesex Yeomanry was in attendance, and the dancing continued until a late hour. The costumes were reported to have been unusually good, with everyone "successfully representing the individual character selected". Ladies were to be found dressed respectively as Evening Star, Frost, Moonlight, Dresden China, Boulogne Fishwife, Neapolitan Fishgirl, Queen Elizabeth, and Duchess of Devonshire. Not to be outdone, gentlemen appeared as a Catalan Peasant, Afghan Merchant, French Cook, Charles Surface, Oliver Cromwell, Gentleman of the time of George III, Brigand, and a "20th Century Masher"... It is hoped that they all got home safely and were able to resume their own characters without any confusion!

Looking back now, it can be seen that in 1895 Banstead, and the country as a whole, were on the verge of great changes. The advance of the motor vehicle, and increasing intervention by central and local government would be notable features of the early years of the 20th century.

Chapter 5

Banstead from 1895 -1913

The New Age

In the late 1890s, there seems to have been a quickening of the pulse at the thought of the approach of the twentieth century. When the turn of the century was followed, in January 1901, by the end of Queen Victoria's reign of more than sixty years, the feeling was increased that a New Age had arrived.

In many ways, changes were in fact afoot in this period. For instance, the County Council and District Councils had, by the beginning of the period, become firmly established, with new powers and duties being regularly given to them. Government departments were replacing a miscellany of bodies and taking over their particular functions. There was also in the latter part of the period a good deal of legislation on new social services, such as old age pensions, national insurance, and labour exchanges. Public intervention had become much more common in ordinary everyday life.

Transport

Motor vehicles, which at the turn of the century were still regarded as a luxury and rarity, had by the end of this period become commonly used. This was another change with far-reaching consequences. It is said that the first cars in Banstead belonged to the two wealthy landowners, the Gartons, who had a Rolls Royce, and the Colmans, who had a Mercedes. To have one's own car was still a special privilege, even at the end of this period; but enough vehicles were on the roads, even by 1907, for complaints to arise about "the dust and nuisance" caused by them. By 1908 the Parish Council was asking for control on vehicles in Banstead High Street. Four years later, in 1912, they asked for a Motor speed limit to be imposed on the stretch of the

Figure 15. Banstead and surrounding area in 1913 / 1914

Brighton Road from Garratts Lane to Chipstead Road. This was turned down by the County Council, but the Automobile Association agreed to put up warning notices of "Concealed Turnings".

Another indication of the new state of affairs was that Mr. Coomber, who for years had carried on the business of "fly proprietor" from premises behind Ivy Cottage, was from 1911 described as "motor car proprietor". Occasional transport by car had become possible for anybody in Banstead who could afford to pay for the ride. For those with cars, Mr. George Weeks was by 1911 available to give them service as "motor engineer".

Most people, however, would have to rely on other kinds of transport, particularly the railways. A development in this respect was the creation and extension of the Chipstead Valley railway line, which reached Kingswood in 1897; Tadworth in 1900; and Tattenham Corner in 1901. The final extension was motivated, as the Epsom Downs line had been earlier, by the hope of profits from the Race traffic; and, on Derby Day 1901, Tattenham Corner received forty thousand passengers. No doubt the hope was also held that residential development would spring up in the neighbourhood of the new stations, giving rise to enough regular passengers to make the line pay its way. This did not happen at that time in the Tattenham Corner area. Eventually regular services were discontinued to that station: the trains terminated at Tadworth, except on Race days.

Property

As to development and ownership of land in the Banstead area, this was a time of relatively little change, with two main exceptions. The Nork Estate remained intact, for although Mr. F. E. Colman died in 1900, his widow survived him. Mr. C. H. Garton remained at Banstead Wood, and indeed slightly increased his landholdings in 1906/7, when he bought what had become known as the Holly Hill estate from Colonel F.A.H. Lambert, and some land on the other side of Holly Lane from the John Lambert Trustees. In 1913 he conveyed most of this estate, to one of his sons, C. L. Garton, who had already built Holly Hill House on the estate. Another son, A. S. Garton, was installed at Wood Lodge, a house built near the Brighton Road. (This is now Aberdour School). John Lambert's Trustees continued from time to time to dispose of other parts of his estate, but a great deal remained in their hands.

Building Developments

Of the two main developments in this period, the first had begun before 1891. Five houses had been built on the part of Shrubland Road which had at that time been laid down; and twenty six houses had been built on the partially laid down Diceland Road. This development continued over the next decade and beyond. Diceland Road was completed, and Ferndale Road laid down, as was part of Lyme Regis Road at the Brighton Road end.

Shrubland Road and Lyme Regis Road remained incomplete and unconnected. By 1905, however, Shrubland, Ferndale and Diceland Roads were adopted and made up by the Epsom Rural District Council, but house owners who had frontage on these roads had to pay the cost of having them made up. By 1913, housing along these roads had been practically completed. Some houses had also been built on the southern side of Chipstead Road, as well as a few on the Brighton Road frontage.

In all there were by this time over one hundred houses in this area, together with a few shops, a grocery/sub-post office, a bootmaker, and a builder's yard. The old Wheatsheaf public house stood on the Brighton Road near the junction with Garratts Lane. (It would in 1938/9 be replaced by the new building, further back from the road). All this amounted to a new community, separate and distinct from the village, which still lay to the east of the church.

It seems probable that a good many of the people living in this new community were employed outside Banstead, since the area was reasonably near to the Banstead railway station. The Parish Council minutes show that complaints about the train service were received in 1903 and 1904 from residents in this area. They were asking for earlier and later trains to be run on the Epsom Downs Branch. In November 1904 the London, Brighton and South Coast Railway agreed to run an earlier train in the morning and a later one in the evening, as from 1 April 1905. This may be regarded as the first specific provision of "commuter trains" to and from Banstead. It indicated, too, a considerable increase in the number of local commuters. That increase would continue until ultimately it altered the nature of the whole village.

The second main development of consequence in this period was the building of houses on the north side of Court Road. The indefatigable schoolmaster, Henry Knibbs, in 1902 had bought from the John Lambert Trustees land on that side of the road. In 1903 Knibbs sold off building sites towards the western end. On these sites a row of houses were built as far as the present line of the footpath from Court Road towards the church. This path, which had formerly run diagonally across to the churchyard from a point opposite Court Farm, had been diverted for this purpose. Two large semi-detached houses, South Lea and Prior's Lea, and one large detached house, Sixways, were also built at the eastern end of Court Road. Until his death in 1908, Henry Knibbs and his family lived in Sixways. Mrs. Knibbs later lived in Prior's Lea.

A piece of land north of Court Road, between the diverted footpath and South Lea, was sold in 1904 by Henry Knibbs to a committee of parishioners, who gave it to the Ecclesiastical Commissioners for an extension of the churchyard. A part of this, in 1973, became the site of a new vicarage.

Another piece of land was also in 1904 acquired for an extension of the churchyard. This was the land between All Saints Church and the High Street. It was conveyed to the Parish by the Earl of Egmont for a nominal sum.

Two major developments of land have been mentioned in this chapter. A third development involved the laying down of the road known as De Burgh Park, southwards from the corner of Court and Avenue Roads, and the erection of four large semi-detached houses and one large detached house between the new road and the Cricket Ground.

Several large houses were also built in or off Park Road beyond The Mint public house. These were Hilden and The Homestead on the western side, and Walworth House on the eastern side. In 1913, Larklands was built on the western side for Sir Henry Lambert, who moved there from The Larches on the Brighton Road. Further along Park Road, on the eastern side, a new private road, Soloms Court Road, led to the house named Soloms Court, erected on land bought from John Lambert's trustees.

Development in the High Street

There were some changes in the High Street. The Metropolitan Police bought a plot of land south of the High Street, on which a new Police Station was built. It stands there today, with extensions made to the original building. They vacated the building on the other side of the road in front of Buff House, which they had occupied since 1852. No doubt they needed more space. By 1907, there were stationed at Banstead, besides the Station Sergeant, five other sergeants and eighteen constables. This may have been due to a policy of sending to Banstead policemen who simply had a few more years to qualify for their pensions. They could hardly have been fully occupied in fighting crime in the area, except possibly on Race days.

Of more direct benefit to the residents was the building in 1906 of the Church (or Village) Institute, on part of the land north of All Saints Church. This was made possible by a gift of one thousand pounds from the brother of the Reverend Duncan Woodroffe. The latter had just succeeded the Reverend E. V. Buckle as Vicar of Banstead, thus ending the line of Buckles who had

Figure 16. Rosehill School, the Garden Front

Figure 17. Rosehill School, The Playing Field

held the Vicarage since 1823. The Institute was to be in the nature of a Parish Club for recreation, games and entertainments, with a room for classes and the like, and a larger hall with a platform. It was to fulfil a need, which had been evident for many years, to supplement or replace the use of the Village School for meetings and entertainments. In 1907, a Working Men's Club was founded at the Institute.

Private Schools

Banstead became recognised at this time as a suitable place for the more expensive kinds of schooling. Banstead Hall was already established and flourishing as a preparatory school for boys, and in 1901 more land in Bolters Lane was acquired to extend the playing fields as far as Bolters Corner. E. J. Maitland, the founder and headmaster, died in 1903; but the school was carried on briefly by his widow, and then, from 1907, by their son, Captain J. E. Maitland.

They were to have new neighbours in 1913, when Sir Henry Lambert, having moved to Larklands in Park Road, let The Larches to Miss A. C. Molyneaux, who for a number of years ran a school there called The Larches Girls' College.

In 1898, Miss Mary Ellen Mason had bought the building called The Lodge, further along the Brighton Road, between what was to become Lyme Regis Road and Chipstead Road. The Lodge had been built in 1860 as a farmhouse, and more recently had been occupied by a Mr. Harrington Hudson, and, after his death, by his widow. Miss Mason made considerable extensions and alterations to the building. One very large room was constructed on the ground floor, and later a further storey was added. Then Miss Mason opened The Lodge as a high-class "finishing college" for young ladies.

Not very far away, Garratts Hall, in Garratts Lane, and the land held with it passed in 1902 from Frederick Lambert to his son, Colonel F.A.H. Lambert, who let it to Mrs. Mary Louisa Davies. She set it up as a Girls' Boarding School which proved highly successful. According to the Reverend A.W. Hopkinson, who, as Vicar of Banstead, knew Mrs. Davies and her school from 1918 onwards, "She had no academic qualifications, no capital, no influence, she had a trying Cockney accent, and latterly was almost blind... Nevertheless, by sheer force of personality and amazing courage she built up one of the most lucrative schools in England." One of her pupils was Megan, daughter of the Liberal Prime Minister, David Lloyd George.[1]

1 A.W. Hopkinson, Pastor's Progress, published by The Faith Press, ed. 1958.

At the other end of the village, another high-class school arrived in 1903. A large house, known as Rooks Nest, belonging to the John Lambert Trustees, stood on the western side of Park Road, on a considerable area of land stretching back westwards to The Green and south-west well beyond The Green. For a short time, around 1900-1902, it was occupied as a preparatory school called Appuldurcome, which owed its name to its origins in the Isle of Wight. When the property was put up for sale in 1902, it was bought by Mr. and Mrs. Percy Browning, who were then running the flourishing Rosehill School for boys in Tunbridge Wells. In 1903 they moved to Banstead with most of their staff and pupils, absorbed Appuldurcome School, and set up a new Rosehill School on the Rooks Nest property.

Rosehill became a leading preparatory school for boarders, with ample grounds, playing fields, a kitchen garden, and farmland which provided milk and vegetables for the school. The whole property contained about fifty acres, including much of the open land between Park Road and Holly Lane.

The author, Rupert Croft-Cooke, whose parents were living in Chipstead, was sent to Rosehill School as a boarder in 1910 at the age of seven, and remained there until December 1914. He later described life in the school as he remembered it.[2] Mr. Browning as Headmaster and his wife as Matron were personally and totally involved in running the establishment. Memories that rankled with young Rupert were the over-frequent use of the Headmaster's cane; the "cramming" system of teaching; and undue restrictions on the young pupils' visits to the outside world. Yet he appears to have retained happy memories as well of the school and the friends he made there. He applied the phrase "merits and evils" to his preparatory school; and probably, for such a school at this period, it was considerably better than the average.

The existence of these schools in the immediate vicinity of the village cannot fail to have provided extra trade for the local shopkeepers and tradesmen, and some degree of employment. They also had an effect on the social life of the village.

Back in 1895, Mr. E. J. Maitland of Banstead Hall had become one of the first Parish Councillors. He was also, along with Tom Gilbert, one of the Overseers of the Parish for Poor Law purposes. His son and successor, J. E. Maitland, followed his father as a very active member of the Council. As for members of the school staffs, their influence was particularly strong in the Banstead Cricket Club, round which much of the social life turned. This applied particularly in the summer, when the Green was the venue for outdoor events of various sorts besides cricket.

2 Rupert Croft-Cooke, The Gardens of Camelot, pub. Putnam, London, 1958

The Green and the Cricket Club

Bernard Knibbs, a son of Henry Knibbs by his second marriage, recalled the sports meeting held on The Green to celebrate the Queen's Diamond Jubilee in 1897. There were running races, jumping contests and tugs-of-war. Samuel Stevens, then licensee of The Woolpack, won the "throwing the cricket ball" competition; and there was a "greasy pole" about twenty-five feet high, with a leg of pork at the top to be won by whoever could climb it.

Among Rupert Croft-Cooke's memories of his years at Rosehill School was the music of the local band, playing for villagers dancing on The Green, while he was in the School dormitory on summer nights. The school groundsman looked after a big acetylene lamp which was put up on a pole, while the villagers danced to tunes such as Alexander's Ragtime Band. The author described the music as "coming mysteriously up behind the great chestnut trees beyond the school gardens".

The Cricket Club itself had become quite ambitious over the years in its fixture list. Mr. Wigram, of Longcroft in Woodmansterne Lane, had as early as 1887 arranged matches against socially high-class clubs such as Incogniti and Oxford Harlequins, in spite of the fact that at that time part of the outfield was neither closely mown nor rolled. In 1891 "Cricket Weeks" were started, and in 1893 a Second Eleven was formed. Following the opening of the Banstead Hall School, there was an influx of playing members from the half a dozen assistant masters on the staff. They had been well coached at school and university. Bernard Knibbs recorded[3] that they played a higher class of cricket than the club had been used to, and they invited friends from their own social class to join them. The First Eleven thus became largely their preserve, and the villagers were relegated to playing in the Second Eleven.

This was bound, in the long run, to create ill-feeling, especially as there was evidently some social distinction drawn between the two teams. In 1898 the ladies of Banstead gave the club a tea marquee and twenty-five chairs. But the marquee was put up only on the days when the First Eleven was playing at home; and it was strictly reserved for the use of first team members and their ladies throughout this period. From 1903 the division between the two teams grew still wider. The staff of Rosehill School now became available, and social class seemed even more clearly to rule the choice of First Eleven players.

The new regime had its advantages. Up till 1905, Tom Gilbert, of the Victoria Inn, who farmed land adjoining the inn, had supplied a man and a

3   In a draft History of the club, and in a taped interview with members of the Banstead History Research Group.

Figure 18. Horse-drawn mower on the Cricket Club Ground

horse to mow the field with the club's mowing machine. In 1905, for the first time, a groundsman was employed for the season. He rolled the outfield with a heavy water-filled roller, and cut it with a mower. Roller and mower were drawn by a horse which had been given to the Club by a member. When working on the field, the horse wore leather boots with flat soles. In 1906, sight-screens were bought; and in 1907 a drink licence was obtained.

The Club had become one of the strongest round London, with a fixture list to match its strength. Amongst the more notable fixtures were matches against the London County Cricket Club. This team had been set up for the Grand Old Man of English cricket, Dr. W. G. Grace, who managed it when he parted company with Gloucestershire towards the end of his career. This former English captain played several times against Banstead at his club's ground at the Crystal Palace, and at least twice he played at Banstead[4]. In the match on The Green on 27th June 1904, at the age of fifty-six, he opened the innings and scored twenty-nine runs. He went on to bowl nine overs and took one wicket for forty runs.

---

4   Records of these appearances are contained in a book, W. G. Grace, The Great Cricketer, by
    G. Neville Weston, published in 1973.   Other information is from B. Knibbs' draft History
    and other people's recollections.

There are many stories about "W. G.'s" occasional tantrums at this time, especially when he was given "out" before the spectators had been given a proper sight of his batting. One such story applies to a match at Banstead from which he is said to have gone home in a huff. A more probable story, which has long been a tradition in the Gilbert family, is that the great man, whose second name was Gilbert, was a relation by marriage of this Banstead family. Tom Gilbert, licensee of the Victoria Inn, was a founder member and for years Captain of the Banstead Club. It is said that W. G. Grace visited the Inn when he came to Banstead, before going on to the Green with one of the Gilbert children.

The minutes of the Banstead club show that on several occasions entertainments were held in the School Gymnasium at Banstead Hall; and a dance was held at Rosehill School. The Club and its incidental activities must have been a very pleasant feature of Banstead's social life for those who could fully enjoy it, though perhaps not quite so pleasant for the villagers who were in part excluded from it.

In about 1908 a hockey club was formed. It played on the cricket field and included some of the cricketers; but it did not last for more than a few years. There also appear in these years to have been teams who played cricket and football in a less formal atmosphere on one of the fields near the Victoria Inn. Sometimes they were dignified with the name Banstead Victoria; but in the village they were more commonly known, for obvious reasons, as The Moppers. No doubt there were other sporting activities of which no records have survived.

Population

No detailed statistics for these years are available to enable trends in population and occupations in Banstead to be accurately stated. The total population for the whole parish, apart from staff and patients at the Asylum, was stated to be 2,338 in 1891 and 2,947 in 1901. In 1911 the total was 4,070. The number of inhabited houses rose from 438 in 1891 to 557 in 1907. By 1911 this total had reached 809. It is unlikely that these increases were due to any rise in employment. They are much more likely to have resulted from the arrival in the parish of new residents: some of independent means; some in retirement; some working elsewhere. The sharper rate of increase in the second decade (1901 - 1911) corresponded with the general trend of Londoners to move further out as better transport and housing facilities became available.

Roads and Public Services

The newcomers would be concerned with the standard of essential services available to them in their houses and streets. New streets could be in a very primitive state until they were adopted and taken over by the Epsom Rural District Council, normally at the expense of the owners of premises fronting on the road. Even then, the surfaces would be fairly rough, consisting of granite chippings and flints on top, rolled in by a steam roller. Flints for this purpose were "knapped" by hand. As late as the beginning of the twentieth century, a "flint knapper" could be seen at work at the corner of Court Road; and farmers would pay one halfpenny for a pail of flints to be knapped, for putting down on the road surface.[5]

By 1899, water mains had been laid in the Brighton Road by the Sutton District Water Company. Besides water, gas, supplied by the Sutton Gas Company, was available by 1903 in Court Road and Bolters Lane. In the following two years the Ferndale Road area was also serviced. Main sewerage, however, would not be available anywhere in Banstead for many years; nor would street lighting. Both were regarded by many residents as unnecessary or expensive luxuries.

In July 1904 a long correspondence started over the provision of telephones in the Banstead area, when the Parish Council wrote to the Post Office Telephone Department. All sorts of difficulties were raised. In 1908 the Post Office reported that the necessary wayleaves for posts and lines over the Common had almost been settled; but there would be a further delay, because the Telephone Exchange was to be at Burgh Heath instead of Banstead. Finally, the Exchange was opened in 1909 at the back of a grocer's shop, Roberts' Stores, at Burgh Heath. Although later the exchange was located in Banstead, its name was to survive as Burgh Heath.

Shops

A number of shops in Banstead which had been open in 1895 were still in operation at the end of this period. In particular, Mrs. Betsy Ann Tonge remained as grocer/sub-postmistress. New businesses included the schools which have been mentioned. Other new businesses in the village included a saddler and harness maker, two firms of builders, a doctor, a hairdresser, a baker, a confectioner, a dairy shop, a motor engineer, and a branch of the London and Provincial Bank. In the Diceland and Pound Roads area, there were two new firms of builders, a bootmaker, two grocers, and a dairyshop.

---

5   This was recalled by the late Mrs. Mabel Baker in an interview recorded in 1988.

There was also a music teacher.[6] Overall, there had been a certain growth in shopping facilities; but no great housing developments.

Public Education

For local children, the Village (or Board) School continued from 1895 to provide elementary education, normally up to the age of thirteen.   In conjunction with the Surrey County Council, a Technical Committee of the Parish Council supplemented this with extra classes for school leavers. These classes included woodcarving, carpentry and drawing, a domestic class, and what were called "Boys' Continuation School Gardens" at Burgh Heath, the Pound and Yewlands. In March 1896 the committee reported that attendances at the classes had not been up to the County Council average requirements of ten for the wood-carving and twenty for the domestic class. Nonetheless, classes were currently being held in horticulture, home nursing, dress cutting, first aid, wood carving, carpentry and drawing.

The Continuation School Gardens scheme had been very successful and prizes had been gained. A "Bee Van", supplied by the County Council, had visited "The Centre" and aroused great interest. A "Travelling Dairy School", of Kent and Surrey County Councils, had come to Banstead in October 1895 from the Agricultural College which had been set up jointly by the two Councils at Wye in Kent. This Dairy School organised a course of lectures and practical instruction in butter-making in a tent put up in a field owned by Mr. Shove. Twelve pupils had passed the examination with credit; and one pupil, Winifred Couchman, had been sent on a six-weeks course in dairy work at the Agricultural College.

As already mentioned, the County Council had set up scholarships to existing grammar schools; in addition, they had begun to found their own County Secondary Schools. For boys, one such was set up at Sutton; whilst for girls, a County Secondary School was founded at Wallington. The bright scholar at the village school in Banstead could hope to win a scholarship to one of these fee-paying schools. Getting to school would probably involve a train journey from Banstead.

In 1902 schools providing elementary education were also brought under the County Council, and became known as Council schools. This led to improved standards of teaching and school maintenance, and a school medical service.

6   Information from Kelly's Directory.

Figure 19. Cookery at the Village School, 1910.
Mary Baldwin, owner of the exercise book below, is in the front row, 3rd child from the left

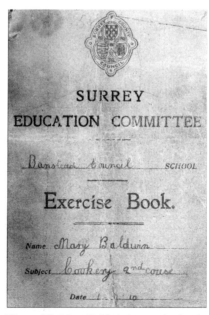

Figure 20. Mary Baldwin's exercise book.

End of an Era

Henry Knibbs was now coming to the end of his long career. He was Headmaster of the village school, Clerk of the Parish Council, Assistant Overseer of the Poor, one of the managers of the cricket ground, and holder of various other posts in the village. He retired as Headmaster in 1904, but remained Clerk of the Parish Council, and was active in other spheres until his death in 1908. The village had for some forty years been accustomed to the considerable influences of the Reverend E. V. Buckle as vicar and Henry Knibbs as schoolmaster and parish official. These two influences both came to an end at a time when village life was entering into a period of considerable change.

Chapter 6

The War Period 1914 - 1918

The World War, which broke out on the 4th of August 1914, interrupted the steady development of the village and seriously affected the lives even of those who were not called up for military service.

From accounts which have been given of life in general at this time, it is clear that at first the expectation was of a short war which need not affect the future too seriously. To boys such as Rupert Croft-Cooke, the war at first was seen as "an almighty football match between the nations, a match which we were jolly well going to win." He wrote of the boys' thrill at their first sight of a column of soldiers marching past the school in September 1914, and their changing feelings as the war went on.[1] As the months passed, the lists of casualties mounted; restrictions and regulations multiplied; and shortages of many kinds resulted in rationing or, simply, "going without". The mood then changed to one of determination to "carry on", to "make do", and to place all hopes on the distant prospect of an end to the fighting. What lay beyond that was too far ahead for most people even to contemplate.

The records of the Parish Council show how the Council coped with the changing situation. Mr. C. H. Garton, owner of Banstead Wood House and the extensive estate held with it, remained as Chairman of the Council throughout these years, and other councillors continued to serve. The older generation had a special part to play in this and other ways in keeping things going.

One of the first problems, with which the Surrey County Council was particularly concerned, was that of unemployment arising from dislocation of trade. To deal with this, one of the measures taken was to provide money for road widening and highway improvements.[2]

---

1 "The Gardens of Camelot" (op.cit.) page 219, which contains an evocative passage.

Figure 21. Pound Stores

For its part, the Parish Council of Banstead, at a special meeting on the 19th of August 1914, considered what steps should be taken to deal with any distress arising from the War. A Committee was set up to collect funds for local needs. A formal appeal was organised for a War Relief Fund. In October 1914 it was reported that seven wives and ten mothers of men with the Colours had been "relieved" in September, and seven wives and fourteen mothers in October, at a total cost of £28. 3 shillings. In November 1914, receipts for the War Relief Fund stood at £455. 13 shillings; and £36. 14s. 3d. had been spent. It was then decided to keep a register of unemployed.

By the middle of 1915, the country had plainly settled down to a prolonged war. Regulations and organisations were set up, both at the national and at local level, to husband resources and to keep production going both in the factories and on the farms. Unemployment was no longer a problem. The War Relief Fund in Banstead had apparently become less urgently needed: £300 of surplus money in the Fund was invested in July 1915.

---

2 A general account of the County Council's activities appears in Surrey through the Century by Dr. Robinson (S.C.C. 1989).

On the other hand, everybody at home was becoming involved in one aspect or another of the "war effort". In October 1915, the Parish Council set up a committee to assist in the formation of a Village War Food Society to increase the supply of home-grown foods. In April 1916, a start was made to acquire land for further allotments. Part of the field called Horsecroft, east of the Brighton Road, and owned by R. W. Shallcross, lent itself to this purpose. On being approached, Mr. Shallcross replied that Horsecroft was "building land" and could not be let at an agricultural rent. Mr. Garton then offered some of his own land "near Pit Barn" for the purpose. This satisfied demand in the Pound Road area. In Court Road, Mr. Adams, of West View, granted shared use of land.

As the War ground on, and more men went into the Services, women were encouraged or required to take on jobs which, up to then, had traditionally been done by men. The services of school children were increasingly used in harvesting, and in growing food in "school gardens" and elsewhere.

Basic needs for the community became the subject of public controls to a degree never before contemplated, but now welcomed. In October 1916, the Parish Council, having received a complaint as to the increased price of milk, instructed the Clerk to write to the Prime Minister, the Local Government Board, and the Board of Trade, to urge that production and sale of milk be placed under Government control. In June of that year, a Sub-Committee of the Parish Council had been set up to consider the purchase of coal to meet the needs of poor people; because, it was said, much suffering had been caused by indifferent supply in the previous year. In reply, the Local Government Board informed them that the supply of coal was made under a scheme by the Coal Controller, to whom the Clerk to the Council was instructed to write.

There were some bizarre proposals to assist the War Effort. In July 1917, the Epsom Rural District Council offered rewards for killing house sparrows to save the crops: three-pence per dozen for fully-fledged sparrows; two-pence a dozen for unfledged sparrows; and one penny a dozen for eggs. After discussion, it was agreed that Mr. Gale, the schoolmaster who had taken over the Village School and become a Parish Councillor, might be authorised to pay for sparrows killed and eggs seized in the parish. But it was insisted that the bodies and eggs should then be sent to Epsom for inspection by one of the officials, a Mr. Jay! The Parish Council considered that this was too much and the Epsom proposal was finally rejected.

Air Raids

A more serious consideration was the potential danger from air raids. These raids were a new phenomenon in World War I. The first raids on this country were by Zeppelin airships in 1915. Although they were intended for London, the airships for the most part failed to reach the capital, and dropped their bombs elsewhere. Some fell on Woolwich and some on Guildford. Another Zeppelin, having bombed Shorncliffe Camp, then passed over South London, Croydon and Tunbridge Wells. The raids were not negligible. In 1915, 209 people were killed, and £800,000 worth of damage was caused.

1916 was the busiest year of Zeppelin raids, aimed at Liverpool and the Midlands as well as London, although London was still the main target. Two or three Zeppelins were shot down in the London area.

Some of these Zeppelins had probably passed over Banstead, and the raids on London were visible from the village. Mr. Edgeler, then a small boy living with his parents and grand-father at the Pound Stores in Pound Road, used to see the searchlights sweeping the skies at night. On one occasion, he was called out of bed to watch the spectacle of a Zeppelin in flames over London. On another night, when the family had reached Banstead Station after a visit to London, he saw another Zeppelin shot down.[3]

From the autumn of 1916 onwards, air raids were made by aeroplanes, sometimes in combination with Zeppelins; but later the planes were largely on their own. These raids were often made by daylight in the spring and summer of 1917. After that, they were mostly by night. They caused many casualties and much damage in London and elsewhere. For Londoners the raids were extremely frightening. On September 30th 1917, at the end of a concerted week of raids, some 300,000 people were sheltering in the London Underground system, causing a state of chaos. Thousands of other civilians fled to the countryside.[4]

It does not appear that Banstead was itself hit by bombs; but by October 1917 the raids over London had become a matter of great concern in the village. A request was received by the Parish Council from the Epsom Poor Law Guardians to provide any accommodation for Londoners that might be necessary during air-raids. In November, it was decided that the Church Institute and the Council Schools could be used as emergency refuges for this purpose. Proper supervision would be provided, in conjunction with the police. There does not appear to be any record of this arrangement having been implemented, but it was obviously a sensible precaution.

---

3   This and other recollections of Mr. Edgeler were recorded on tape by B.H.R.G.

4   General information as to the raids is contained in "The Bombers" by Rupert Cross. Bantam Press, 1987.

Climax of the War and Plans for Peace time

At the beginning of 1918, whilst the catalogue of wartime shortages and wartime measures continued to dominate affairs, thoughts were beginning to turn to post-War requirements. Consequently, on the 28th of January 1918, the Parish Council had a diversity of items on their agenda. First, they made a complaint to the Epsom Rural District Council about the state of the roads during recent frost and snow. This was rejected by the Rural District Council, who described the complaint as "unpatriotic and unfair". The second item on the Parish Council agenda concerned the prospects of setting up a Communal Kitchen in the Parish. Possibly it was as a result of this that a Soup Kitchen was set up in a tin hut next to the Village School. Item three on the agenda, on the other hand, was to enquire of the Epsom Rural District Council what action was proposed for "Housing the Working Classes" after the War. In February 1918 another pest-killing exercise was proposed, this time by the County Council, concerned to get rid of rats. It was agreed to publish notices offering one shilling per dozen of rats' tails. The results of this are not recorded.

In April 1918, land for allotments in Horsecroft, to the west of the footpath, was finally obtained from Mr. Shallcross.

In May 1918, consideration of post-War housing problems reached a positive stage. In that month the Epsom Rural District Council stated that in their opinion fifteen "cottages" should be erected in Banstead, including ten already provided for; and recommendations as to sites were requested. In June, the Parish Council considered four possible sites. The first was of about five acres, consisting of Horsecroft and adjoining land. The second suggestion, made by the Vicar, was glebe land north of the High Street, opposite the Vicarage. The third suggestion was the west end of the Town Garden, belonging to Lord Egmont, and lying south of the High Street at the Bolters Lane end. The fourth suggestion made, despite the disapproval of Sir Ralph Neville of Banstead Place, was land near Apsley Cottages in Park Road. The Parish Council recommended purchase of the Horsecroft site; but, as will be seen, other land became available in 1919, and none of these four sites were taken.

All this time, the havoc of war continued, with tragic consequences for many of those who had been "carrying on" and beginning to plan for the peacetime to come. In October 1916 the death on active service of one of Mr. Garton's sons had been recorded; and in October 1918 another of his sons was killed.

Figure 22. The War Memorial, High Street

During the War, the Vicar and congregation of All Saints' Church had endeavoured to obtain news of men at the Front, and to make this news known in the Parish through the Church Magazine. The issue of the Magazine for December 1918, the month after the War had ended, contained revealing and poignant items under the heading of "War Notes".

One man had served in France since October 1914, and had been awarded the Military Medal; three men, now home on leave, had been in France since early 1915; one had been in France for three months and then in Salonica for three years; two more had gone to India in November 1914 and had recently come home from Mesopotamia; one man had died on 13 October from wounds received in action, and after receiving the Military Medal for bravery; and another had been killed in action on the 14th of October, less than a month before the Armistice. One man had died in Palestine from malaria, the second in his family to die on active service; and another man had died on the 12th of November, the day following the Armistice, as a result of pneumonia contracted on active service.

The Magazine also contained a long list of subscribers in 1918 to the Banstead and Burgh Heath Sailors' and Soldiers' Christmas Fund, to provide parcels to be sent to those on active service. This amounted in all to £101. 14s. 4d. A Receipt and Expenditure Account for Red Cross Work for the year showed money raised, in a variety of ways, amounting to £192. 10s. 8d. The community's feelings for those in the Services are clearly underlined.

When it was possible to assess the cost of the War years in terms of lives lost, Memorial Panels in All Saints Church recorded the names of 82 men of the Parish who had died on active service.

Wartime Changes in the Village

In the village itself, it was not to be expected that there would be many positive developments under war-time conditions. The list of trading firms in 1918 remained much as it had been before the War, though in a few cases businesses had changed hands. Mrs. Betsy Ann Tonge continued to preside over the grocery and post office in the High Street; and Edgar Pushman still ran the grocery and post office in Ferndale Road. Samuel Stevens remained landlord of the Woolpack Inn.

One or two of the tradesmen appear to have widened the scope of their activities, perhaps as a result of the shortage of manpower in the village. Walter Oakshott, at No. 1 Shrubland Road, was now advertising himself not only as a carman, contractor and coal and coke merchant, but also as a builder, decorator, plumber and wheelwright. He was also now conducting the business of Undertaker, advertising in the Church Magazine "Funerals personally conducted to all parts. All orders promptly attended to." Thomas Balchin, saddler in the High Street, was agent for three makes of cycles. In addition, he repaired portmanteaux and travelling bags; supplied cricket requisites; hired out cycles by the day or week; and sold Pratt's and Shell Motor Spirit.

The Cricket Club

The sale of cricket requisites must have been principally to the Schools which continued to operate in Banstead throughout the War, for Club cricket had ceased. The Banstead Cricket Club had on the 4th of August 1914 been due to play a match against a Navy team from "H.M.S. Excellent". That match was cancelled, and the club ceased to exist as such for nearly five years. According to Bernard Knibbs, practically every man of military age joined one of the Services in the first month of the War. He added that, whilst the strength of the Club membership in 1914 was not precisely known, it was probable that the number of playing members did not exceed forty at that time. Of those, fourteen died on active service.

Bernard Knibbs went on to say that those members who returned in 1919 found that the Cricket Ground was a hay-field. The first thing to be done was to get it back into playing condition. They attacked the grass with every sort of mowing machine they could lay their hands on. Such good progress was made that they were able to arrange a match for the First of May 1919.

Re-organisation of the Club went on during the year. The men who returned had very different ideas from those held by the members in 1914. They were determined that control of the Club should be exercised by Banstead men; and that the class distinction which had prevailed before the War should be abolished. To this end, a new rule was introduced, which laid down that only residents, past and present, in the Parish of Banstead should be allowed to play for the Club on Saturdays.

General

Looking at the general situation in the area at this time, one sees that, just as there had been little building development during the War, there had been little change in the ownership of land in the Parish. The larger estates remained practically intact. However, the Parish Council had, as has been mentioned, begun consideration in 1918 of post-War housing needs. There would soon be many other changes, to emphasise that the pre-War state of affairs had gone for ever.

Chapter 7

Peace and the First Stages of Development

With the end of the 1914 - 1918 War, there was an evident need to make urgent provisions both to house the very large number of Servicemen to be demobilised and to provide employment for them. The Parish Council, with the Epsom Rural District Council, had made progress towards providing some "cottages", but this took a long time to bear fruit.

Meanwhile, the Parish Council were much concerned with proposals for "Welcome Home for our Fighting Men, Peace Celebrations and a War Memorial". In this connection, there arose what may be called the affair of "The Large German Gun".

A scheme had been proposed for such guns to be displayed in places throughout the country by way of War Memorials. The Tadworth representative on the Parish Council proposed that the Council should take advantage of this scheme. The Council took this up with enthusiasm, asking to be given three large German guns, to be placed in different parts of the Parish. The reply stated that only one such gun was available. It was decided to offer it to the Tadworth War Memorial Committee. Unfortunately, when it came to the point, the Committee had to admit that they had no place for the gun. So the Council had to tell the War Office that "in changed circumstances" they were after all unable to accept it.

In the meantime, a more practical proposal had been made for a conventional War Memorial, to be erected on a small piece of common land at the eastern end of Banstead High Street; and this was implemented in due course.

Land - Purchases for development

As to housing, in October 1919 the Parish Council resolved to ask the Epsom R.D.C. for compulsory purchase of the land at Horsecroft unless a site could be found elsewhere. The reply from the Rural District Council was of great significance, not only as to the site for Council housing. They said that they had purchased part of Winkworth Farm, and had applied for approval to use it as a site for "cottages". In fact, the land which they had bought included very much more than what was needed for the Council's housing projects. It was one item in the list of properties being sold off by the Trustees of the Will of John Lambert, which represented the residuary estate remaining in their hands more than forty years after his death.

The extent of this residuary estate was remarkable. It included about 672 acres, spread widely over the Parish, east of the Brighton Road. Amongst the larger properties were Banstead Place Farm, with two cottages and about 186 acres; "Longcroft", between Woodmansterne Lane and Croydon Lane, at that time a large residence with twelve bedrooms, dairy, stables and grounds, occupying some sixteen acres in all; and Well and Sheep Farms, lying between Croydon Lane and Woodmansterne Lane east of Longcroft with a total area of about 218 acres. Also included were Park Cottage, Wilmot Cottage and Nos. 1 to 4 Jireh Cottages in Park Road; a number of fields described as "fully ripe for building"; the Winkworth Farm buildings adjoining the High Street on the northern side; and about fifty-one acres of Winkworth Farm land, described as "offering an exceptional site for development as a Garden Suburb". It was this last item which was purchased by the Epsom R.D.C.

Winkworth Farm comprised much of the old Commonfield, which had included most of the land from the High Street northwards to Banstead Downs. It lay between Bolters Lane to the west and a track on the east which ran north towards Cheam. In one way or another, John Lambert had acquired the Farmhouse and also some seventy-four acres of the Farm land (not directly adjoining it); whilst A. Uvedale Lambert, of the Buff House branch of the Lambert family, had become entitled to the rest of the Farm land as well as Buff House itself and its grounds.

The purchase of fifty-one acres of John Lambert's land by the Epsom R.D.C., which was completed in 1920, was ultimately to prove to have been the first step towards the conversion of all the Winkworth Farm land into building land, roads and allotments; but for some years most of the land would remain open farm land, with nothing to interrupt the view of Banstead Downs and Belmont to be had from almost any part of the High Street.

The Epsom R.D.C. seem to have been very far-seeing in buying this land in 1920, since it was much more than was needed to meet housing requirements. Part of it was in fact used to dump sewage collected by sewage carts or vans from the village, where no main drainage was at that time available.

The District Council were not the only Council to seize on the opportunity afforded by the sale of John Lambert's Residuary Estate to buy land for purposes assigned to them. When, towards the end of the War, consideration was given to the problems of resettling into civilian life those serving in the Forces, one of the proposals accepted was for County Councils to buy agricultural land, divide it into blocks of smallholdings, and let these to ex-Servicemen in the hope that they would live there and produce crops which, perhaps on a co-operative basis, they could sell locally. This would provide them with housing and jobs. It would also continue the local provision of food, which had been produced in wartime by requisitioning gardens and open spaces for allotments. There were two suitable areas of land available in the auction of John Lambert's estate. The County Council bought these areas, and created on them smallholdings on both sides of Croydon Lane. These were to remain a feature of the district for a great many years.

In 1923 there was held another auction of land in the neighbourhood which was to have far-reaching consequences. Mr. Frederick Colman, owner of the combined Nork and Great Burgh Estate, had died in 1900; but his widow and children had occupied Nork House, and the whole Estate had until then been retained intact. It amounted to some 1320 acres, and included almost all the land bounded by the Brighton Road on the east, by Fir Tree Road on the north and north-west, by Epsom Downs and Walton Downs on the west, and on the south by Corner Farm, Tadworth and the Tadworth Court Estate. With the exception of the small village and common of Burgh Heath, the Estate extended almost as far as what is now Shelvers Way.

Apart from Nork House and its outbuildings, a house called Great Burgh built about 1911 for one of the Colman sons, a riding-school, and a few farmhouses and lodges, the whole area was open land. Some of it near Nork House was parkland; much of it was farmland; and the rest of little use except for recreation or field sports such as shooting or hunting. The Reverend A.W. Hopkinson described it as rough farm land, harbouring so many hares that, when the Beagles met there, every dog had a hare to chase.

Along with the Commons, the Banstead Wood Estate, and the land forming part of John Lambert's Estate, this land had in effect formed a sort of Green Belt protecting Banstead from building development which might otherwise have taken place well before the 1914- 1918 war, since the building potential of the district had been recognised at least as early as the 1870s.

The result of the auction of the Nork Estate, following on the auction of John Lambert's land north of the village High Street, was to open the floodgates to large-scale building developments, both in Nork and in the village. The first part of this remarkable phase of development took place in Nork, starting in 1923. Building development started in the area north of the village High Street in 1926. After that, rapid development continued both in Nork and in the village up to the outset of the Second World War.

The Development Drive

It is of interest to consider the reasons why all this development occurred and continued, as it did, throughout the 1920s and 1930s, years which saw in the country as a whole a series of economic depressions and peaks of unemployment. One obvious factor in the early 1920s was the effect of the complete cessation of house-building throughout the period from 1914 to 1918. This meant, not only that no progress had been made towards improving bad housing conditions existing in 1914, but that the situation had necessarily worsened. In 1923 Banstead Parish Council reported that many cottages in the Parish were unfit for habitation. Closure orders had been made for some, but not carried out. Seventy-two cottages were inhabited by two or more families.

Another general factor was the perennial outward surge of Londoners which had persisted for centuries, assisted by improvements in transport. The 1920s were particularly notable for improvements in public transport in the South East, and especially in and around London. The London General Omnibus Company and others ran larger and better buses and greatly extended their Routes. The London Underground was extended to Morden in 1926; and the Southern Railway (having taken over the earlier competing companies) improved the rail service south and southwest of London enormously, especially by the electrification of lines and co-operation with developers in providing stations expressly to serve newly developing estates, such as Worcester Park and Stoneleigh.[1]

Banstead did not get quite the same boost in public transport services as did some of these areas, but the improvements were sufficient to make it reasonably accessible to the new band of commuters. The attractions of the neighbourhood were coupled with the availability of houses which were relatively lowly priced because labour was cheap and plentiful, as were materials, both British and imported. Employment and salaries amongst

[1]   The whole subject is discussed in Alan A. Jackson's book "Semi-detached London".

office workers and others in financial or administrative jobs in London did not suffer to the same extent as was the case in other parts of the country, where manufacture was the principal source of employment. So the flood of building in the South East continued throughout the years of economic depression.

The Development of Nork

The development of what had been the combined Nork and Great Burgh Estate had its inception when, at the auction in 1923, the whole Estate was bought by a development company called Halden Estates Limited, whose managing director was Mr. G. M. Humphrey. He was a remarkable man. In a brochure, circulated to architects and others potentially interested, he spoke in almost visionary terms of his dreams for the community who would live in the new "garden city" of Nork, "thirteen hundred and twenty acres unspoiled, favoured by nature... as no other... in this lovely England of ours... now to become a land of a thousand homes." He added that he wanted to be able in the future "to look at Nork from Tumble Beacon as the dusk falls on some October evening and see lights twinkle out one by one." It was a vision of "a Nork of happy homes, where men and women live happily, where children scamper, breathing the life-giving oxygen of these uplands, where no prospect is marred by semi-detached and terraced houses."

In a slightly more down-to-earth view, the brochure promised that between two and three hundred acres would remain as open spaces for the health of the residents on the Estate; that all houses would have large gardens; that trees would be preserved; and that every house would be fitted with a telephone at the builders' expense. There would be fields for cricket and football, a Birds' Sanctuary, children's playgrounds, an Open Air Theatre, a Village hall, and "Porcelain Dairies" erected on the Estate to ensure the provision of pure milk. There was also to be a school for children from the kindergarten age up to eight or ten years of age on a lovely ten-acre garden site.

The brochure stated that all the houses at Nork would be detached. Purchasers might employ their own architects and builders, if they so wished. The houses might be small, but they "must be such as will suit the surrounding scenery and differ from but not clash with the design of nearby property." The whole Estate was to be developed in this fashion. Nork was "no ordinary Estate", Halden Houses were "no ordinary houses" and the developers were "no ordinary people". The whole emphasis was on the superiority of the intended development over those with "avenues of ugly suburban roads".

Figure 23. Nork Park Estate looking north, 1930s.

There were a few special properties "available for sale with their original surroundings". These comprised "the existing Nork Park Gardens, Nork Park Mansion itself, some Orchards, a gardener's cottage, and a Gamekeeper's cottage."

It should also be mentioned that the developer had agreed with the Vicar of Banstead to donate a site for a church on the Estate and to pay half the cost of building it.

It is impossible now to judge how far the brochure stated practical possibilities or how far it represented hardline salesmanship. If the developers had succeeded in selling plots as rapidly as they appear to have contemplated, and thereby financed their own building plans, perhaps the Estate would actually have taken shape on the lines laid down in the brochure. But this was not to be. As the Reverend A.W. Hopkinson put it, "The director, though truly a man of imagination, was lacking in other qualities, lacking, most of all, in financial discretion." [2]

Before the development of the Estate had proceeded far beyond its beginnings (for instance, with the building of houses at the top of Nork Way), the Company fell into insuperable financial difficulties and was wound up. Various parts of the Estate had been mortgaged to different sets of mortgagees; and the result was that parts of the Estate were sold off by the mortgagees to a considerable number of builders and development companies, and its development proceeded in a much less planned or organised way than might have been the case, and was spread over a longer period. Indeed, although the main core of the development was still built rapidly, at least one part of the Estate (off Headley Drive) was still being developed in the 1990s.

The story of the actual development of the Nork Estate can be given here only in summary form.[3] Building started in that part of the Estate near Banstead Station and along the existing roads such as Fir Tree Road and the Reigate Road. What was to become Nork Way was the first planned new road, with shops at the northern end. Then followed the building of the upper part of Warren Road, and development on The Drive. As the main drive leading up to Nork House, this had up to then been known as Nork Drive. The upper parts of Tumblewood Road and Beacon Way were also developed.

Houses on the Estate were not necessarily built in continuous blocks or series of plots, but according to the plots which particular builders or developers had bought, and the wishes of particular purchasers. The first

2 Pastor's Progress", op.cit.
3 It is given in much more detail in a series of articles by Geoffrey A. Robinson headed "Nork in the 1920s", in the Nork Quarterly magazine, 1976.

houses had been built in accordance with the original plans. These were detached, with large plots for gardens, and plenty of room for garages, if these were wanted. Later houses were much more varied in character.

From 1924, the development proceeded rapidly. An Association of residents and prospective residents was formed in November 1925 to protect their interests, and membership rose from 138 in September 1927 to 205 in 1928; to nearly 350 by the end of 1929; and to over 600 by the end of 1930. These figures probably indicate fairly the number of houses occupied in the Estate. At first only detached houses were built; and although in 1928 some semi-detached houses were built in Warren Road, Town Planning continued to limit the number of buildings to six per acre, so that each house had ample garden space, and the general aspect was considerably more open than on most suburban estates built at that time.

A row of shops was built on part of Nork Way, near its junction with Fir Tree Road, mostly in the 1920s, and this was continued round the corner in 1930. But in the early days, services to Nork were mostly provided by tradesmen from Banstead village or Burgh Heath, though milk was produced at North Tadworth Farm by the dairymen, F. and E. Hodges, on part of the Estate not then developed, and delivered twice daily in horse-drawn carts. Bakers and other tradesmen made regular deliveries, either by van or by delivery boys on carrier bicycles. Most houses used coal for heating, and this was delivered by the coalman from Epsom.

The proposed gift by Halden Estates Ltd. of a site for a Church on the Estate, and of half the cost of building it, failed with the collapse of the company. Consequently, the Estate had no Church until 1928, when a site in Warren Road was donated by a member of the Church Council. What the Reverend A.W. Hopkinson described as "a modest but adequate church building" was erected there and dedicated on 6 March 1930. A Church Hall and a Vicarage were added some time later.

As the Nork Estate expanded, a new dimension was given to its development in 1929 by the making of a new road linking the Brighton Road to Tattenham Corner. At first this was called Great Tattenham Road, but later it was split nominally into Tattenham Way and Great Tattenhams. Along and off this road, building would spread extensively to further parts of the Estate bought by Halden Estates Limited. The Estate, as has been seen, extended well beyond what is now regarded as Nork, as far as Tattenham Corner and on towards Tadworth. In January 1930 the layout of new roads at Tattenham Corner was put before the Epsom R.D.C. This was followed by the building of the Tattenham Grove Estate.

Hillside, Green Curve etc	About 86 acres
South of Warren Road, up to Plantation at Nork Park Wood	About 107 acres
Nork Park proper up to north of Tattenham Way	About 103 acres
Both sides of Tattenham Way	About 47 acres
Land from Tattenham Corner to Nork House, including Great Tattenhams	About 180 acres
Tadworth to Burgh Heath, south of buildings near to Great Tattenhams	About 260 acres

Table 1. Description of Interim Development Order
for all Perrys' Nork Park Estate,

Further developments were in hand, particularly by Perrys (Ealing) Ltd., who had become much the largest of the developers involved. In January 1932 the Epsom R.D.C. recommended the making of an Interim Development Order for all Perrys' Nork Park Estate, which is described in Table 1.

In November 1932, this was followed, after a Public Inquiry, by approval of plans for the Company to build 2300 houses on land between Tattenham Corner and the Brighton Road. This left sixteen acres to be allocated for shops, and forty acres for Open Space for the Council.

The original plans of Halden Estates Ltd. for the Estate which they bought could now be regarded as obsolete, though they had by no means been entirely discarded.

The Development of Banstead Village

The first area to be developed in the vicinity of Banstead High Street was, as has been mentioned, on part of the land bought by the Epsom R.D.C. in 1920. By 1926 some Council houses were occupied in what became Lambert Road. The Council had, however, no hope of making use of most of the land for Council housing, which they could undertake only on a very limited scale.

There was a proposal, first put forward by the Ministry of Transport in 1923, for a "Banstead by-pass road" to run through the land, connecting Croydon Lane to Fir Tree Road, with junctions at Sutton Lane and the Brighton Road respectively. But this project hung fire for some time; and in the meantime most of Winkworth Farm remained open land.

The rural aspect of the village itself, even at that time, is well illustrated by the story told by the Reverend A.W. Hopkinson, who was Vicar from 1919 to

1928. He related that when Mr. Wesson, the fishmonger in the High Street, told him that there was a covey of partridges in the Winkworth Farm fields opposite, he dashed to the Vicarage, seized a gun, crossed the High Street and shot a brace of them. "Five minutes quick work", he called it.

The general development of Winkworth Farm began in earnest in 1928. The first private houses on it were on land at the western end, belonging to Mr. Uvedale Lambert (formerly of Buff House). A new road, later named Wilmot Way, was laid over this land. Approval was given by the Rural District Council to a layout plan for houses on this road in June 1928; and in November 1929 the erection of twenty-two houses on the road was approved.

There was also building on some of the eastern part of the former Buff House Estate. In 1923 Uvedale Lambert had sold Buff House itself and the grounds and land adjoining it, except for a small plot adjoining the High Street. No immediate development occurred there; but in 1926 the eastern part of the High Street frontage was sold off to builders; and most of Buff Avenue was laid and houses built on it by about 1928.

Buff House itself and its grounds were bought in 1927 by another private person, Mrs. H.N. Armitage, and did not become available for development till later. This is the area now comprising Harbourfield Road, Garden Close and the shops in the High Street at this point.

Development of the Winkworth Farm area was accelerated by a decision taken by the Epsom R.D.C. in February 1928 that, once the by-pass road and the necessary sewer had been laid, they would dispose of any of the Winkworth Farm land not then required for Council housing "to the best advantage". They followed this up by extending Lambert Road to join up with Wilmot Way in 1929 and building some more houses in the extension of that road. From that time onwards, it became plain that development of the whole of the old Winkworth Farm was about to take place.

The division of ownership of the Farm land must have been mainly responsible for the haphazard development which left awkward gaps in the network of roads. The next area of development in the High Street vicinity was of some more of the western part of the former Buff House grounds, and of a three-acre plot behind Buff House. This land was acquired in 1928 by Charles Lewin, then described as a builder, but subsequently better known as an Estate Agent. It was developed by him as the Glenfield Estate, comprising what became Glenfield Road and Sandersfield Road, and the bottom end of Buff Avenue, together with shops in the High Street on either side of the junction with Glenfield Road.

Figure 24. Little Garratts

The remainder of the old Buff House Estate formed part of a fairly continuous development. It included what became the full length of Wilmot Way; the shops in the High Street on either side of its junction with Wilmot Way; The Oval; and the western end of Lambert Road. The Oval layout was approved in 1933 and houses were built there in 1933 to 1934. A piece of land off Lambert Road had been conveyed to the Parish Council for allotments in 1931; and the Oval abutted these allotments.

Two features of the High Street disappeared during this period. A large pond, which was on the southern corner of the High Street - Bolters Lane junction, opposite the Victoria Inn, was filled in. This made way for a crescent of shops. Another large pond at the western end of the Buff House grounds was also destroyed. In December 1929 French and Foxwell Ltd., who had been running their garage business from the yard behind Ivy Cottage, were given permission to drain the pond and use it as the site of a new garage. The garage was later taken over by Brew Brothers Ltd., and is now the site of a block of offices and shops called Traceway House.

All this time negotiations had been going on about the intended by-pass road. In June 1931 agreement was reached between the Epsom Rural District Council and the Surrey County Council on outstanding matters. The District Council urged that construction should start immediately, and offered to surrender to the County Council the land in their ownership required for the road and also to contribute towards the cost. In September 1931 the District Council put into action resolutions which had been passed in 1928 to dispose of all the land not required for the road; and they agreed to sell this land, amounting to about thirty-nine acres, to the United Kingdom and Overseas Development Ltd. for £17,650.

No Conveyance was made at this time to the Company, though in December 1931 they put the property up for Auction in a number of plots, as if they were the actual freeholders. They had in fact followed the practice of the Nork Estate developers, Halden Estates Ltd., in buying an Estate without having the money to pay for it, in the expectation that they could sell it off in bits, quickly enough to pay off their Vendors. They had the advantage of an Estate with a new public road under construction on which much of the Estate would front; and they proved more successful in their venture.

Applications for approval of houses to be built fronting on the by-pass road came in from December 1931 onwards. The first application was for thirty houses to be built by E. Best and Co. Later houses fronting on the road were built by a number of firms.

A major step in the development of the Estate was the approval in February 1932 of a layout plan for what was to be called the Winkworth Farm Estate (North). Apart from the plots actually fronting on the new by-pass, soon to be named Winkworth Road, this new Estate comprised almost all the land between the new road and Banstead Downs. This included what were to become Palmersfield Road, Commonfield Road and Follyfield Road. The developers were Onyx Property Investment Co. Ltd., to whom all this land had been sub-sold.

As a result of the various developments, by 1933 very little open space was left in the area north of the High Street. There were a few buildings which had been on that side of the High Street for many years. These included the Victoria Inn and Winkworth Farm buildings at the western end; Buff House and grounds in the middle; and, beyond Buff Avenue at the eastern end, the Smithy and some old cottages, with shops in the corner block between Salisbury Road and Sutton Lane. In between, there were now several new parades of shops and the new Garage.

On the other hand, south of the High Street there had been little change. Six semi-detached houses had been built between the Baptist Church and the Bank on the corner of Avenue Road. Otherwise, on and beyond that side of the High Street, things were for the time being much as they had been for many years.

There were other new estates in the course of development in the village area. In 1930, Mrs. Davies, the proprietor of Garratts Hall School, died. The School was closed and the Hall and land were put up for sale and bought by a Company calling itself Garratts Hall Estate Ltd. At first the Hall itself and its gardens, Little Garratts, and the Stable Block were kept back. The remainder of the Estate was laid out as a Building Estate, with new roads to be known, on the recommendation of Sir Henry Lambert, as Colcokes Road, Monks Road and Garrard Road. Four houses were built in Garrard Road in 1931, and a further eight houses in that year or 1932. Little Garratts was sold off, and the Stable Block sold with it as a Riding School. By 1934 hopes of selling the Hall and gardens as such were abandoned. The hall was demolished, and houses were built on the Garratts Lane frontage as well as on the original Building Estate.

A similar fate awaited Greenhayes, a large house on the eastern side of Bolters Lane. Plans for redevelopment of the Greenhayes Estate were passed early in 1932, and plans for ninety-three houses were approved in December of that year. These would be built fronting on the higher part of the road which would become Greenhayes Avenue or on roads leading off it. Lower down Bolters Lane, the large house itself, Castleton, did remain, converted into a Nursing Home, but its grounds were developed as the Castleton Estate in 1933 and 1934. This included construction of the bottom part of Greenhayes Avenue as far as, but not leading on to, Winkworth Road.

General view of Developments

Looking at the Banstead area as a whole, the pace of development over the years before 1933 seems to have been almost frantic. One thing that affected those on new estate roads, either at Nork or in the village, was that commonly houses were built, sold, and occupied long before the roads had been properly made up. Private cars were uncommon, but tradesmen's vans and contractors' vehicles churned up such surfaces as existed. As the development and provision of services such as gas, electricity, and main drainage spread, the surfaces were often dug up and only roughly restored. There were usually no footpaths, and at first no street lighting at all, though after a few years lights were supplied at key points.

It was commonly several years before purchasers enjoyed the benefits of all the amenities which are nowadays taken for granted, such as electricity, main drainage and clearance of domestic refuse. Mains water and gas were, however, generally available from the start.

That any sort of planning and control of development was maintained through these early years, was due to the exercise by the Epsom Rural District Council of the powers which they had under the existing Town Planning Acts and the Public Health Acts. The Planning legislation of the 1920s was not universal in operation nor as comprehensive as it later became. But in the hands of a determined local authority it did enable control to be kept over the type and number of buildings to be erected. Houses also had to comply with certain requirements relating to Public Health.

The Nork Estate development marked the beginning of a change in the nature of the whole district. Up till 1924 it was still possible to regard Banstead mainly as a village community, with a certain number of "commuters" forming an exception to the general pattern. The size of the Nork development and the fact that its appeal was plainly directed to families who were at the time London-based, and whose bread-winners would continue to work in London, meant that the Banstead area became in reality as much a residential one for people working elsewhere as one for those whose interests were entirely local. The balance was bound to be still further tilted as the Nork Estate and the developments in the village continued. They confirmed that this was now primarily a residential area housing "commuters" and their families.

Other Aspects

It is convenient here to take a pause and look at other aspects of Banstead in the period up to 1933.

The massive developments had not been welcome in all respects; not even to all of those who had come to Banstead as a consequence of their inception. In the Nork Quarterly, the magazine published by the Nork Association of residents on that Estate, a resident wrote in October 1929 of his dismay that "in quite a short time we shall be fully equipped with made-up roads and pavements, street lighting and all the so-called improvements which are the bane of anyone who has a real desire to live in the country".

The "improvements" were not to arrive as quickly as he expected; and for some time there remained much open, undeveloped land on the Estate. In fact, only a few months before that, the magazine had reported representations to Perrys (Ealing) Ltd. about shooting being allowed in the

Estate, citing one case in which a resident had actually been hit; another in which a house had been damaged; and several other "near misses'.

There was also apparently some hope that a golf course would be constructed on the Estate, which would at least have meant the preservation of open space. The Chairman of a meeting of residents, on 19 February 1929, had announced that Nork House and one hundred and nine acres were to be acquired for the purpose of a clubhouse and golf course. In January 1930, however, it was admitted that the project had "petered out".

As to the village itself, Sir Henry Lambert could be sympathised with for raising objections, in May 1929, to the cutting down of trees in front of the Buff House Estate in the High Street, in order to make way for the building of shops. No doubt many of the long-established residents regretted the changing nature of the neighbourhood.

The population of the district had spiralled as the spate of building continued. In March 1930 a Parish Meeting was informed that in the previous seven years the number of houses had apparently doubled, and the population was then over ten thousand and rapidly increasing. One of the effects of the developments round the village itself was that the balance between the number of residents there and those in the Nork Estate had evened out, and it had become only sensible that they should all have a common body to represent their interests. So in January 1931 the separate Nork Association was merged into the Banstead Association, covering the whole of the Parish. The first President of the new Association was Sir Henry Lambert. This was a conscious effort to create a community spirit throughout the new and old-established population. Whether that was feasible in the changed situation only time would tell.

There were many common elements during these early years. As has been mentioned, the Nork residents were at first very dependent upon Banstead shops and Banstead tradesmen. Shops on the Nork Estate, limited to one Parade at the top of Nork Way, were slow to come into being; though by 1929 there were a useful number there, gradually increasing over the next two or three years.

At first there was no available hall on the Nork Estate for any sort of combined entertainment or social activity, and so these were held at the Church Institute in Banstead or at the War Memorial Hall at Burgh Heath. As the numbers of residents on the Nork Estate grew, several Societies were formed; and in 1928 a barn on Warren Farm was made available to the Residents and with a great deal of effort converted into a centre for community use. Some activities such as the drama group, known as the Nork

Players, continued to give their performances at the Banstead Church Institute; but The Barn was used for monthly dances and a number of other purposes. By 1929 there was a Nork Musical Society; a Nork Badminton Club; a Nork Literary and Debating Society; a Nork Dance Club; and a Concert Party, "The Blackbirds".

The Nork Association actively pursued the question of sufficient representation of the Nork population on the Banstead Parish Council; justifiably so, since by July 1930 it was stated that, of 2127 persons in the Parish eligible to vote in local elections, 539 were members of the Nork Association. Their efforts were at least partially successful: one of the eight Parish Councillors elected in March 1931 was an active member of their Association.

Another aspect of the integration of Nork with Banstead was in Town Planning. There had always been some control of building by the Epsom R.D.C., but it was not until 1930 that a draft Banstead Town Planning Scheme was published, dealing with developments of land both east and west of the Brighton Road. The scheme stipulated that, west of the Brighton Road, no more than six houses should be built on one acre of land. To the east of the road, there were to be not more than eight houses per acre, except that on the Glenfield Estate there could be up to twelve houses per acre.

The Scheme also allocated areas to be developed for shops: on both sides of the High Street; at the Drift Bridge; at Tattenham Corner Station; and at the junction of Tattenham Way and the Reigate Road. Open spaces would include the Cricket Ground in the village; a Children's Playground behind Chipstead Road; and hopefully further areas on the Nork Estate. Roads would be widened: Nork Way would be connected at its southern end with Beacon Way; Burgh Wood, a road through the actual Wood which had been authorised in spite of strong opposition to the necessary felling of trees, would be linked to Buckles Way. Later in the year the actual Banstead and Woodmansterne Town Planning Scheme was published.

In a still more down-to-earth way, the two areas of population had in November 1929, after a great deal of delay and some changes of plan, been connected in a comprehensive drainage system under what was called the Banstead and Woodmansterne Drainage Scheme.

Another subject of practical importance was to make arrangements for the disposal of domestic refuse. In March 1924 it had been agreed by the Parish Council that an incinerator should be erected on the District Council's Winkworth Farm land, and in May of that year it was agreed to accept an estimate from a contractor to collect house refuse. In September 1924 the contract was signed, though by then it had been decided that the refuse was to go to a pulveriser on land outside the Parish. In March 1926 the contractor died, insolvent, and the District Council maintained the service temporarily. Subsequently a contractor, suitably named Mr. Lavender, was employed to provide this service.

Local Government

The Parish Council, representing the whole of the Banstead area, had up till 1927 continued annually to re-elect as their Chairman Mr. C.H. Garton, owner of the Banstead Wood Estate. He had served as such since 1911, even though he had told the Council in 1920 that he might have to ask to be relieved of his office on account of his deafness. In April 1927 Mr. Garton finally announced his retirement from that office and Mr. Edward Gale, the Headmaster of the Village School, who had for some years been a Councillor, was appointed Chairman.

The relationship between the Banstead Parish Council and the Epsom Rural District Council had at times been a difficult one on particular points. Sometimes this was because the Parish Council wanted some provision for the Parish, such as Council housing, which the Rural District Council refused. More often, it was because the Rural District Council wanted to make improvements, such as main drainage and street lighting, to which the Parish Council objected, usually because of the cost involved. On the whole, however, the arrangement worked reasonably well.

So in 1931, when tentative proposals were made by the Surrey County Council for the constitution of a Banstead Urban District Council, to be responsible for the Parishes of Banstead, Woodmansterne, Walton-on-the-Hill, Chipstead and Kingswood, the Banstead Parish Meeting rejected the proposals "by an overwhelming majority".

Nevertheless, the proposal took shape. This was probably inevitable in view of the enormous increase in the population of the Epsom Rural District Council's area. Consequently in April 1933 the new Banstead Urban District Council came into being. After holding its first meeting in Epsom, the Council looked for premises in Banstead, and found what they wanted in what had been, first The Lodge, and then Miss Mason's high-class Finishing School for Girls in the Brighton Road. Some alterations were made to the interior; the large room made for school purposes became the Council Chamber; but the exterior was at first little affected.

Schools

Garratts Hall School and Miss Mason's School in The Lodge, two prestigious Girls' Schools, ceased to exist in 1930. But the two high-class schools for boys, Banstead Hall and Rosehill School, remained. Then in 1932 a new Girls' School was inaugurated. Mr. Maynard Taylor's house in Sutton Lane, known as Heath House, had been renovated since his death in 1927 and was put up for auction in 1932, with about three acres of land in Mellow Piece. Two ladies, Miss Pasley and Miss Wagstaffe, bought the property, and in the next year opened there a private school for girls, to be known as Greenacre School. Some of the school furniture was bought from the closed school at The Lodge.

At about the same time, another private school was closed. This was The Larches Girls' College, which had been run by Miss Molyneaux since 1913. The premises on the Brighton Road were in 1933 taken over by a preparatory school for boys and girls called "Aberdour", which had been founded by Miss Roberts in 1927 in a house in the High Street, and had moved to buildings in the stable yard of Court Farm in Court Road in 1931. In 1934 the new owner and headmaster, Mr. R.M.D. Grange, changed the school to one for boys up to the age of 13, and the school grew rapidly.[4]

Two other private schools should be mentioned.For a short time there was at Banstead House on the Brighton Road what was called A Childrens' Hotel and Nursery Home School.The other private school, The Priory, had been established in the 1920s as a preparatory school for boys and girls aged between five and twelve.In the early 1930s it was transferred to a large house in Bolters Lane known as The Red House, which up till then had been occupied by the Jaques family.Mr Jaques had owned a sweet factory and, being generous to local children with his products, had been known as Peppermint Joe.

The great increase in the population both in Nork and in Banstead had given rise to a need to supplement the provision of publicly provided School education. Only the old Village School in Banstead High Street was available in the Parish, though there were two small Church Schools at Burgh Heath. But this need remained unresolved until some years later.

Several private schools had been established in Nork, including one called Bluegates in Nork Way near the shops, and the Nork Preparatory School in Warren Road, which later moved to Eastgate. But those children living in Nork whose parents could not or would not pay for them to attend one of these schools had to make the long trek to the Village School. Some of

---

them could catch a bus, but others simply had to walk, crossing the already busy Brighton Road on the way.

Shops and Businesses

Trade in Banstead High Street was very much in a state of transition in the early 1930s. Some of the old-established businesses remained at the eastern end, notably the old Woolpack Inn, managed by Samuel Stevens and, after him, Robert Putman. Cunnington's butcher's shop was carrying on, and Hodges still ran the Dairy. The Oakshott family business had changed from carpentry to that of "Carman" in the lifetime of Mr. Oakshott; and after his death to that of Coal Merchant, carried on by his widow. Mr Palmer had succeeded Mr. Shaw in the Smithy. The Aldridge family ran a Hairdresser's business; and the Tonge family continued the business of Grocers and Sub-Post Office.

At the Western end of the High Street, the Victoria Inn had been managed by Mrs. Ella Maria Gilbert since 1918, when she took over from Mr. Thomas Gilbert.

There were other well-established family businesses in or near the village: for instance, Gurney (Confectioner) and Head (Butcher) in Diceland Road; Pushman (Grocer) and Bellows (Bootmaker) in Ferndale Road; and Rickett Cockerell and Co. Ltd. had long operated as Coal Merchants from the Railway Station.

On the other hand, by the early 1930s, both on the north side of the High Street and in the parade of shops at Nork Way, there had appeared a large number of shops and offices which were then quite new to Banstead, and provided a much greater variety of services. In 1915 there had been only about a dozen shops in the High Street and a few in the Diceland and Ferndale Road area. As might be expected, there was very little growth in the 1915 to 1918 period. Between 1918 and 1922, there was still little growth, the most notable addition being French and Foxwell, motor engineers.Then between 1922 and 1927, about fourteen new shops appeared in the High Street and two in Nork Way; between 1927 and 1930, nine in the High Street, and about fifteen in Nork Way; and between 1930 and 1934, about twenty-six in the High Street, sixteen in Nork Way, and seven in the new Drift Bridge Parade.

There were also new firms of builders and other tradesmen; professionals, such as doctors, dentists and solicitors; and motor engineers, including Watkins Garage in the High Street.

There were three Tea Rooms in the High Street. One, popular with cyclists out for the day and called Ye Olde Tea Rooms, was at the corner of

Figure 25. Greenacre School, 1935

Park Road. Another, west of the Village School, with a large garden, was called The Tudor Tea House and run by a Mr. and Mrs. Buckle. The third, known as The Old Cottage, said to be some 300 years old, was on the Northern side of the High Street, some 200 yards east of the Victoria Inn.

Wingfield House, nearer the Victoria Inn, housed a football betting business, run by Mr. V.S.Stevens, which had started in a small way in a house in Salisbury Court Road in 1919, and grown enormously, under the name Wittons.

The list of shops and businesses in the area had greatly lengthened; but it would still prove insufficient to cope with the growth to come.

Recreation

Some recreational facilities had been provided, but they lagged behind what would be adequate for the mass of new residents. The Banstead Cricket Club, having succeeded in reinstating the ground after the War, had resumed its activities on the Green. Two teams were run, and in 1928 an attempt was made to raise a third team, to play on a field opposite the Church Institute. This was to cater for the great increase in population, particularly in Nork. The scheme failed, however, for lack of playing members.

In 1931 Mr. Garton made a gift to the Parish of land on the northern side of Garratts Lane, to be managed as a recreation ground by the same Board of Managers as the main Cricket Ground, and to be available for junior elevens of the Cricket Club.By this time enough support had arrived for a third eleven to be run, using the new ground, which became known as The Garton Recreation Ground.

This ground was also used for football by a team called the Banstead Football Club. Their shooting may sometimes have been rather inaccurate, since the adjoining householder complained in 1933 about the number of footballs being kicked into his garden, and it was decided that the football pitch might have to be moved further away.

Apart from the cricketers and footballers, the Village in 1925 enjoyed the benefits of another gift of land for recreation - the piece of land between the Cricket Ground and the buildings in the High Street. This had been sold off by John Lambert's Trustees to a builder named William Taylor and put up by Taylor's Executors in 1895 for sale as building plots. At that time five public-spirited gentlemen, including Sir Ralph Neville, a High Court Judge then living at Banstead Place, joined to share in buying the land to preserve it as open space.

After the death of Sir Ralph, and that of his son, also called Ralph, his daughter, Miss Edith Neville in 1925 bought up three of the shares in the open space and persuaded the other two holders of shares to join with her to offer to convey the land to the Parish for a Recreation Ground; and she made a gift of money for the purpose. The Parish Council gladly accepted the offer, and the Ground was dedicated to the memory of Miss Neville's mother, Lady Neville. When fully laid out a few years later, the Lady Neville Recreation Ground included five tennis courts and a bowling green, as well as open space for general recreation.

Two Tennis Clubs were formed on the Nork Estate in the early 1930s: The Banstead (Hard Courts) Tennis Club in The Drive; and later The Shelley Hard Courts Tennis Club in Roundwood Way. Golfers had the old-established Banstead Downs Golf Club available; the Cuddington and Kingswood Courses nearby; as well as the prestigious Walton Course, said to be a favourite visiting place for Edward, Prince of Wales. The Walton Club

Figure 26. Hodge's Dairy Milk Delivery Cart, Mr. Touzel driving

had an "artisan club", with limited facilities, for "people of the working class type", which seems to have been liberally interpreted.

With the Commons and the underdeveloped mass of the old Nork estate open to them, and the Epsom Downs easily accessible, there was little lack of open space for those who wanted to get away from the dust and noise and general confusion caused by the builders and contractors engaged in the rapid developments.

Social Life

Most of the social functions in Banstead took place at the Church Institute, including notable contributions from Nork Societies. The Nork Players put on theatrical performances and the Nork Operatic Society provided musical performances. The combined Banstead and Nork Residents' Associations were now constituted as The Banstead Association, in three groups: Banstead Village, Nork, and Surrey Downs. Its membership ran up from one thousand to fifteen hundred, and it organised entertainments as well as representing the interests of residents in local government and other matters.There were regular dances at the Church Institute run by the Association and others.

The Banstead Horticultural Society was active. There were occasional functions, such as Dances and Fetes organised by the Cricket Club, sometimes in the Gymnasium of the Banstead Hall School or in the grounds of that School or Rosehill School.Small functions took place at the Tudor Tea House. During the summer evenings there were open-air dances on the Green, with music from the Banstead Silver Band. Other events were organised by the Churches in the village. One of the most popular forms of entertainment, the cinema, was to be had by going to Epsom or Sutton; but although twice in the 1930s there were proposals put forward and approved for a cinema in Banstead, for some reason they came to nothing.

Transport

Transport to and from Sutton, and so on to London and other destinations, had become easier. Since the First World War, regular bus services to the Village and to Burgh Heath had been laid on by the London General Omnibus Company and the East Surrey Traction Company. There were periodical complaints about both the numbers and the timing of the buses as well as the standard of the driving. As early as May 1922 the Parish Council had written to the bus companies to say that less damage would be done if buses rounded such corners as Bolters Corner at less speed. In October of that year they complained that the existing hourly service was insufficient, and asked that a half-hourly service be resumed. The L.G.O.C. replied with a proposal to extend one of their Services (No. 113) from Sutton to Banstead Village.Further extensions of bus services continued.

One of the hazards for the bus drivers (and their passengers) was the narrowness of the road from the eastern end of the High Street to Sutton Lane. The corner itself was sharp, because Hodges Dairy building jutted out on one side, whilst on the other side overhanging trees from the Well House garden could threaten the front windows of the buses. There was no room for buses to pass in this stretch, so that the conductor had to get out and run in front to give the "All Clear" to the driver.

Apart from these "Red Bus" services, there was for some time an express motor coach to London run by the Skylark Motor Coach Company. This lasted until the L.G.O.C. started a "Green Line" service in 1931.[5]

The Epsom Downs - Sutton railway line was a main artery for "commuter" traffic, and the service was improved by the electrification of the line from London to Sutton in April 1925, and of the Epsom Downs Branch

---

5 A more detailed account of the Bus Services is contained in Chapter 15.

Figure 27. Mowing in Blakes Field (Garton Recreation Ground)

line in June 1928. Other commuters used the Tattenham Corner line, or went by bus to Sutton to catch trains there.

The number of private cars had by 1933 greatly increased since the early post war days. Besides the established garage and hiring businesses in the High Street, run by French and Foxwell, another garage was opened by Mr. Richard Chandler in the Brighton Road by 1930. This was followed by the Nork Service Station, the Drift Bridge Garage, and Watkins Garage in the High Street by 1934.

The opening of Winkworth Road in 1932 eased traffic problems in the High Street for the time being. The High Street, Holly Lane, and other roads in the vicinity of the village remained comparatively peaceful for at least several years.

Chapter 8

From 1933 to 1938 - The New Community Established

Whilst there was no actual pause in the process of development in the area in 1933 or at any other time in the 1930s, a fresh impetus in certain directions arose from two events in 1934. The first was the decision of the Church authorities to dispose of the old Vicarage. This stood just to the west of the Church in the High Street, and its gardens and grounds occupied the southern side of the High Street almost as far as Bolters Lane. The second was the death on the 19th June 1934 of Charles Garton, owner of the large Banstead Wood Estate.

The Vicarage

The old Vicarage had, no doubt, like many others throughout the country, become altogether too large for the modern parish clergyman. It was a three-floor building, with nine bedrooms, drawing room, study, dining-room, kitchen, larder, parlour, and scullery. It had been much enlarged in 1824 at the beginning of its long occupation by successive members of the Buckle family; and the garden was as extensive as it had been in the seventeenth century, when John Aubrey wrote of it as having "a fine collection of Laurels, Ivy's and Holly's formed into Grottos, Caves and Arbours"[1]. Celia Fiennes, in a book published in the early eighteenth century,[2] described this remarkable garden at some length, as well as some of the contents of the house.

The Reverend A.W. Hopkinson wrote that even in the 1920s he was able to live in some style in the Vicarage. The Vicarage "had a good name". Visitors were "glad to stay in a house where there is a reasonable calm, and

1   In his book 'Antiquities of Surrey'.
2   'Through England on a Sidesaddle in the time of William and Mary'.

Figure 28. The Vicarage c.1910

their room is clean, and they got hot water, and their shoes are blacked in time for them to go out in the morning ... Maids have stayed and been content." It was perhaps as well that this Vicar of the old school left Banstead in 1928, before the old style of the village had disappeared.

The Reverend A.W.Hopkinson was succeeded as Vicar by the Reverend F.N. Skene; but in 1933 there began a progressive disposal, first of the grounds of the Vicarage and finally of the Vicarage itself, making room for the development of the southern side of the High Street with shops, banks and other premises.

The first piece of land sold off, in 1933, was a site for a purpose-built Post Office.

In December 1934 more of the land in the High Street was sold to a builder. It was to become the site of shops at the time called Post Office Parade and a Bank in the High Street, with an Express Dairies Depot at the rear. In 1936 the remainder of the Vicarage grounds and the Vicarage itself were sold off to V.S. Stevens in his role as a developer, with completion of the sale of the Vicarage itself set forward to March 1937. This was no doubt to allow for the completion of a new Vicarage which was being built in Garratts Lane, just above the Garton Recreation Ground.

By 1938 most of the old Vicarage land had been redeveloped. Some more shops and premises had been built on vacant plots on the northern side of the road, particularly on the site of Buff House, which had been demolished. The High Street had become almost entirely urbanised on both sides.

The former Vicar's style of life had, by his own account, owed a great deal to the favours of the Garton family, who since 1893 had owned and occupied the Banstead Wood House and Estate. He wrote revealingly about their life style.[3]

It seems that, some years after Mr. Charles Garton bought the Banstead Wood Estate, he to some extent took on the patriarchal role in relation to the village which had in the past been played by the old-established landowners, such as the Lamberts and the Buckles.

In about 1910 he became Chairman of the Parish Council, a post which he held for seventeen years. On more than one occasion he gave practical assistance, by lending tractors to help to remove heavy snowfalls, or during the 1914-18 War by providing land for allotments. He later gave to the Parish the recreation ground in Garratts Lane which is named after him. His wife also took an active part in doing good works for the villagers, in a slightly old-fashioned matriarchal style.[4]

At the time of Mr. Charles Garton's death in 1934, his surviving sons were both resident in the Parish. A.S. Garton was at Wood Lodge in the Brighton Road, and C.L. Garton owned Holly Hill House with seventeen acres of land in Holly Lane. After the death of his father, the Banstead Wood Estate passed to A.S. Garton. He made available Banstead Wood House and its grounds for the creation there of what was intended to be a Children's Hospital to be known as The Princess Elizabeth of York's Hospital for Children, of which he was to be Vice-President. Within a few years the rest of the Estate had been disposed of. So Mr. Charles Garton was the last of the series of big private landowners who for long had exercised so much influence over the affairs of the village.

The disposal of the Banstead Wood Estate, which included about 790 acres, did not give rise in itself to building development, apart from that required to adapt the House for use as a hospital; and much of this was delayed until after the 1939-45 war.

---

3 'Pastors Progress'.
4 A more detailed account of the Garton Family and their activities appears in Chapter 13.

There had recently been enacted legislation enabling Local Authorities to declare land round London to be "Green Belt" land, and to acquire land for its preservation as open space. In February 1935 the Surrey County Council informed the Banstead U.D.C. that the London County Council had offered to make grants of up to two million pounds for the purpose, and invited the U.D.C. to come to a Conference on the subject.

The Banstead U.D.C. then put forward a proposal for acquisition of Banstead Woods "for the benefit of the people of urbanised London", except for the proposed Hospital site and grounds. Negotiations followed with A.S. Garton and the owners of land to the south between the Wood and the Chipstead Valley. Eventually in November 1936 the purchase of 314 acres of land in the Parish of Banstead and a further 75 acres in the Chipstead Valley by the Surrey County Council was agreed.

The bulk of the agricultural land held as part of the late Charles Garton's Estate, including Canons Farm and Perrotts Farm, was sold in 1938 to the Ecclesiastical Commissioners for England (now the Church Commissioners), who regarded the land as an investment and continued to lease it for farming.

Holly Hill and other Developments

The Holly Hill House and Estate owned by C.L. Garton since 1913 had by 1938 been sold by him to the enthusiastic businessman and developer, V.S. Stevens, then living at Court House. The property included land on both sides of Holly Lane. The house itself was preserved, along with the drive leading to it from the top of the access road from Holly Lane. This became known as Holly Hill; and the lodge in Holly Lane was converted into a modern house. A Convalescent Home was built at the top of the hill. The rest of the Estate, on both sides of Holly Lane, was developed as housing, though a plan to drive a new road to join the track leading from Chipstead Road to Holly Lane failed to materialise. This was because of a proposal then current for an Orbital Road from Croydon to Leatherhead, which would have crossed Holly Lane by a flyover bridge at the end of the track. That proposal was eventually dropped.

Banstead Hall, Walton Lodge, and Bentley Lodge

The Banstead U.D.C. were informed by the Surrey County Council in November 1936 that the County Council intended to acquire all the property belonging to Banstead Hall School, which Captain Maitland had decided to close. As well as the school building, this comprised most of the northern part of the area between Bolters Lane and the Brighton Road, and also some land on the Western side of the Brighton Road, up to the end of the gardens of houses in Green Curve. The County Council proposed to use the School buildings and most of the land as a Short Term Approved School for Boys, selling off any land not required.

The land west of the Brighton Road was in due course to be exchanged with the Lords of the Manor to become "common land" to replace strips of Banstead Downs which would be needed to widen the Brighton Road. This exchange did not take place until 1944.

The new school would be of a very different character from the high-class private school it replaced. Of the buildings which had been held along with Banstead Hall itself, Banstead House was to be used as an annexe to the Approved School. The Nursery School which had been carried on there was to be closed.

The character of the area between the northern part of Bolters Lane and the Brighton Road was about to undergo further change. In 1930 three ladies had bought Walton Lodge and its grounds, and in 1935 they also bought Bentley Lodge and the grounds held with it north of the access road, which

Figure 29. Walton Lodge, Brighton Road, 1930s

Figure 30. Staff of Banstead Village School, early1930s.
Standing from the right: Mr Bullard, Mr Carpenter, Miss Staddon
Seated: Mrs Woods, Edward Gale, Helen Day.

was itself slightly north of the Priory School. It appears that this was an investment with a view to development, because in 1937 they sold both properties to R.F.H.Watts, a builder, of Streatham.

That part of the Bentley Lodge Estate which lay south of the access road, including a bungalow and poultry farm and Norgrove Cottage, was sold to V.S. Stevens in 1938 - no doubt also with a view to development.

There was a house called The Orchard between the poultry farm and the Garton Recreation Ground with some grounds and an access road to the end of the High Street, and this was bought in 1936 on behalf of the Provincial and Town Lands and Property Company.

Nork and Great Burgh

Development of the combined Nork and Great Burgh Estate continued throughout this period, having spread out in several directions, but especially in the area around Tattenham Corner and south of Great Tattenhams including Merland Rise, Chapel Way and St. Leonards Road.

One purchase by the Banstead U.D.C. in 1937 was of about 39 acres of land at the Tadworth Farm end of the old Great Burgh Estate, between Merland Rise and the railway. 34 acres of this were to be used for a cemetery but the project, as will be seen, never took shape. The other five acres were to be used as a Council depot.

Education

Apart from the houses and shopping parades built in the Banstead area at this time, there were new provisions for educational and recreational needs. It had been acknowledged as early as 1932 that a Central (or Secondary) school for the enlarged community in the area was required; and at first it was suggested that this should be in Garratts Lane. However, the Parish Council preferred to have the new school located on the Nork side of the Brighton Road. In 1933 it was agreed that the Surrey County Council would acquire a site on a proposed new road which was to run from Tattenham Way to The Drive, and which was to become Picquets Way. The Banstead Central School was opened on that site on the 17th February 1936, the first Headmaster being Mr. Edward Gale, up to that time Headmaster of the Council School in the High Street. It started off as a mixed school for boys and girls, with 322 scholars between the ages of eleven and fourteen, from Banstead, Tadworth, Burgh Heath, and Kingswood. At least 120 of them came to school by bus or charabanc. By 1937 a new building had been added, and separate boys' and girls' schools had been created. Mr. Gale and Miss Adams were the respective heads of these schools, which had in total much larger numbers. In 1937 there were 285 boys and 284 girls; and by 1939, 330 boys and 316 girls.

Recreation Grounds

Negotiations were also started by the Banstead U.D.C. in 1935 to buy some fourteen acres of land between Church Lane and Tattenham Way for a recreation ground, together with about four acres of land adjoining, which was to be used as allotments.

The purchase was completed by June 1937. It took some time for the ground to be prepared, but by the spring of 1939 cricket pitches had been laid and were allocated - one of them to the Burgh Heath Cricket Club.

It was also recommended that eight to ten acres of land near Preston Hawe, south of Great Tattenhams, should be reserved for a playing field.

Village Entertainments

Val Randall said in his book[5] that there was a far greater "amusement content" in the village in the 1930s than there was in the 1970s and that there was always some form of entertainment going on. The Church Institute was very heavily booked. There were regular dances run by the Banstead Village Association, and by various other bodies. The Nork Players and Banstead and Nork Amateur Operatic Society appeared there, and there were concert parties and a minstrel group (perhaps that from Nork).

Elsewhere, there were weekly evening open-air dances on the Green to the music of the Banstead Silver Band, and whist-drives at the Wilmot Cafe in the High Street. There were several cinemas at Sutton, two at Epsom and one at Cheam, though the proposals for a cinema at Banstead had fallen through.

The Banstead Cricket Club prospered, using both the Green and the Garton recreation ground in Garratts Lane. There was no public swimming bath in Banstead but at Burgh Heath there were two pools available to the public, at establishments known in those days as Road Houses: the "Sugar Bowl" on the Brighton Road, and "The Galleon" on the corner of the Brighton Road and the Reigate Road, now a garage. These were privately run and had restaurant facilities, a dance hall in the winter and a swimming pool in the summer.

There was a long-established local golf club, the Banstead Downs Club, and several other courses in the district. There were Riding Stables for lovers of horse riding, and the Epsom Race Course for those who preferred to watch the horses running.

---

5 "Focus on Banstead", published in 1970.

There were now many more private cars and an ample bus service, together making other parts of the district and country much more easily accessible.

A Special Event

One event referred to by Val Randall must have stirred up memories amongst some of the older generation in the village. In 1897 Queen Victoria's Diamond Jubilee was celebrated in Banstead by a Sports Meeting on the Cricket Ground.[6] On 6 May 1935 it was the Silver Jubilee of King George V and Queen Mary which was marked by a public holiday and various celebrations. There was a Combined Church Service at the Council House. A conifer tree was planted in the Lady Neville Recreation Ground.[7] The Bowling Green on the ground was officially opened. A fete and sports meeting was held in the new Garton Recreation Ground in Garratts Lane, and in the evening a bonfire was lit as one of a chain of bonfires on high places right across the country.

Banstead in 1938

A general impression of the state of development of the area around Banstead at the end of this period is that the bulk of the tremendous building programme which had been running since the early 1920s had been completed, so far as the immediate village area was concerned. There would be some more building to come in the Banstead area, but the village itself had been largely urbanised.

Much of the former Nork and Great Burgh Estate still remained to be developed, as did some of the smaller areas. On the other hand, very important additions had been made to the areas of open land protected from development, thanks to the implementation of the Green Belt powers in relation to the Banstead Woods and to the provision of Recreation Grounds.

The open nature of the countryside on almost every side of the extended built-up area had been preserved in such a way as to rule out any likelihood of the district becoming wholly suburbanised in the manner suffered by many areas on the former outskirts of London. Also a good deal of open land remained even within the village area itself. Besides the Green, the Walton Lodge Estate and all the land held with Rosehill School between Park Road and Holly Lane still remained open. The continued presence of the Church, the Village School, the old Woolpack Inn, old shops and cottages, the Forge

6   See Chapter 5
7   Unfortunately, the tree was destroyed by the hurricane-type wind in 1987.

Figure 31. Banstead 1932-1933

and Well House all ensured that the old village environment had not been altogether destroyed.

To a considerable extent the late 1930s had seen the arrival of a more settled state of affairs after the frantic rush of expansion which had reached its peak in the mid 1930s. Perhaps benefiting from the direct attention of a Council based in Banstead, roads had largely been taken over and made up. It was now taken for granted that electricity, water, gas, and main-drainage would be available to house-buyers; and by the end of 1937 street lighting had been installed. With the new Central School and private schools available, education was much improved. With the Garton Recreation Ground in Garratts Lane and the Tattenham Way Recreation Ground supplementing the Green and Lady Neville Recreation Ground, ample provision had been made for cricket and other games. The High Street now contained a vastly increased number of shops and there were also parades of shops at Nork, at the Drift Bridge and Tattenham Corner. A new kind of community had gone through the stages of formation and had become reasonably well established.

By 1938 the worst of the economic crisis which had dominated the nation in the 1920s and 1930s had passed; but now there had succeeded a series of international crises created by invasions of different countries. These were perpetrated by the Italians under Benito Mussolini and the Germans under Adolf Hitler, reaching a climax in March 1938 with the German invasion of Austria. Britain and France recoiled from the menace of a Second World War. In September 1938 they settled for assurance by Hitler of his future intentions, in what became known as the Munich Agreement. But preparations for the eventuality of a war had in fact begun in earnest. Little of these preparations may have been apparent at the time in Banstead. But one aspect of those preparations was indicated in the month of the Munich Agreement, when Mr. Gale, Headmaster of the Picquets Way School, was called to County Council Headquarters for a Conference labelled "Action in International Crisis". The community was approaching a new and prolonged period of disruption.

Chapter 9

The Second World War Years

Preparations for War

By the early months of 1939, the possibility of a war with Adolf Hitler's Germany had become very nearly a probability and there were open signs of preparations for such a contingency as well as a great deal of work being done behind the scenes.[1]

Perhaps the most obvious application of those preparations to ordinary people in Banstead was the issuing of gas masks, which were supplied to every person in the country, including children. About thirty eight million gas masks were then issued.

The fear of air raids with the use of poison gas was at this stage as strong as that of bombing with high-explosive or incendiary bombs, though active precautions against that kind of bombing were also evident. In November 1938 domestic air raid shelters, the "Anderson" shelters, were put into production. Each consisted of an arched shell of corrugated steel, six feet high, four and a half feet wide and and six and a half feet long, and each was to be buried in the earth to a depth of four feet, with at least fifteen inches of soil to be heaped over the curved roof. They were to be installed free for those with an income of less than £250 per annum and at a cost of £7 to those of higher income.

In April 1939 the Banstead Urban District Council, on instructions from the Government, appointed an Air Raid Precautions Committee; and in the same month they received instructions to accelerate Civil Defence measures, showing that by then the crisis was regarded as imminent. In May 1939, the

---

1 General facts of this kind are to be found in "Life in Wartime Britain" by E.R. Chamberlain (Batsford 1972) and "A People's War" by Peter Lewis (Methuen, London, 1986).

Committee reported that shelter trenches had been completed in the Lady Neville Recreation Ground.

Also in that month the Council were told that five employees of the Council had been "called up" for military service in peacetime. By June the A.R.P. Committee had delivered circulars about the provision of air raid shelters to some six thousand households. About two thousand responses had been received and inspections of houses were being put in hand.

On the 26th of August, in view of the immediate emergency, a Special Meeting of the A.R.P. Committee was held, which put into effect necessary wartime measures, such as the continuous manning of Council telephones, masking of traffic lights, setting-up of Wardens' Posts, and the digging of Public Shelter Trenches. The Home Office had by then given notice that Anderson Air Raid shelters were available, and particulars of requirements had been sent to them.

On the First of September 1939, the Council appointed Committees for the rationing of coal and of food; and later that month a small "Emergency Committee" was appointed with wide general powers to deal on their own authority with matters arising from the impending wartime situation.

On the other hand, in the months leading up to the beginning of the War, people were still for the most part concerned with normal peace-time activities. The house-building programme continued. Applications were made and accepted for the making-up and taking-over of roads on the developing estates, and the Council gave permission for the building of new houses on those estates, for instance, in May 1939 for houses in Tattenham Grove, Colcokes Road, Holly Lane East, Yew Tree Bottom Road, Hillside, Tudor Close and Beacon Way.

In June the Council approved plans for a further batch of houses. It agreed a layout for housing to be built on the Walton Lodge Estate. In July, it approved actual plans for some houses on that Estate. The Council also considered how "The Orchard" and some adjoining land, which was at that time being used as a poultry farm, should be "zoned". It was projected that this land would ultimately be used for shops and business premises and for a car park.

The Parks and Open Spaces Committee allocated pitches on the Tattenham Way Recreation Ground for the summer to the Burgh Heath Cricket Club; and in July 1939 the Banstead and District Silver Band were granted permission to give performances in the Council's Recreation Grounds.

There were other unexciting, yet important matters for the Council to consider, such as a Scheme for a South Orbital Road to pass north of Woodmansterne. This was to cross Holly Lane by a flyover bridge and to pass on across the Brighton Road. Objections were made that it would "destroy a large part of Banstead Heath". This was "business as usual".

The War begins

The war began on the Third of September 1939. One effect of this was strict control of all sorts of materials, building and engineering works, bringing to a stop almost all housing developments as well as projects such as the South Orbital Road. Some of the developments remained incomplete, and were resumed at the end of the war. Others simply failed to materialise. Among these was the proposed development of the Walton Lodge Estate.

After a long period of rapid expansion which had continued since the mid-1920s, Banstead was to undergo practically no further development for more than six years. Engineering and building work would be confined to things related to the war: defensive measures against invasion; protection from air raids; and repair of damage from such raids. The general shape of the village was not to change during the wartime period, apart from the loss of a few familiar landmarks.

From September 1939, action on air raid precautions proceeded with ever greater urgency. By the First of October 1939, the Council had received 450 out of a batch of 600 Anderson shelters promised by the Home Office; and it was agreed that eleven extra trenches should be dug in the Lady Neville Recreation Ground. These would accommodate 960 persons. The Anderson Shelters continued to arrive for supply to householders at a good rate. By 7th May 1940, it was reported that shelters had been delivered to all the households requiring them, numbering in all 1960.

By then, gas masks were generally being carried; wardens were enforcing the black-out of any naked lights visible from outside; domestic shelters and public trenches for protection against air raids were commonplace. The mobilisation of emergency services was complete. These included Air Raid Wardens; the Auxiliary Fire Service; the Rescue Service and the Women's Voluntary Service.

A great many statutory regulations and controls of supplies and resources had come into force. Although food rationing did not start on the outbreak of war, from the 8th of January 1940 bacon, ham, sugar, and butter were rationed, followed within a few months by meat and tea; and later many other items were rationed or unobtainable.

The direct impact of the war on Banstead was undramatic in the first few months, in the period which came to be called the "phoney war". Banstead was generally regarded at that time as a safe place. Even as early as April 1939, a firm of Coal Merchants had applied for and been granted permission to use the premises of Rosehill School as offices "in the event of and during any hostilities"; and once the War started, there were many other similar applications from London firms who evidently felt that Banstead in wartime would be a safer place than London.

Officially Banstead was categorised as a "neutral area". Consequently there was no official evacuation of children from Banstead. From London, however, over a period of three days, about one and a half million children were sent off to "safe" places in the country. Some adults, with their families, did move out of the Banstead district, either from choice or because their offices or workplaces were "evacuated". Two of the private schools also moved out of the district.

The Rosehill School Headmaster had made up his mind, by the spring of 1939, that in the event of hostilities the School would move to a safer area. At the beginning of the war, the School was moved to a Country House at Alderley in Gloucestershire. (It was a move intended to continue for the duration of the war; but in fact after the war the School remained at Alderley and its premises and land in Banstead were sold off.)

Another private school, the Greenacre School for Girls, in Sutton Lane, also decided to lease the school premises in Banstead to a Nursing Federation, and to take a lease of a large house in Dorset to which the School would go for the duration. Most of the "day girls", as well as existing "boarders", moved there two days before the actual declaration of war. "White Cottage", a part of the premises owned by the School in Banstead, had not been included in the lease to the Nursing Federation. Before long, as the "Phoney War" period continued, it was converted into a small school for young children whose parents had remained in Banstead or wished to return there. This was run by two of the staff who had stayed in Banstead. (The main school remained in the West Country until it returned after the war). On the other hand, Aberdour School in the Brighton Road, and the Priory School in Bolters Lane both remained open throughout the war.

As for the Village School, the Burgh Heath School, and the Picquets Way School, there was no question of evacuation. The problem was to provide all possible protection for the pupils against air-raids before re-opening for the Autumn term 1939.

The same was true for a new Primary School in Nork, officially known at the start as Nork Council School, but later as Warren Mead School, which was actually due to open on the 4th of September 1939. The opening of this school was not long delayed. By the 19th of September, three concrete air raid shelters, with curved roofs banked with soil and chalk, about twenty to thirty yards long, were constructed beyond the playground. The School then opened; and a fourth shelter became available in October.

Arrangements for the existing schools were more complicated. Neither the Village School nor the Burgh Heath School re-opened on the normal date in the Autumn of 1939. Their pupils were ultimately sent to share the premises of the Picquets Way School, which re-opened on the 23rd October, after the completion of air raid trenches. Overcrowding was thus added to all the other wartime problems at that school, though some relief resulted from the departure of the children from "Beechholme", who had been moved to the Reigate and Redhill area. It was not until March 1940 that the Village School was re-opened, air raid shelters having been provided there; and even then the Burgh Heath pupils remained at the Picquets Way School.

For the residents in general the situation was one of steadily increasing restrictions: rationing of food (and later of fuel); and shortages of things no longer manufactured or imported. Coupled with this was a steady drain of manpower as the Armed Forces and other wartime services increased in numbers.

The Battle for Britain - Preparations

The whole situation changed suddenly and radically with the Germans' "blitzkrieg" in the spring of 1940, when their armies surged into Holland, Belgium and France, occupying the whole of the Continent facing England. The arrival of the German Army and Air Force on the coasts across the English Channel left the country in a desperately weak position, with a very real danger of invasion and conquest.

This demanded the immediate mobilisation of all the resources of the nation for the war effort, to a degree which had never before been attempted. In one day, 22 May 1940, Parliament passed through all its stages an Act which gave the Government the widest possible powers over the nation's industry, assets of all kinds, property and the occupations of individuals. One salient feature was the power of compulsory direction of labour. The utmost priority was to be given to restoring the equipment of the Armed Forces, much of which had been lost in the evacuation of the Army from the

Figure 32. Tank Traps at the Drift Bridge

Continent. It was vital to increase the country's defences to cope with the much greater threat now being faced.

One of the most critical of the new menaces was that of air raids from a German air force now flying from bases only just across the Channel. This meant that no part of the Southern Counties could any longer be regarded as "safe", and places like Banstead were obviously now not free from risk.

Some provisions were made for "evacuation" of children from Banstead, though this was not on a large scale.

On the other hand there were also schemes for reception in Banstead of "evacuees" from London or the South Coast. In May 1940 some refugees from the Continent, mostly Belgians, were "allotted" to the Banstead district and accommodation was found for them, either by "billeting" them on families or by placing them in unoccupied houses. The Women's Voluntary Service helped them by obtaining furniture, and in other ways. The atmosphere was tense, with everybody having to face up to all sorts of grim possibilities in the near future.

There were ample physical signs of the seriousness of the situation to anybody going about the Banstead area at this time. Everything was geared to measures intended to hold up or delay enemy invaders. The railway from Belmont to Epsom Downs, including the deep cutting near Banstead Station, was regarded as a potential defensive line; and a mixed force of soldiers and civilians was brought in to strengthen it as a defensive feature. They dug tank traps adjoining the Brighton Road, heaping up the excavated chalk to create a wall to prevent tanks advancing from the south from fanning out over the Downs. Slots, in which curved steel rails could be inserted, were made in the road surface of the bridge over the railway, to block the passage of tanks. A concrete blockhouse was built near the Brighton Road bridge to command the approaches. This was camouflaged to give the impression that it was a refreshment kiosk. A smaller "pillbox" was built near the Banstead Road railway bridge, and this too was camouflaged. Other pillboxes were built at intervals along the railway line. At the Drift Bridge, there were similar works. These included slots in the roadway under the railway bridge to take steel girders; and groups of pyramid-shaped obstructions, two feet in height, which were known as "dragon's teeth".

In the fields between Drift Bridge and Longdown Lane; in a garden in Higher Drive; in Holly Lane opposite Park Farm; near the junction of Burgh Wood and the Brighton Road; and at other points in the district regarded as strategic, there were more concrete blockhouses, deep trenches intended as tank traps, dragon's teeth, and such-like defences.

The home of Ernest Hilton, on the corner of Winkworth Road and Commonfield Road, became not only a centre for Air Raid Precautions, but a potential armed strongpoint. Mr. Hilton was a builder who had been responsible for a good deal of development in Banstead, including houses in the Winkworth Road area. He was an Air-Raid Warden, with a hut at the side of his house as Air Raid Post No. 29. He was also Bomb Reconnaissance

Officer, which meant that he was called out to view places where bombs had fallen, and to decide whether action was necessary to deal with any danger remaining from them. This was a highly dangerous and responsible job, particularly as there were many types of bombs, some of them designed to injure or kill anyone who disturbed them. Besides these antipersonnel bombs, there were conventional bombs that could fall without exploding, and these provided a continuing menace. One example was a 1,000-pound bomb which fell at number 104 Greenhayes Avenue on the 15th October 1940, crashed through the bathroom and finished under a pile of rubble eight feet high. This bomb was ultimately made safe and removed.

The front bedroom of Mr. Hilton's house, No. 55 Winkworth Road, and the room below it were requisitioned in 1940. The ground floor room was strongly reinforced with supports for a machine-gun post in the bedroom, which consisted of a concrete wall built behind the bay windows, with gaps for firing positions. The bay windows were left in position, and the curtains left up to disguise the existence of the post. The object was to provide a field of fire in either direction along Winkworth Road in the event of an invasion. The post was never regularly manned, and, like other such defences, was never called into action.[2]

One of the major fears at that time was of landings by German paratroopers and glider-borne infantry. To counter this, the Downs were cleared of undergrowth so as give a clear field of fire for the defenders. Large concrete sewer pipes, old motor cars and lorries, and other large obstacles of all sorts were placed on any area of the Downs large and flat enough for landings. Such areas included the fairways of Banstead Downs and Cuddington golf courses; which must have presented golfers with unprecedented hazards! In addition to all these defence measures, heavy steel cables, secured to pylons, were placed across the Brighton Road at a suitable height to prevent landings on the roadway.

All this amounted to an impressive display of anti-invasion works. Whether they would have proved sufficient is another matter. Other measures taken to hamper invaders included the removal of direction signposts at the Banstead crossroads and elsewhere. Nameplates were removed on the station platforms. The name on the roof of Banstead Station was obliterated. (This had, in fact, in earlier days, been painted there in large letters with the very intention of aiding air navigators heading for Croydon Airport.)

2   Facts provided by Mr. Arthur Hilton in an interview on 3/9/92.

Each household was issued with a Government booklet advising people what to do if an invasion came. This was largely concerned with avoiding panic flight, since this might choke those roads needed to be used for defending forces, as had happened in France.

On the 14th May 1940, to make up for the shortage of available troops, the Secretary of State for War had called for volunteers for the L.D.V. (Local Defence Volunteers: later called the Home Guard). These were all drawn from able-bodied men not serving in the Armed Forces, and included those too old or too young to be conscripted. They were to be used to defend their own locality. Hundreds of thousands immediately responded, though most at first lacked arms or uniforms.

By July 1940 these volunteers had received half a million First World War rifles from the United States. By August 1940 the volunteers numbered more than a million men.The local contingent exercised on the Banstead Downs; and for rifle practice they took over an area formerly occupied by railway sidings near Banstead Station (and used after the War by the Gally Hills Shooting Club).

It would be misleading to leave the impression that the normal life of the village was entirely displaced by these warlike preparations. There was strong encouragement to "keep the Home Front going": by extra efforts to grow vegetables in gardens and allotments; by making home-grown fruit into jam; by use of appropriate cooking recipes; and by salvaging "scraps from the dustbin" to be put into "pig bins".

There were still social events: a Summer Garden Party organised by the parishioners of St. Paul's Church,Nork, in July 1940; and a "very successful" Banstead Horticultural Society's Summer Show. The Banstead Cricket Club continued to run one Eleven "on terms of the most rigid economy". Other societies and sporting activities continued to operate as well as conditions would allow. There was still no complete ban on using cars for pleasure purposes, and people still occasionally found time to make trips up to London or to the seaside.

Life could not be limited solely to pursuing worthy causes and to waiting for the enemy to arrive. There were amateur film shows in a backroom of Geoff Pushman's shop in Shrubland Road; and the pubs were as busy as ever, with a great mixture of people in uniform and others in civilian clothes.

The Battle for Britain - The Air Battle

There were a number of air raid warnings in the months following May 1940; but the first actual bombing "incident" in the area was when two bombs fell at

Great Burgh House on 17th July 1940. Even then no damage or casualties resulted. This was the lull before the storm.

As is now known, Hitler and his staff had decided that the Luftwaffe was to attack England; and invasion would follow only if the air attack succeeded in making invasion a viable proposition.

The Luftwaffe's attack was to move forward by stages, starting with Channel shipping, and ports and radar stations on the south coast. These were attacked between the 8th and 11th of August 1940. The next stage was to attack R.A.F. airfields near the coast. By the middle of August, raids were being made by daylight on R.A.F. airfields further inland; and at night on aircraft production factories as far away as Belfast, Liverpool and Birmingham.

On the 15th of August Croydon Airport was bombed. The war had come very much nearer to Banstead in grim reality.

A lady then living in Wallington has recalled her memories of that day, and of the days which followed.[3] Her sister with her three young children had come to stay in Wallington for a rest from the bombing in Southampton. She and her husband decided that, as it was a fine summer's day, the three young Southampton cousins should be taken with their own three children on a trip to Chessington Zoo. The family party were on their way back to Wallington, when they stopped at a smallholding in Woodmansterne to buy fruit. Whilst they were doing that, a fierce air battle broke out overhead. Bombs fell on Croydon Airport. They took shelter in an Anderson shelter in the nearest house; and eventually got home, relieved to find their own house untouched.

From then on, she added, they had intensive daily raids from midday till about half past six in the evening. After this, evening raids were likely to follow. Since the family were spending much of the day and most nights in the shelter at the bottom of their garden, her sister decided it would be better to return to Southampton. This was to prove a mistaken decision. However, after the departure of her sister, the children's beds were moved down to the lounge of the house; and she and her husband also slept there, on the floor. It was a strange and unsettled sort of existence, and not untypical of what people faced in Banstead.

The air raids continued to be very fierce, and the strain on R.A.F. Fighter Command was becoming almost intolerable. By the beginning of September, however, it had become vital for the Luftwaffe to achieve command of the

---

3   In a letter which appeared in the Banstead Herald on 28th August 1989.

air. Unless this was quickly achieved, autumn weather would rule out the possibility of an invasion.

The Battle for Britain - The Blitz

At this stage, the German High Command changed the whole course of the Air Battle by deciding to concentrate on bombing London. The afternoon and evening of the 7th of September 1940 saw the first mass attacks of the "London Blitz", causing terrible damage and casualties in the East End and Dockland areas of London, as well as slighter damage in central and western London.

The bombing of London by heavy masses of bombers then continued. However, R.A.F. Fighter Command now had a chance to re-equip and reorganise for what was to become the decisive day of the Air Battle. This was on the 15th of September 1940. Both sides lost a number of aircraft and pilots; but the Germans lost at least twice as many aircraft and about ten times as many aircrew as the R.A.F. This proved a crippling blow.

On the 17th of September the German High Command decided to postpone operation "Sealion" (the codename for the invasion) for an indefinite period.

The postponement of "Sealion" was not, of course, known here, nor did it mean a pause in the bombing attacks on England. On the contrary, the "blitz" on London was intensified and continued every night from the 7th of September to the 1st of November; and then from the 2nd to the 13th of November. London casualties were 6,000 killed in the first week, falling to rather less than 3,000 in the fourth week. On the 14th of November there was substituted a major attack on Coventry, which caused great damage and killed more than 550 people. After that, while attacks on London did continue, heavy night bombing was spread to major cities all over the country.

The Luftwaffe made a final attempt to devastate London in April and May 1941 with three attacks, of which the last, on the 10th of May 1941, was the worst raid of all. Made by 550 bombers, it killed 1,400 people, caused over 2,000 fires, and destroyed 30 factories and 5,000 houses. After this time, although some bombing continued, it was on a much reduced scale.

Life for the people of Banstead during 1940 and 1941 naturally reflected the different phases of the campaign. The most direct involvement of Banstead came in the period when enemy bombers were attacking R. A.F. aerodromes as near as Kenley and Croydon, and aircraft factories at places such as Kingston and Weybridge, whilst the fighter planes of both sides were engaged in aerial battles over most of southern and south-eastern England.

At this time, apart from the constant state of readiness necessary for those with Civil Defence duties, everybody had to put up with alerts, day after day, and night after night. The air-raid sirens sounded again and again, warning that people should take shelter in the nearest available place.

The logbooks of the schools which remained open in Banstead at the time illustrate the sort of interruption of normal daytime activities which resulted. For instance, the logbook of the Picquets Way School shows that between the 16th of September and the 8th of November 1940 there was at least one air-raid on 28 of the 35 school days, numbering 59 air raids in all. Often there were three or four warnings during one day.

It can well be imagined how unpleasant it was to spend these lengthy times in the shelters; and how difficult for a tired and reduced staff to try to provide some kind of normal education for a swollen number of pupils. The schools would, of necessity, strictly adhere to the rule of taking shelter when the sirens sounded. All the same, there were times when the warning system did not prevent the pupils from being in danger. On one occasion a teacher in charge of girls gardening outside the school realised that an aeroplane overhead was German.At once she ordered the girls to lie down. The plane attacked the Epsom Downs Grandstand. Schools in the area during this period did sustain actual damage as well as suffering from near misses.

As to the general population, quite apart from those whose duties compelled them to be about during air raid alarms, most people did not automatically take shelter every time the sirens sounded. Indeed, on a day like the 16th of September 1940 it would have been impossible for them to carry on business, or shopping, or any normal activity during the day, if they had taken shelter. There was a great deal going on in the skies above and there was plenty of danger. A large number of bombs were dropped in the Banstead area in these months, both by day and by night, and there were aircraft crashes. But in the wartime atmosphere people had come to accept a certain amount of risk. They would take shelter only if the danger became obvious and immediate. At night they might be more cautious; but it was said, probably with some truth, that travelling in the blackout was in itself sometimes a greater risk than being bombed.

There was an ammunition depot at Courtlands Farm; most of Banstead Woods was requisitioned by the War Department as soon as the war started; and by 1940 there were a number of Canadian troops in the neighbourhood. Some of these were at a camp at Park Farm, some in what was left of the Nork

House buildings, and others in huts at the back of Beacon Way. But Banstead had no airfield and no factories, and was not on any main line of communication. It seems safe to assume that most of the bombs which fell on Banstead during the period were planned to fall on other places. The bombers had either missed or been driven off their intended targets by the fighters, or by the 'barrage' put up by anti-aircraft guns.

Even haphazard bombing can kill or cause much damage; but in Banstead neither a high explosive bomb nor a bunch of incendiary bombs was likely to damage more than two or three houses, whereas in a city, incendiary bombs could start extensive fires which would devastate a whole densely packed area. That it was safer to live in Banstead than it was to live in London was demonstrated when in September 1940 thirty homeless persons from East London were temporarily accommodated in flats in Banstead High Street.

A few items from the official record of bomb "incidents" in the Banstead area may illustrate the sort of random bombing which occurred are listed in Table 2.

Bombs were not the only hazard for people in the Banstead area at this time. The aerial combat was not always high up in the sky; and aircraft on both sides were shot down. On the 9th of September 1940 a Hurricane crashed on Burgh Wood; and on the 30th of September a German plane was shot down in flames on the Common near the junction of Mill Lane with the A 217 at Tadworth. In another incident on the 25th of September the front of a house in Green Curve was damaged by an anti-aircraft shell, and an old lady in the house suffered shock.

It could also be perilous to venture out by car, since warnings might not be heard. In September 1940, Father Dockery, resident priest at the Roman Catholic Church in the Brighton road, Banstead, was killed when he was taking his mother and sister to a quiet part of Sussex for a week-end away from the air raids. The incident occurred when the car was hit by a bomb as they passed through Forest Row. He was buried in the churchyard of All Saints, Banstead, on the day after a bomb had dropped there, disturbing many graves.

In view of the very real dangers experienced over some nine months, it seems almost incredible that there were so few people either killed or injured. The damage, though widely spread, was not as heavy as that in many urban areas. But the strain on the people of Banstead was heavy enough. It has to be borne in mind that many of them were working for firms or institutions that continued to operate in London. These people faced danger and difficulties both at home and in their journeys to and from work in a transport system

Date	Time	Place	Attack	Consequences
1940				
9 Sept	17.50	Hillside, between GreenCurve & Tudor Close	H.E.	Damage to houses & water service pipe. No casualties.
15 Sept	02.00	Banstead Churchyard & adjoining garden	H.E. & I.B.	Damage to graves & windows in shops & flats in the High St.
	22.35	Banstead Downs, Burgh Wood, Tumblewood Rd.	I.Bs.	"The whole of the Downs alight". House in The Drive damaged by fire. Car burnt out in Tumblewood Rd.Damage to roofs in Hillside & Burgh Wood.
2 Oct	00.25	10 roads in the High St. - Winkworth Road area	I.Bs.	Many reports of damage to roofs. Several cases of I.Bs. entering rooms through roofs & causing damage & fires. No casualties.
27 Oct	19.17	Wilmot Way, between Nos. 39 & 41	1000kg H.E	This bomb was defused & removed in pieces.
17 Nov	05.55	Priory School, Bolters Lane	H.E & I.B.	Extensive damage by fire to the school. Tile & window damage in Bolters Lane.
	05.55	Eastgate, Nork	H.E.	Extensive damage to property & to gas main, sewer etc.
29 Nov	21.20	ShelversWay, Tattenham Cnr Station area.	I.Bs & H.E.	Train on fire at the Station.
1941				
16 April	21.45	Warren Rd. & Fir Tree Road	H.E & IBs.	Damage to several houses Fire in Warren Rd. 7 "casualties", 4 of whom were taken to hospital. An air raid warden injured by the blast.
28 May	02.17	Warren Rd. & Fir Tree Rd. area.	11 H.Es. 2 U.X.Bs	6 houses were hit. 3 H.Es. landed in playing fields, and one on the railway track. One of the U.X.Bs. was on the playing fields, and one in a house. A piece of rail 20 feet long from the railway track pierced the roof of 24 Warren Road and entered a bedroom.

Table 2 . An official record of a few of the bomb "incidents"

Note: H.E - is a High Explosive Bomb, I.B is an Incendiary bomb. U.X.B is an H.E. Bomb which failed to explode..

often seriously disrupted. On arrival in London itself, of course, they were still facing danger.

The War drags on - 1941 to 1943

After May 1941 there followed a long period in which the direct impact of the War through aerial bombing practically ceased to affect Banstead and the surrounding districts. The log book of the Warren Mead School (or Nork Council School, as it was then called) records that there were only six air raid warnings between Spring 1941 and the Summer of 1944. But this could not be foreseen. Indeed the immediate reaction to the "Blitz" was to redouble efforts to protect the civilian population against the consequences of air raids.

"Anderson" shelters were impossible to install in closely-packed areas of housing, and large surface shelters were vulnerable. So a new Home Secretary, Herbert Morrison, sponsored the provision throughout the country of a new "indoor" type of air-raid shelter, which inevitably became known as the "Morrison" shelter. Each consisted of a sort of massive steel table, with steel mesh at the sides for protection and a wire mesh bed a few inches above the floor. These shelters, whilst even more constricted in space than the "Anderson" type, had obvious advantages for the crowded areas, and proved very popular even in the area of the Banstead U.D.C. By January 1942, 1,000 had been received. At the same time, large numbers of bunks were being provided for "Anderson" shelters.

Another thing which had been learnt from the "Blitz" was the necessity for all sorts of business premises to have "fire watch" parties, who could tackle incendiary bombs and extinguish them. This was often done quite simply with buckets of water and a stirrup-pump or buckets of sand, before the flames spread through the premises and on to adjoining premises. Compulsory fire-watching for business premises was ordered; and the Banstead U.D.C. had by May 1941 instructed 520 people, who were to be leaders of "supplementary Fire Parties" for this purpose. There were other measures to tighten up "Civil Defence"; and by June 1941 two "Field Kitchens" had been established: one at the Picquets Way School, and the other at the Banstead Hall School, which was by then an "Approved School" run by the Surrey County Council. These could prepare food for 1,000 people in an emergency, and one week's food was kept in reserve.

In 1941 the Government found it necessary to call on the services of something like two million more people for the Armed Forces and Civil Defence, and about one and a half million workers for the munitions industry. All women aged 20-21 had to register for "war work". At the end of 1941,

Figure 33. Civil Defence Personnel, 1942

Back Row: Darby, Killick, Williams, Maple, Bailey, Evans, Antill, Couzens, Reekes, Ruffer, Jack, Coles, Worsfold, Polden, Ixen.
Middle Row: G. Smith, Dalbourne, Ray, O 'dell, Herman, L. Couzens, Trumper, Armstrong, Hayes, Jameson, Dobinson, Morris, Nott, Willatts, Entwisle, Harding.
Seated: Acland, Rignall, Roberts, Carter, Gale, Whitehead, Allan.

conscription of unmarried women between the ages of 19 and 30 was introduced, with a choice between the Services, Civil Defence and industry; whilst women up to the age of 40 had to register for war work, though there were a number of exemptions. (In 1943 registration was extended up to the age of 51.) Although there was relief from the danger of bombing, it had been accompanied by an ever harder grind for the civilian population as greater demands were made upon it, whilst shortages of all sorts of things were becoming more acute and rationing and restrictions more severe.

In coping with this situation, there was a very notable contribution from voluntary organisations typified by the "Women's Voluntary Service". W.V.S. activities in Banstead in 1941 included First Aid Classes; a "Housewives' Service"; a Canteen Service providing seven canteens; staffing an emergency transport service; Mobile Kitchens; Rest Centres; and an Enquiry Office for the newly introduced clothes rationing.[4] In fact, throughout the war, the W.V.S. (like other voluntary organisations) constantly helped out in all sorts of ways where official provision was lacking, or a flexible and human touch was required. As their chief said, they were "regarded as a pair of hands asking to be used". Evacuees, refugees and air raid victims had particular cause to be grateful for their efforts.

The second half of 1941 was a crucial period of the war, and for the moment the news worldwide was bad. For this reason, a good deal of attention was being given in Banstead, as elsewhere, to sustaining both the war effort and general morale. On the 4th of August 1941, a Sports Gala was held on the Tattenham Way Recreation Ground, organised by the Home Forces and the Canadian Army. In October, a Civil Defence Football League was set up, to play on the Council's Recreation Grounds.

In January 1942, a proposal was made to set up a "British Restaurant" in Banstead. This was one of many such restaurants to be set up by the local authorities, with Government support, to "provide simple but adequate meals at a reasonable price". The first proposal was to enlarge the Village Institute for the purpose, with space for 89 persons. When this ran into difficulties, it was later decided to convert three lock-up shops in Buff Parade in the High Street for the purpose. The restaurant was formally opened on 16th January 1943, providing an average of 220 main meals per week. By April 1943, this figure had risen to 289. One incentive to use this or other restaurants was that having a meal there did not involve the surrender of Ration Coupons.

4   Recorded in the Banstead Quarterly, October 1941.

There were other practical measures to meet wartime shortages. All over the country, the need for scrap iron was being met by compulsory requisitioning of such things as railings round parks and houses. In March 1942 nearly 39 tons of iron railings, which had bordered the Tattenham Way Recreation Ground, were handed over. As in so many other cases, they were never to be replaced.

A survey had been carried out in the spring of 1941 of all the Council's Recreation grounds and open spaces. The result had been to add to the considerable amounts of land already being used for allotments or farming. Part of Banstead Downs was put down to crops; as were seven acres in the Tadworth Farm area which formed part of a site that had been bought in 1938 for cemetery purposes. These seven acres had been reserved in the early stages of the war "for civilian dead". Fortunately, the civilian casualties had been fewer than anticipated.

There was little warlike activity in Banstead in the years 1942 and 1943 compared with the days of the Battle of Britain and "the London Blitz".The general picture was one of ever tighter rationing, restrictions, controls and compulsory direction of whatever workforce was available. Food and furniture were rationed; and petrol was available only for "essential journeys". Where things were in short supply, there were inevitably queues: it might be for fish or offal; or it might be for ladies' stockings. The country was being wholly mobilised to hit back at the Germans and their allies; and locally there was much to be done and fewer people to do it.

The war situation had visibly changed by the end of 1942. In England the American Army and Air Force had arrived in some strength. The combined R.A.F. and U.S.A.A.F. now increasingly out-numbered what was available of the German Luftwaffe; and the war planning was directed to attack rather than defence.

In 1943 the R.A.F. and the U.S.A.A.F. in England began a campaign of bombing German cities as well as military and industrial targets, which dwarfed the German raids. The other task of the R.A.F. and the U.S.A.A.F. was to prepare to give support to plans for the invasion of France: which was the objective of the Armies now mustered in the south of England. These allied forces included British, Canadian, American, French, Polish and other units.

The people of Banstead had become well accustomed to the presence of the Canadian troops. Since 1940 they had occupied a camp set up at Park Farm in Holly Lane, and the adjoining Banstead Woods. More had been accommodated in other places. They were well known in the village.

Volunteers ran a canteen for them at Park Farm, and they held dances there, appropriately in the Long Barn.[5] Now American and other troops were also in the district.

Social Activities in Wartime

Amidst all the military activity, there was an effort to dispel what was called "war weariness" by the organisation of entertainments in Banstead. The Council, in April 1943, set up a Committee to encourage "Holidays at Home". This was very much to the point, because access to many south coast areas and other holiday resorts was barred. They produced a provisional programme in May. There was to be an Opening Ceremony ; Bands at Recreation Grounds on two Sunday afternoons and evenings; a Boxing Tournament; Civil Defence and Children's Sports; a Swimming Gala; two Concert Parties; two Concerts; a Punch and Judy Show; and open air Dancing; all organised by the Committee. There would also be privately arranged Fetes, Bowls, Cricket and so on.

Also in April 1943, the Banstead Youth Council obtained permission to hold a Sports Day on the Tattenham Way Recreation Ground on the 19th of May, as well as a pageant on the 22nd of May. Clearly they were confident that there was no danger of such events being interrupted by enemy action.

The Banstead Cricket Club, which had completely closed down during the First World War, managed to keep going throughout the 1939-45 war in a limited fashion. One team continued to play throughout 1940 and 1941, though there were interruptions and gaps in the fixture list. By June 1942 the position had so much changed that it was felt possible to hold a Centenary celebration match with the Twickenham Cricket Club, whose records showed that there had been a match between Banstead and Twickenham in 1842. Bunting and flags were slung between the lime trees adjoining the ground, and two bands played during the tea interval. The day ended suitably when the last two Twickenham batsmen were dismissed in successive balls, leaving Banstead as victors with six minutes to spare before "close of play". For the moment the war and the perils of air raids must have seemed at a distance. In fact, confidence in the future of the Club was sufficient for an attempt to be made in 1942 to buy the field in Rosehill Farm, which until 1939 had been the Cricket Field of Rosehill School. For the moment, those negotiations failed. Yet a full fixture list was arranged in 1943 for both first and second elevens, and nineteen new members were elected. The Club was much nearer normality than it had been at any time since 1939.[6]

5   See "World War II - The Banstead Wood Camp", BHRG, 1995

Signs of a return to something more like normality were not limited to the Cricket Club, though there was no let-up in restrictions and controls of food and materials, nor in demands on the labour force, both male and female.

The tide of war had now turned, and the Allies were on the attack. The cities of Germany were being hit by "saturation bombing"; the war in Africa was over; Mussolini was overthrown in Italy, and Allied landings were made in that country.

Thoughts about Post-war Affairs

In spite of all the extra demands on the population, there were increasing reasons for optimism, and thought was already being given to the problems which would arise after the war. In April 1943 the Banstead U.D.C. was asked by the Ministry of Health to review the needs for "Housing for the Working Classes", and to concentrate on preliminary arrangements for this. In September 1943 they were given power to requisition houses for families inadequately housed.

In October 1943 a Food Control Committee was appointed for the Council's area. It consisted of ten Consumers, five Tradesmen and one Trade Union representative. Whilst there was evidently no expectation that food shortages would be overcome for some time, this appears to have been a move towards a more lasting, democratic kind of control for the future.

Preparations for the post-war situation were indeed pursued in the Spring of 1944 in a remarkably active fashion. The invasion of the Continent did not take place until June of that year; yet in February 1944 the Council had appointed a "Post-War Reconstruction Committee"; and preparations for post-war housing were going ahead. In March the Council settled on sites to be purchased or developed for Council houses "in the two years following the cessation of hostilities in Europe"; and in May a layout of the proposed sites was produced. By June, land at Tadworth had been acquired for housing and the layout of sites had been discussed with the Ministry of Health; the purchase of about nine acres of land at Holly Hill had been recommended; and plans for a "Horsecroft Meadow Estate" had been approved.

A "Mini-Blitz"

These preparations had gone ahead in spite of a renewal of German bombing attacks, admittedly on a much smaller scale than those of 1940-41. On 20 February 1944 a number of incendiary bombs fell in Chipstead; part of the

6   This information about the Banstead Cricket Club was given by the late Mr. Bernard Knibbs.

wing or cowling of an enemy plane fell on Banstead Downs; and three enemy airmen were captured at Woodmansterne. In the same month, the roof of the Girls' School at Picquets Way was damaged. In March some forty windows at the School were blown out by the blast from a bomb which fell on the edge of the recreation field; and blast from a high-explosive bomb, dropped at the junction of Reigate Road and Yew Tree Bottom Road, caused widespread minor damage there. Though the "mini-blitz" must have come as a considerable shock, after a long period of freedom from air raids, it was not enough to cause major damage or disruption.

Danger did not always come from enemy raids. On the 31st of May 1944 an American Lockheed Lightning fighter plane piloted by Lieut. Andrew Jackson got into difficulties, and looked like crashing on Banstead. The pilot succeeded in diverting his course and crashed on the Banstead Downs near Belmont. He was killed and his plane disintegrated.

A plaque has been placed near the spot to commemorate the event.

Attacks by Flying Bombs

From the time when the Allies landed in France, on the 6th of June 1944, it must have seemed that Banstead would be less directly involved in the war. The Canadians and other troops had departed, to join the forces invading the Continent. The former Canadian camp at Park Farm had been turned into a Prisoner of War camp for Italian prisoners, who were allowed a considerable amount of freedom, as their country had ceased to be a combatant. Air raids had practically ceased.

By this time, the Germans did not have either the aircraft or aircrew to mount the sort of raids common earlier in the war, and our air defences were much stronger. But on the 13th of June a new kind of aerial attack on the South of England started. This was made by "flying bombs", also known as the "V1's", "buzz-bombs", or "doodle-bugs". They were shaped like an aeroplane and powered by a pulse-jet engine mounted on their tail-end. They were launched from sites in the Pas de Calais and aimed at London, though many of them fell elsewhere. The name "buzz bombs" arose because the engine noise was a harsh vibrating buzz, which came to an end either by a timed explosive control or when the fuel ran out and the aircraft then either dived or glided.

Each flying bomb carried 1400 pounds of explosives at a speed of 400 miles per hour; and up to a hundred could be fired each day. They caused a great deal of damage and many casualties; and their arrival was quite unpredictable and could spread over the whole day and night. It took time

Figure 34. Flying bomb damage to the Woolpack Inn, 1944

Figure 35. Flying bomb damage to the Forge and cottages, 1944

before anti-aircraft guns and fighter aircraft could develop techniques to attack them, and even so, more got through than were intercepted.

The first flying bomb in the Banstead area fell on the 16th of June 1944 near the Banstead Mental Hospital. During the night of 16th-17th of June several more fell in the area, most notably one which, at about 5.40 a.m. on the 17th of June, landed in a field to the side of Warren Mead School in Nork. This caused extensive damage to the School and houses in the Parsonsfield Road and Partridge Mead area. One house was demolished and twelve were seriously damaged in Partridge Mead. The official report mentions one casualty. Twelve people had to be provided with temporary accommodation.

Flying bombs continued to fall on the Banstead area in the following weeks. One fell at Great Burgh Wood on the 24th of June, damaging houses and shops at Downs Wood, Yew Tree Bottom Road and elsewhere. Another, at Tangier Way, on the 29th of June, damaged about 300 houses, though miraculously there were no "casualties". The campaign was obviously mounting in intensity.

The biggest single blow to the village was caused by a flying bomb which fell near the eastern end of the High Street, just before nine o'clock on the morning of the 8th August 1944. This killed one man, an off-duty soldier, and injured 32 others. It created widespread damage to the buildings at that end of the village. A number of properties, including the old Woolpack Inn, the Forge, and other old shops and houses, were damaged beyond repair. Altogether 28 houses and shops were severely damaged, and about 200 more slightly damaged. About 200 people were made homeless, at least for the moment, and were given meals in the British Restaurant.

For the population of areas such as Banstead, on the "flying bomb" path to London, as well as for those in London itself, protective measures had to be taken which would equal, or in some respects exceed those taken in 1940 and 1941. In Banstead the number of air raid shelters was increased. More than 1800 extra "Morrison" shelters were delivered in the Banstead U.D.C. area; and for the first time there was an official Government evacuation scheme for the area. Some evacuees were in organised parties: 99 adults and 435 children. But the majority of people moved out under private arrangements with the assistance of Travel Vouchers and/or Billeting Certificates. 1096 adults and 1774 children were "evacuated" in this way.

An "Emergency Works Organisation", with the co-operation of Civil Defence personnel and builders, made "first aid repairs" to houses, and were assisted in the clearance of debris by soldiers in the locality and by the Home

Date	Time	Location	Damage and Casualities etc.
1944			
3 July	12.25	Junction of Nork Way & Eastgate	Extensive damage to houses, shops & food stores. 11 casualties, 5 taken to hospital,of whom one died
19 July	11.26	Fir Tree Road & Ruden Way	10 houses seriously damaged, 200 buildings (including shops) slightly damaged. 10 casualties, including one taken to hospital. "Rest Centre" opened at Drift Bridge Hotel.
21 July	11.24	Warren Road	Serious damage to 30 houses. Minor damage to about 100 houses. 13 casualties, 5 taken to hospital.
8 Aug	09.05	Buckles Way	Severe damage to 2 houses, minor damage to 200 houses. 6 minor casualties.

Table 3. More bomb "incidents"

Guard. "Emergency feeding" was supplied when necessary. The "Holidays at Home" programme was postponed indefinitely.

The "flying bomb" campaign went on until the launching-sites were captured by the Allied armies in September 1944. Some "flying bombs" were later launched in the air from planes, and fell scattered over England; but for Banstead the ordeal from "flying bombs" was practically ended in September. It had been a severe ordeal. Besides those "incidents" already mentioned, a few more examples listed in Table 3 may illustrate this.

On 12 September 1944 the Banstead Urban District Council were given a report about the "flying bomb" incidents which had occurred between 13 June and 29 August in the Council's area. 37 bombs had fallen in the area, and there were 192 casualties. These comprised 2 deaths, 57 hospital cases and 133 minor injuries. 67 houses had been or would have to be demolished; 85 were seriously damaged, and 3,785 slightly damaged. About 80 shops were damaged, some seriously. A number of people had been rehoused, and additional properties had been requisitioned for them. It was an impressive list for such a short period.

Attacks by Rockets

Another shock followed. From the 8th of September 1944 new and even more deadly weapons were launched by the Germans, this time from bases in Holland which were still beyond the advance of the Allied armies. These were huge rockets , the V2's: steel canisters 45 feet long and carrying one-ton warheads. They were more powerful than the flying bombs (Vl's); they were supersonic (4 times the speed of sound), and arrived completely without warning, so that no avoiding action could be taken. They were aimed at, and mostly fell in London, where over six months they killed 2,700 people, badly injured 6,000 more, and at times damaged houses at the rate of 20,000 a day. Had they come into operation earlier, or had the Allied armies not overrun the launching sites towards the end of March 1945, the consequences hardly bear thinking about. Fortunately, only two V2's are recorded as having fallen in the Banstead area. One of these fell on the 2nd of November 1944 on a Villa building annexe at the Banstead Mental Hospital, causing serious damage to the nurses' hostel, farm buildings and out-houses. Three people were killed; eleven were seriously injured; and sixteen received minor injuries. Another V2, on the other hand, fell in a field at Chipstead and caused only six minor casualties.

It was just as well that no more V2's hit Banstead because, in spite of Government advice to the contrary, a good many families, who had moved out of the area during the flying bomb attacks, and some of the children who had been officially "evacuated" during that time, had already returned to the area.

Summary of Air Raid incidents

A post-war summary of all "air raid incidents" in the Banstead U.D.C. area during the war showed that there were 204 such "incidents". About 600 high explosive bombs and many incendiaries of different types were dropped, 97 houses were demolished, 138 badly damaged, and no less than 5,753 houses slightly damaged. It appears that, in spite of all this, only a handful of people were killed, in stark contrast to the terrible list of casualties in the bombed cities. The open nature of most of the built-up areas in the district, and the lack of large buildings, factories or industrial plants must have been an important factor in this respect.

Preparations for the Post-War period

The new waves of bombing in 1944 did not stop preparation for the post-war period. In August 1944 a significant new move was made by the Banstead U.D.C. towards meeting the coming housing demand. It asked the Government for priority for an allocation of *"temporary houses"*. These were small bungalows of a standard pattern whose component parts were made in factories, ready for assembly on site. They were soon to be known as "prefabs". They were intended to have a life of twenty years at the most, though in practice many of them survived much longer.

The idea was to make use of available factory capacity to provide accommodation speedily and without demands on traditional building resources. These resources would be fully employed on creating "permanent" housing and on many other tasks, including especially the repair of War Damage to existing buildings.

On the 13th of September 1944 the Council confirmed proposals for "permanent" houses at Horsecroft Meadow and Holly Hill. "Factory-made" houses (pre-fabs) were in principle to be erected at a number of sites. On the 27th of September the Housing Committee recommended the erection of at least 250 prefabs. These were provisionally allocated to Banstead (75), Nork (50), Tadworth (75), and Woodmansterne (50). The Committee asked for authorisation to be obtained for a further 50 pre-fabs. In November 1944, the Ministry of Health informed the Council that 100 pre-fabs were already available, and more would follow according to the rate of production. Four sites had been agreed for the pre-fabs, and the Council were considering plans for a further 3.9 acres.

In December 1944, the Council gave detailed instructions to the architect for the Horsecroft Meadow estate of "permanent houses". There were to be eight dwellings for aged persons, twenty-two three-bedroomed dwellings and ten four-bedroomed dwellings.

In April 1945 the Council approved a lay-out for pre-fabs on land in the Tattenham Corner area; in Merland Rise, Chetwode Road and St. Leonards Road; and they asked the Ministry for authority to take rapid possession of the necessary land.

By the beginning of May 1945, the provision of 300 pre-fabs had been assured, and discussion was going on as to sites for them. So a good deal of really practical progress had been made before "V.E. Day", marking the end of the war in Europe, on 8 May 1945. But there were already homeless people to be housed, and others who had been "evacuated" and would wish to come back. Soon there would be a stream of people returning from the Services; so that before very long there would be a demand for even more houses than had up till then been contemplated.

Such traditional building resources as were available had for some time been almost entirely engaged on the repair of war damage to houses, under a Government scheme administered by the Council. By the 17th of October 1944, the Council had spent about £14,000 on the repair of war damage from the flying bombs, and this rose to £20,000 by November. In that month a comprehensive programme of repairs was settled, hopefully to be completed within six months. In fact this target date was improved upon. By the end of

March 1945, it was reported that 1,467 houses had been repaired; and it was recommended that the current scheme for carrying out such repairs should be terminated as soon as possible.

Other emergency provisions were being scaled down or ended now that the main dangers appeared to be over. In November 1944, the Ministry of Transport were asked to remove all road-blocks and obstructions on the highways; and the War Department gave notice of their intention to remove anti-tank trenches and to restore the land. In December the number of air raid wardens was reduced from 24 to 17, and the "Home Defence Organisation" was closed. In March 1945, the Fire Guard Plan was suspended and compulsory Fire Watching abolished. On the 2nd of May 1945 the whole Civil Defence Organisation was dissolved.

A number of allotment holders would soon be displaced by the Horsecroft Meadow housing scheme; and in January 1945 they were given notice to quit. In December 1944 there had been available 143 permanent and 1,045 war-time allotments, of which 905 were let. The number would now be considerably reduced.

Anticipating traffic problems to come, the Council had written to the Surrey County Council in October 1944 asking them to consider widening the High Street at the eastern end. This had been made easier to contemplate through the destruction of properties by the flying bomb on the 8th of August. A particular example was that of the old Woolpack Inn, which had greatly restricted the width of the High Street.

Victory Celebrations

At the beginning of May 1945, attention turned to arrangements for the celebration of "V.E. Day" on the 8th of that month. In Banstead, as everywhere in the country, this was a day long awaited and to be long remembered. V.E. Day and the next day were declared national holidays and the schools were closed. Accounts given by some of those who were children at the Warren Mead School at that time afford a vivid impression of their feelings:

"On V.E. night, there were bonfires up in the cornfield in Nork Park. People were burning everything and anything to keep the fires burning, for it was a night to remember."

"It seemed to be a permanent summer after that and always a blue sky. Then our father came home for good, and we didn't have to get up in the middle of the night any more, grab our dressing gowns and slippers and rush down to the underground shelter. The war was over."

Figure 36. Victory Party at The Junipers, Croydon Lane

In truth, though, the war in the Far East was far from over, and even in Europe there were many dangers and problems spilling over into peacetime. But this was certainly a moment for great relief and great rejoicing.

Chapter 10

Years of Reconstruction 1945 - 55

Though the defeat of Germany made the ultimate defeat of Japan inevitable, it was still entirely possible that the Japanese would fight on to the last. But it was not to be. On the 6th and 9th of August 1945 atomic bombs were dropped on Japanese cities, and the appalling destruction which they caused brought the war in the Far East to a rapid end. The Japanese Government officially surrendered on the 14th of August 1945.

This final act of the Second World War came nearly six years after the beginning of the war in Europe. The news was received in a mood more sober than that on V.E. Day. A two-day "V.J. Holiday" was declared for the 15th and 16th of August, and there were in some places street parties and the like. But in Banstead the Council decided that there should be no public celebrations organised by them. The Churches would be holding appropriate services, and a general service of Thanksgiving would be held later.

The official day of celebration was in fact not until the 8th of June

8th June, 1946

TO-DAY, AS WE CELEBRATE VICTORY, I send this personal message to you and all other boys and girls at school. For you have shared in the hardships and dangers of a total war and you have shared no less in the triumph of the Allied Nations.

I know you will always feel proud to belong to a country which was capable of such supreme effort; proud, too, of parents and elder brothers and sisters who by their courage, endurance and enterprise brought victory. May these qualities be yours as you grow up and join in the common effort to establish among the nations of the world unity and peace.

Figure 37. King George VI's letter to schoolchildren

1946, when an Open Air United Service was arranged at the Picquets Way School. King George VI, in a message addressed to school children, referred to "the courage, endurance and enterprise which had brought victory". He expressed the hope that these qualities would be theirs as they grew up and joined in a common effort to establish unity and peace among the nations of the world.

An unfortunate feature at the time was in fact a common feeling that laws and controls were made to be broken or dodged without loss of conscience. Two cases in Banstead, which were brought to court, demonstrated this. In one the temporary manager of a car hire service bought from a soldier petrol belonging to the U.S. Navy and the War Department. He was caught and fined. In another the foreman of a bomb damage repair group working on a house in Fir Tree Road was charged with stealing wine glasses from the house. He was acquitted on the facts, but only after he had said to the court frankly that it was "quite simple to take anything from bombed premises".

Housing Developments in 1945 and 1946

One of the urgent demands of peace-time which had been foreseen was that for new housing. As has been mentioned, a good deal of thought had been given to that as early as 1943 and 1944, and some plans had been made; but the scale of the problem was to prove much greater than any of those plans had anticipated. Above all, shortage of materials and manufacturing capacity was to prove a limiting factor.

In 1945 there were five million people in the Armed Forces: by 1947 four million of these had been returned to civilian life. Hundreds of thousands of people who had been working in munitions or aircraft factories or in other war-time occupations had also to be re-settled, not only into other jobs, but often into new localities. The more fortunate ones were those who had homes, families and jobs to return to. There were many of them, but a great many other people had to be "re-settled" in almost every sense. The decade after 1945 would come to be known as "the Reconstruction Period".

During the first half of 1945, whilst planning for new housing needs continued, an officially organised building force in Banstead concentrated on repairs to war-damaged houses. By the end of June, more than 1800 such houses had been repaired, and action was on the point of switching to the building of new housing. It was, however, not until September that the "Emergency building force" was disbanded, having by then repaired 2,085 war-damaged houses.

The "pre-fab" era effectively began in August 1945, when the first "temporary house" was erected on what was known as the Tattenham Corner No. 1 Site. Other sites in the Tattenham Corner, Chetwode Road and Merland Rise area were successively taken over for pre-fabs. So were two sites in Nork: one east of Hillside and one on the northwest side of Fir Tree Road. The first proposal for "permanent" Council houses was for houses on a 39-acre site at Merland Rise; and the Council followed this by an application to the Ministry of Town and Country Planning in October 1945 for permission to buy about three acres in Picquets Way for permanent housing.

The provision of accommodation in Banstead was now about to go ahead in a number of different ways. A "Housing (Emergency) Committee" had been set up by the Council in July 1945, in place of the all-purpose wartime "Emergency Committee", which was winding up its affairs. Various "war organisations" had been disbanded on the 1st of July 1945. For instance, canteens at the Council House and at the Tadworth Court and Sutton Lane Depots had been closed; and shelter bunks had been put up for sale. The new committee was to deal with the requisitioning and management of houses for people who were homeless, either through enemy action or inadequate housing. It would deal with the licensing of building work, conversion of unoccupied houses, and the repair of war damage.Ordinary housing matters, such as the acquisition of sites and the erection of pre-fabs and permanent Council Houses, would be dealt with by the normal Housing Committee. Both these Committees would have plenty to do .

The Housing (Emergency) Committee reported, at the beginning of November 1945, that there were eighty-nine houses and flats then held under requisition by the Council. Twenty-six of these, including Walton Lodge (which had been divided into eight flats), had been transferred to the Council by the military authorities. Most of them were occupied by families who had been made homeless, but six of them accommodated families who had been "inadequately housed". A few were not yet occupied. Licences for building work had been issued in 211 cases, and refused in 49 others.

At the same time, the pre-fab programme was beginning to achieve results. By December 1945 tenancies of twelve pre-fabs in Merland Rise had been granted, and three in Chetwode Road. By February 1946 about thirty more prefabs had been let, at Merland Rise, Chetwode Road and St. Leonards Road.

As for permanent housing, a tender for building fifty-three Council Houses on the Horsecroft Meadow Estate was accepted by the Council in January 1946. In February 1946 a number of applications for planning permission to erect privately-owned houses were considered by the Council. These were for houses to be built in Shawley Way, Garlichill Road, Downs Wood, Beech Grove and Shelvers Way.

Approval was also given for the purchase by the Diocesan Authorities of land in Great Tattenhams for a Church Hall, a Church and a house.This was the go-ahead for the foundation of St. Mark's Church.

By the end of March 1946, seventy-four pre-fabs had become available on the first two sites on the Tattenham Corner Estate; a layout plan for five pairs of Council Houses in Sutton Lane had been provisionally approved; and tenders had been invited for erection of Council Houses at Picquets Way.

The pace of applications to the Council to approve plans for private housing accelerated in April 1946; but in May there came a hold-up. The Government forbade the Council to issue further building licences for new houses without express Government consent, saying that the number granted by the Council had exceeded that allowed by Government policy. Licences could, however, still be granted in relation to "cost-of-works" houses. These were war-damaged houses where the owners had chosen to take a lump sum of compensation from the War Damage Commission and to carry out whatever works they wanted themselves. The Government agreed to the building of thirty-six Council Houses on the Horsecroft Meadow Estate; but for the time being they refused permission for sixteen bungalows for old people on the Estate.

Some local authorities were finding that, even if they could command enough funds and materials, they did not have enough land available for their housing projects. In June 1946, the Banstead U.D.C. agreed in principle to grant reasonable facilities to the Mitcham Borough Council and the Merton and Morden U.D.C. to build houses in the Banstead area. This would be a co-operative development with the Banstead U.D.C. itself.[1]

There was some private development. A.J.Wait Ltd. built 33 houses at Kenneth Road and Cunningham Road. But in June 1946 the Council had a list of 1,772 applicants who had been accepted as having genuine grounds for claiming to be housed. It was considered that about 2,000 houses would ultimately be needed; that the immediate programme should be increased to 1,450 houses; and that other sites should be found.

It was a large order. Temporary expedients would be required to meet the most pressing needs, in addition to the pre-fab programme, although that was continuing at a good rate. In September 1946 the Council took over for

---

1   This was to result in the building of the large Preston Hawe Estate.

housing purposes several camps by then declared redundant by the War
Department. These included thirty huts at Nork Park, which were in various
states of disrepair, and a flat over the stable of Nork House. Between them,
these eventually produced fourteen dwellings. Seven huts adjoining the
ammunition depot off Park Road were also taken over. Some of these huts
were already illegally occupied by "squatters". Later the Council provided
accommodation for four more families in huts at Yewlands Close which had
been used as "Rest Centre Huts".

General Constraints

The disruption of the economy and the shortage of materials, equipment,
food and fuel after six years of war were becoming constantly more evident.
Rationing and controls were mostly still in place; but even so, serious
difficulties occurred. In May 1946 the Ministry of Fuel and Power instructed
that, owing to the grave shortage of fuel, street lighting should be
discontinued generally from the 2nd of June to the 17th of August. The
wartime collection of salvage continued in Banstead. Waste paper, kitchen
waste and bones were collected. Tubs were put out for people to put pig food
in; and some pigs were kept at the Council's Sutton Lane depot. In June 1946
the Ministry of Fuel and Power gave instructions for the sale of the
emergency stocks of logs which had been stored during the war. Then, on the
22nd of July 1946, bread rationing had to be introduced. Bread had never
been rationed during the War itself, but it was now to be rationed for just over
two years.

Social Matters and Recreation, 1945-1948

Social and sporting activities in Banstead soon picked up in spite of all
difficulties. As early as June 1945 the Banstead Cricket Club, with thirty-four
new members, decided to bring the Garton Recreation ground in Garratts
Lane into use in the 1946 season. It would be used by two teams, in addition
to the two teams who played their home matches on the Green. The
swimming pools at the two Roadhouses at Burgh Heath, The Galleon and
The Sugar Bowl, were regularly used by the schools as well as by the general
public. People would also go there for a meal, or in the winter for a dance.
Local societies of various kinds were revived or evolved.

A feature of these years was the keen desire of the residents, with support
from the authorities, to establish Community Centres and the like. In May
1946 a deputation from the Banstead Village Community Association,
consisting of a Mr. Russell Lewis, Mr. J. Brace (British Legion), and Mrs.
Muller (Banstead Communist Party), spoke to a Council Committee, asking

Figure 38. The Galleon Swimming Pool, Burgh Heath
at junction of Reigate Road and Brighton Road (A217), 1934

for the reservation of a site in the village area for community centre purposes. They were assured of the Council's goodwill, though the Council did point out that they were not the only authority concerned.

In January 1947 the Association came up with a positive proposal. It was for the purchase of the empty Rosehill School building for £25,000, to be used as a Community Centre, for the County Library, the Citizens Advice Bureau and so on. Unfortunately, they could not themselves raise one third of the cost, which was a condition for financial support by the local authorities; and although the suggestion was put to the Surrey County Council, the opportunity was lost.

The following year the demand for a centre for the people of the Tattenham Corner - Merland Rise area was in principle more successful. A site of 2.65 acres at Merland Rise was approved for the erection of a Community Centre, clinic and welfare centre.

Another pleasant happening was the re-opening of Banstead Woods to the public, after their occupation throughout the war by the military authorities. The formal opening was made, on the 5th of April 1947, by the Right Honourable J. Chuter Ede, an M.P. with Epsom connections, and a notable Government Minister.

About the same time the Council decided that they would like to buy Park Farm, in Holly Lane adjoining the Woods. During the war this had been converted into a Canadian Army camp and then into a Prisoner of War camp, first for Italians, and then for Germans. In May 1948 the property was released by the War Department and discussions were held with the Ministry of Health as to adapting the huts in the camp for housing purposes or building new houses there. These discussions fell through; but in 1951 the Council bought the property. They demolished the old house, which had in the late 18th and early 19th centuries been the home of Mrs. Spencer, Lord of the Manor. They also demolished most of the wartime buildings, and converted the remaining barns and other buildings into a depot for their Parks Department. Parts of the Long Barn and the adjoining field were made available for use by the Banstead Boy Scouts.[2]

The rehabilitation of the Banstead Woods was furthered by the long-delayed opening of the hospital, which had been planned before the war, and developed from and around the big house that the Garton family had occupied until 1934. The fulfilment of the proposal agreed in 1936 had been thwarted by the war and by a serious fire. During the latter years of the war a military hospital had been carried on there. But now the hospital was fully established for civilian use. It was officially opened in June 1948 by Princess Elizabeth. It was at that time a branch of the Queen Elizabeth Hospital for Children in the east of London.[3]

Housing Developments 1947-1950

In what appears to have been a more relaxed mood in the Spring of 1947, the Ministry of Health agreed that the sixteen Old People's Dwellings, proposed for the Horsecroft Meadow Estate, could go ahead. The Council approved a Surrey County Council proposal to use part of the Walton Lodge Estate, which by this time was a term used to include the former Bentley Lodge land, for Old People's Homes; and most of the Wood Lodge property on the

---

2 The clock in the Long Barn's clock-tower, which dates from between 1750 and 1800, was later repaired and restored to working order through the generosity of a Councillor, Miss V. Rhys-Davies.

3 The hospital was later transferred from use as a Children's Hospital to use for residents with learning problems. It retained the title of Queen Elizabeth's Hospital, but it was closed, and in 1997 put up for sale. (No sale has so far resulted)..

QUEEN ELIZABETH HOSPITAL *for* CHILDREN

Hackney Road, E.2 · Shadwell, E.1 · Banstead Wood, Surrey, and
Bexhill-on-Sea, Sussex

Opening of

THE HOSPITAL AT BANSTEAD WOOD, SURREY

by

H.R.H. The Princess Elizabeth Duchess of Edinburgh
(President)

28TH JUNE · 1948

Figure 39. Opening of the Queen Elizabeth Hospital for Children, Banstead Wood. Ward
blocks in foreground, Nurses' Home in background.

Brighton Road was requisitioned for conversion into flats, on being vacated by the firm which had occupied it during the War.

So in 1947 the Council's housing efforts did result in notable acceleration. Between February and May forty more pre-fabs were completed and occupied in Hillside Close, bringing the total for the site up to fifty. In June plans were put forward for 109 dwellings at Preston Lane, Tadworth; and the purchase of four sites in the Merland Rise area for housing, amounting to about 19 acres was approved. In July the Surveyor reported that 62 permanent houses were likely to be completed in 1947; whilst 119 more, started in 1947, would be completed in 1948.

Perhaps it was inevitable that in August 1947 the Ministry of Health once again put a general damper on the granting of licences for new dwellings. This "Stop-Go" situation would persist for much longer than had been anticipated.

The Council's own housing development programme continued throughout 1947 and 1948 in several areas. Private builders were now being employed to build for the Council, and fresh sites were being acquired. One of them was in the Pound area off Chipstead Road, and another in Merland Rise. The Old People's Dwellings in the Horsecroft Meadow Estate were at last opened in March 1948. Approval was also given for further sites in Nork and for a block of eight houses adjoining Sutton Lane.

In 1948 a spate of new legislation came into effect. One of the new acts was the Town and Country Planning Act 1947, which substituted for the rather limited scope of the existing planning laws a more comprehensive planning control. Powers and duties in this connection passed to the Surrey County Council; though, in practice, consideration of applications was delegated to an Area Committee comprising representatives of the Banstead U.D.C. and other local councils.

People proposing to build a new house in Banstead at this time were faced by a number of obstacles. They would need bye-law permission from the Banstead U.D.C.; planning permission from the Area Committee; a building licence, normally from the Banstead U.D.C. acting on behalf of the Ministry of Works; and probably consent from the County Council as Highway Authority. They would also have to sort out questions of a "Development Charge" payable to a body called the Central Land Board.[4] The fact that developments went ahead at a rapid pace in spite of all this showed the strength of pent up demand.

4   In one case, concerning a site in Yew Tree Bottom Road, Banstead, it took almost five years, from 1947 to 1952, to obtain all the necessary permissions.

In July 1948 the Ministry of Health did relax controls as to housing. They "allotted" two hundred houses to the Banstead U.D.C. for the following twelve months, in addition to 91 houses already under contract. Up to one-fifth of the allocation could be used for private housing.

By October 1948, twenty-one licences for the erection of private houses had been issued by the U.D.C.; and a further eighteen were issued by February 1949. Hopes were growing of a more normal situation, in which demand would be met by a combination of private and public building, without resorting to compulsory measures.

It will be recalled that the Banstead U.D.C. had agreed in principle in June 1946 to provide land for housing for the Mitcham and the Merton and Morden Councils. The discussions about this were prolonged; but in April 1950 agreement was reached with those Councils and the Borough of Sutton and Cheam as to the development of about seventy acres adjoining Merland Rise, Preston Lane and Shelvers Way at Tadworth. This would become the Preston Hawe Estate.

Development of the Nork Estate was going on all the time, both by the Council and privately. In October 1949 a Company called Universal Estates Limited applied for permission to build sixteen residential flats on the west side of Green Curve and forty-eight residential flats on the island site at Nork Way and East Gate. In February 1950 agreement was given in principle for the use for Council housing of twelve acres at Shawley Way and thirty-two acres at the junction of Reigate Road and Yew Tree Bottom Road. In July 1950 a revised layout plan was agreed for what was called the Nork (Middle) Site. This was to accommodate 220 houses, including twelve Old People's Dwellings, with a road junction at Shawley Way and Garlichill Road.

The Nork Estate proper was reaching something like a definite shape. On the old Great Burgh Estate, the Riding School created by the Colmans at Little Burgh on the Reigate Road was taken over by Kinloch Limited for a provision depot and store.[5]

Social, Educational and Recreational matters, 1949-1952

Leisure and other social facilities had not been ignored during these developments. In June 1949 the Banstead U.D.C. had recommended to the Surrey County Council the purchase of about 107 acres of the Nork Estate for playing fields and other recreational purposes. In 1950 agreement was reached for the use by the Banstead Athletic Football Club of an enclosed ground at the Merland Rise recreation area.

5   Later it would become the site of the ASDA superstore.

Planning consent was recommended for what was to become Roselands, a residential club for elderly people in Garratts Lane, on the application of Mr.S.W. Rose on behalf of Banstead and Carshalton Housing Limited. This was followed a little later by another such club, Roseacre, on the Holly Hill Estate.

New schools were being planned: a Primary School at Merland Rise in December 1949; a school, which would become de Burgh School, on part of North Tadworth Farm in October 1951; and a school at Shawley Way in April 1952. A proposal was also put forward for a primary school on the Walton Lodge Estate, to replace the Village School in the High Street. This was to prove a very long-term project.

Plans for building St. Ann's Catholic Church in the Brighton Road were approved in May 1949; and plans for a Methodist Church in Great Tattenhams followed in June 1952.

In 1950, the Ambulances and staff which had been housed at the Fire Station, near White Lodge, in the Service Road adjoining the Brighton Road, moved to a detached garage block at Walton Lodge. The County Fire Brigade decided to stay at White Lodge. Plans were made for a Telephone Exchange building to be provided in Garratts Lane to replace the Exchange which had for many years been in Diceland Road. The County Library, temporarily housed in shop premises in Buff Parade in the High Street, was to be moved to a site in Bolters Lane, though the County Council were not yet ready to implement the move.

An allotment site was bought in Holly Lane, to replace a number of temporary wartime allotment sites, and in 1951 plots were allocated there.

Discussions were going on as to re-development of the area at the eastern end of the High Street, widely damaged by the "buzz bomb" in 1944. These plans and developments were evidence of a community trying hard to settle down into a more lasting pattern and to get away from wartime expedients.

Rationing and Controls

An important resettlement initiative was the termination of wartime controls and powers, from food rationing and control of building materials to requisitioning possession of property. This process continued, with some hiccups, over the whole post-war decade, and even beyond that.

The retrograde step of being forced to introduce bread rationing from 1946 to 1948 has already been mentioned, as well as the shortage of fuel for heating houses at that time. Petrol was another item that caused a lot of problems. Wartime petrol rationing ended in May 1950; but, looking ahead for a moment, it was to come back for six months from December 1956.

In October 1951 the food rations were much the same as they had been in July 1945. Tea, bacon and margarine rations were the same; slightly more butter, cooking fat and sugar were allowed; and slightly less meat and cheese.[6] Items of food were after this de-rationed from time to time: tea in October 1952; sweets in February 1953; and sugar in September 1953. But it was not until July 1954 that Food Rationing was abolished.

The National Registration identity cards, which it had been obligatory to have and to carry during and since the war, had been abolished in February 1952. As the Chancellor of the Exchequer of the time said in 1954: "In the last three years we have burned our identity cards, torn up our ration books, halved the number of snoopers (i.e. government inspectors), decimated the number of forms, and said good riddance to nearly two-thirds of the remaining wartime regulations."

The Coronation and the spread of Television

Events of national importance in these years included the death of King George VI in February 1952, and the accession and coronation of Queen Elizabeth II. The Coronation Ceremony in June 1953 was seen on television by many millions of people, marking the arrival of an age in which, in Banstead as elsewhere, television in the home became a principal form of entertainment and information. During the 1939-45 war the radio had been a vital factor, enabling morale-boosting broadcasts to be made as well as providing much-needed entertainment and information. Television had made a small start before the war in the London area, and after the war it began to spread; but for many people the prospect of seeing these impressive State events was one of the inducements to decide that a T.V. set was now one of the normal household necessities. A sprouting of T. V. aerials in the village would mark the new age, though luckily the height of the area, much of which is more than 500 feet above sea level, meant that reception in most cases would be adequate without outside aerials.

New Housing initiatives

Apart from the fact that the new Town Planning regime was more comprehensive than its predecessors, problems as to housing and building were too great to hope for a speedy solution or a total relaxation of controls. There was a lot of pressure in Banstead for the ending of emergency

6   Details from "Prospect and Reality" by T.E.B. Howarth (Collins, 1985).

arrangements, such as the use for housing of the huts at Nork Park and Yewlands Close and at the Park Road Ammunition Depot; and these were successively taken out of use and demolished. Other properties under requisition were gradually released as the Council's building programmes took shape. These showed acceleration whenever permitted by the Ministry, with private housing beginning to take an increasing part. For 1952 the Ministry provisionally allocated permission for the building of 250 houses in the Banstead area, including both Council houses and private houses built under Council licensing. Half this allocation was made available for private houses, and licences for them were taken up by May 1952.

The formation of a Banstead Self-Build Housing Association meant that there was a third category of potential house-builders. In May 1953, the Council took a look at future housing policy, and decided that at Chapel Way 53 houses should be built by the Council, 40 by the Housing Association, and then a further 26 by the Council. There were modifications later to this decision, but the principle was established. It was also decided that there would be 12 new Council houses at Headley Drive, and 18 at Merland Rise; and more building land would be bought at Shawley Way.

The licensing of housing work had been much relaxed in 1953 and 1954; and it was abolished in November 1954, leaving bye-law and planning consents as the main hurdles for intending builders.

Preston Hawe

The biggest public building project in these last years of the post-war decade was the joint development of the Preston Hawe Estate by the Banstead U.D.C. with the Sutton and Cheam, Mitcham, and Merton and Morden Councils. In 1953 the go-ahead was given for roads, footpaths, and 532 houses to be built on that estate; and in January 1954 for 14 blocks of flats.

Rose Bushes and Pound Road

Two other large council building plans were for 200 houses in the Rose Bushes area of the Nork Estate, and for a considerable new estate in the Pound Road area. The Rose Bushes project was delayed for a long time (see Chapter 11). But the way was cleared for the development of the Pound Road area by the purchase of seven old cottages in Pound Road from the enterprising Mr. V.S. Stevens. This was completed by January 1954. In May of that year, plans were produced for an estate of eleven Old People's Dwellings, twelve Old People's Flats, thirty-three three-storey flats and twelve three-bedroomed houses to be built there. The Pound Stores, which had been open there since before the First World War, and four other buildings in Pound Road would for the time being remain. When the recently built estate at the end of Chipstead Road joined up with the new Pound Road Estate, this area would be more or less fully developed, though room could be found for some private houses to be built at Wellesford Close, off Chipstead Road.

Developments in the High Street

In the High Street, approval was given in 1953 for a block of shops, flats and garages adjoining the churchyard to the west. More fundamental proposals were taking shape for "comprehensive development" of the area at the eastern end of the High Street, where the flying bomb had done so much damage. Negotiations were going on with Mr. V.S. Stevens and other owners of properties on both north and south sides of the street. Re-development on the south side was to include the old Woolpack Inn site as well as the house called The Cottage on the corner of Park Road. Chucks Meadow was to remain an open space. Re-development on the north side would stretch as far as Buff Avenue, including the site of the old Forge. The negotiations on these proposals were concluded near the end of 1955. Approval was then given for the building of a new "Woolpack Public House", and plans were considered for a block of flats on the corner of the High Street and Park Road.

The "urbanisation" of open spaces on the rest of the south side of the High Street continued actively, with approval in 1954 of the building of eight shops and sixteen flats at the corner of Bolters Lane and the High Street, opposite the Victoria Inn. They would occupy the space where a large pond had formerly been a rural feature of the village.

Problems resulting from the end of Requisitioning

A good deal of progress had been made before 1955 in releasing premises which had been occupied under requisitioning powers, mostly for ten years or more. For instance, Banstead Place had been released in October 1952. In December 1952 its owners, the Skinners' Company, applied for permission for it to be used either for housing or for an old people's home or a similar institution. The proposal for housing was rejected, but the alternative proposal was thought to be suitable.

Other releases followed; and matters came to a head in September 1955, when the council discussed its housing policy, including the requisitioning situation. The waiting list was stated to be 1,400, and housing proposals would cover only one quarter of this. Re-developing sites of pre-fabs for permanent housing would be considered; and a scheme was recommended for 246 houses and 32 flats at the Pound Estate, and 24 flats at Tattenham Corner.

Just a fortnight later the Ministry of Housing and Local Government asked the Council to state how many requisitioned houses were needed to be held vacant as a "pool" to meet needs, and directed the Council to ask owners of requisitioned premises to accept the present occupants as "statutory tenants". The Council decided to retain Wood Lodge in the Brighton Road, which had eight living "units", for the "pool", and to put out requests to owners as suggested. No fresh occupiers were to be taken on after the 1st of April 1956; and only people from existing requisitioned premises could be put into any such premises which became vacant.

In December 1955 the main building of Walton Lodge was released. By then, some of the owners of requisitioned premises had accepted the occupants of their properties as their own "statutory tenants". The problem had by no means gone away, but some progress had been made. The requisitioning powers expired in 1960.

The Fate of Wartime Services

Throughout this decade, coping with the shortages and restrictions which everybody had hoped would disappear rapidly in peace-time was a steady grind. One wartime activity which persisted for most of the period was the collection of salvage. Waste paper in fact became increasingly in demand.

Some services, developed for the emergencies of wartime, carried on to meet the changing needs of peacetime. The Women's Voluntary Services, later renamed the Women's Royal Voluntary Services, had been formed to meet the consequences of air raids. In wartime, as has been seen, they dealt with many sorts of needs and problems; and after the war they found new scope for their zeal. Amongst other things, either alone or in conjunction with other voluntary bodies, they helped old people, through Darby and Joan clubs and residential clubs. Another important aid to the sick and elderly, the "Meals on Wheels" service, was in Banstead started and run by the Banstead and District Council of Voluntary Social Services from 1955, with some financial help from the Banstead U.D.C. The Citizens Advice Bureau, which proved its value in wartime, continued to be the first port of call for many of the public faced with housing and other problems. At this time, ex-Service organisations, such as the British Legion, also played a prominent part in the re-settlement of people coming out of the Armed Forces, in Banstead as elsewhere.

Summary

By 1955 there was considerable hope that most of the economic troubles arising from the war had been overcome, and the Chancellor of the Exchequer of the time ventured to prophesy a dramatic and imminent rise in the standard of living.

One of the features of economic recovery was a great increase in the ownership and use of cars and commercial vehicles, giving rise to the inevitable difficulties of traffic congestion and lack of sufficient parking space. In August 1955 the Banstead U.D.C. concluded that car parking in the High Street needed to be relieved by the construction of a car park at the rear of the Woolworth shop premises. However, by November 1955, they had suspended action on their proposal, having met opposition to it from residents.

Many of the hopes and expectations held in 1955 would not be fulfilled rapidly or at all; but it seems reasonable to take this as marking the end of the period of rehabilitation from wartime constraints and restrictions, and the beginning of a new era.

Chapter 11

Settling down in a Changed World 1956-1975

General Trends

The post-war decade had been characterised by "Stop-Go" periods economically, and by continued rationing. Much of the following period involved not only similar "Stop-Go" periods, but several economic emergencies resulting in even more drastic Government measures, which were described as "Freeze and Squeeze". These national ups and downs were reflected locally in the ability or inability of the local authority to deal with the continuing shortage of housing and to support other socially desirable activities.

At times, failure of basic supplies and services, such as electricity, through industrial strikes and stoppages, had more direct effect on householders and businesses alike. But there were big gains for the majority of people in the shape of more freedom of choice and movement and a better standard of living. By the 1960s many more people had cars, television sets, washing machines and refrigerators. Foreign holidays were commonplace.

There were differences in the degrees of prosperity in various parts of the country. For people living in the South-East of England, and especially in places such as Banstead, within "commuting" distance of London, the situation was reminiscent of that in the 1930s, when the Industrial North had suffered heavily from closures of firms and loss of jobs, whilst in the South-East many more jobs were created.

One problem in the South-East was the movement of population into the area, so that housing shortages and transport difficulties persisted. Between 1951 and 1961, though the population of Inner London declined by 2.3 per cent, that of the outer suburbs increased by 39.7 per cent. By the early 1960s, one and a half million people were living within London's Green Belt. This compared with one million in 1938.[1]

The population of the Banstead U.D.C. area followed the trend and rose sharply. In 1947 it had been about 30,000; in 1953 it was about 34,300; in 1963 41,350; and in 1973 45,030.[2]

Building Development in the Village

The development of Banstead continued, both through public and private building, at a fair though uneven rate. Part of the expansion was needed to replace "Emergency" measures. Premises which had been "requisitioned" had to be given up; and although, as has been mentioned, some of the occupants were accepted as tenants by the owners, most of them had to be found other accommodation. Later it was decided that the temporary bungalows (pre-fabs) had had their day and needed to be demolished and replaced by conventionally built houses or flats. This meant that a good deal of the Council's efforts at providing accommodation had to be directed to meeting existing needs, rather than to the extra demand which continued to arise. Both public and private building also continued to be affected periodically by the financial effects of "crisis" measures.

One of the most notable changes in the Village in the late 1950s and the 1960s was the long-delayed redevelopment of properties at the eastern end of the High Street, partly, though not entirely, as the result of damage done by the "flying bomb" in 1944. This had been the subject of much discussion in the early 1950s; and now it was put into effect. The old Woolpack Inn was replaced by a new one set back from the High Street; and on the other side of the street, blocks of flats called "Forge Steading" were built on the sites of the old Forge and the old cottages and shops.

Another property whose future came into question at this time was Well House, the former home of Sir Daniel Lambert and his descendants, which adjoined the eastern end of the High Street, with a frontage on Woodmansterne Lane. In September 1960 it became known that this house, virtually the only large and venerable house left in the High Street, was likely to change hands with a view to re-development; and the Council reacted to this by proposing to make a Building Preservation Order for the house, and Preservation Orders for trees in the garden. This was the start of a prolonged

---

1   The figures for London and the South-East are taken from "Britain 1945-1970" by L. A. Monk (Bell and Sons, Ltd., 1976).
2   Figures taken from Official Guide issued by the Banstead U.D.C.

struggle, since both the Council and the Residents' Association were strongly opposed to the destruction of the house.

One idea was that a suitable use of the house for the benefit of the community might be found. Unfortunately, this had no more success than earlier suggestions with regard to Rosehill in Park Road. In February 1961 the Council reluctantly decided not to proceed with the proposed Building Preservation Order.

Re-development was now sure to be proposed; and in December 1961 an Outline Planning Application was submitted by MJ. Gleeson (Contractors) Limited for re-development of Well House and its grounds. This was provisionally approved. The proposal to demolish the house and erect flats, maisonettes and garages on the site was still vehemently opposed, amongst others by Marshal of the Royal Air Force Lord Tedder, who was living in retirement at Well Farm, just round the corner in Woodmansterne Lane. But the battle was lost. In November 1962 planning permission was finally granted. There continued to be minor skirmishes with the developers on details of proposed alterations; the old house was damaged by fire; but ultimately it was demolished and replaced by a block of flats, named after it. Another Banstead landmark had disappeared.

These were not the only items of change at the end of the High Street. On the corner of Park Road and the High Street, there had been for many years a large house called, rather misleadingly, The Cottage, with gardens and a pond in its grounds. This was also to go. In 1958 it was replaced by a three-storey block of flats and maisonettes which was given the name Cheyne Court. With some much needed road widening, this end of the High Street had now assumed a very different appearance.

The permitted demolition of existing premises made room in this period for more developments on the southern side of the High Street. In 1963 permission was given for a block of shops and flats to be built between the Church Institute and the Village School; and in 1973 for a cul-de-sac to be created with Town Houses adjoining it where a coffee house called The Well Coffee House had recently stood, towards the eastern end of the street. This would be named Chiltons Close. At the western end of the street, a Waitrose Supermarket was opened in a block of shops and offices replacing the former Wingfield House, next to the Victoria Inn.

Developers were also very conscious of opportunities for building on spaces left open within residential areas south of the High Street. In Avenue Road demolition of two houses created a gap in which a block of flats, Tyrolean Court, was built, with an archway forming the access to an area of land at the rear, on which were built maisonettes to be known as Cheviot Close.

Even more extensive development took place in the area south of Court Road. Here, in a rather unusual scheme, two developers were in 1959 each granted permission to build an estate road leading off Court Road at a different point, and blocks of maisonettes and flats adjoining that road. The condition for this permission was that the two roads should be joined up at the rear, so as to form a continuous road linked at each end to Court Road. This was later named Courtlands Crescent. A block of flats was also built in 1960 on the site of what had been a house called Little Court in Court Road, near the new easterly junction with Courtlands Crescent. In the grounds behind Rosehill an estate of terraced houses called The Tracery was in 1967 created round an open area.

There were other developments not very far from the main part of the village. Houses were built in Holly Lane; in the grounds of what had been The Grange in Sutton Lane; and at Dutch Cottage at the corner of Court Road and Bolters Lane (Clifton Place).

The chief features of the developments in the Village area at this time were that a large proportion consisted of maisonettes, town houses and flats, and that to an overwhelming extent these were private developments.

A little further afield, another housing estate was privately built, following permission given in 1967. Houses north of Garratts Lane, near its junction with the Brighton Road, known as Beech House, Northacre and Highlea, together with their gardens and grounds, were replaced by the Northacre Estate, with an access road to Garratts Lane.

The Community Hall

Things were also stirring in Park Road, where the future of the open space known as Chucks Meadow, stretching back from Park Road just north of the grounds of Rosehill, was at stake. In 1956 the Lambert Trustees applied for permission to build on this site; and when this was rejected, they compelled the Council to buy the land under Town Planning Act provisions. It was specified that all this land should be held as public open space; but there were other ideas about this, which would come to fruition.

The Banstead Community Association had been formed in 1946. Various groups had operated successfully. From 1948 they had made use in the evenings of the old British Restaurant premises, by then being used in the daytime as the local Schools Canteen. A Book Circle, an Arts Group, a Chess Group, a Horticultural Society and a Film Society, as well as other activities, were carried on there and at the Church Institute. From 1963 onwards a Gramophone Society held sessions at the Central Library. But more permanent and adequate accommodation was plainly needed.

The idea of a proper Community Centre remained very much in mind throughout the 1950s and into the 1960s, especially as in Nork a similar project was being pursued. The obvious place to build a new Centre for the Village would be on the County Council's Walton Lodge Estate, next to the Central Library, which had been built there and opened in 1961.

By October 1961 the Banstead U.D.C. had approved a scheme put forward by the Association for erection of a Community Centre, a large part of the cost of which could be covered by grants from the Government and local authorities. This was put forward to the County Council, with a request to make a site available on the Walton Lodge Estate. Unfortunately, they named a price for the land there which was far too high to be considered. There followed three years of frustration for the Association, who had to seek another site before launching an appeal to raise at least £10,000 towards the cost of building.

After protracted negotiations with the Banstead U.D.C. and the Ministry, it was agreed in the summer of 1964 that the Council would lease to the Association two and a half acres of Chucks Meadow for the proposed Community Hall. The remaining ground would be left as public open space adjoining the Lady Neville Recreation Ground.

At a meeting in April 1965, an appeal was launched to raise the sum required. It was a mountainous task for an Association which at that time had only just over two hundred members. At least a thousand members were needed, as well as all sorts of fund-raising activities. This was not the only difficulty. There was opposition to the use of Chucks Meadow for this purpose.

The objections were overcome; but it was not until 1971 that the funds reached the necessary level; and even then the essential grant from the Government was threatened by one of the usual economic crises. But further grants were made by the Banstead U.D.C. and a contract for the building was signed in November 1973. The building was officially opened by the Mayor of the newly-created Borough of Reigate and Banstead on the 10th of May 1975.

Council Housing

In this period, Council housing was mostly built some distance away from Banstead Village itself. Some was built in the western part of the main Nork

Figure 40. Aerial View of Housing Development near Tottenham Corner, mid 1950s. (Railways Stations between arches)

Estate, stretching now down to the Reigate Road; some was between Yew Tree Bottom Road and Great Tattenhams; some in the vicinity of Merland Rise and Chapel Way; and some more in such space as was left in the Shrubland Road and Pound Road neighbourhood. The demolition of pre-fabs and the closure of allotments in various places provided sites for other Council houses. Part of The Oval allotments was the only new site for Council houses in the village area itself.

The need for Council housing remained obvious throughout the period, and the programme was an active one though punctuated by occasional restraints. The differing attitudes of Central Government as political power changed hands was inevitably reflected in the Banstead U.D.C.'s own housing policies. In spite of occasional setbacks, the Council's efforts were very considerable; and in Nork and elsewhere they were accompanied by a lot of private building. By the beginning of 1959, the Council had added 1,148 Council houses to 309 which had survived the War. They had a three-year programme for 1959-62 which envisaged the replacement of all the prefabs by permanent buildings (except at Hillside) and involved the construction of 144 dwellings in 1959-60; a similar number in 1960-61; and 187 in 1961-62. The first year's developments would be on sites on the Pound Estate, at Partridge Mead and at Chapel Way, Ferriers Way and North Tadworth Farm. The latter area would also see further extensive development in the third year, making 192 dwellings in all; whilst a further 75 dwellings would be built in the Merland Rise - Chetwode Road area to replace pre-fabs. These plans underwent modification and delays, but the general thrust did not change.

In September 1961 the Government gave instructions for slowing down building in 1962. In Banstead, the large development at Chapel Way could proceed. Apart from that, only sixteen dwellings could be built, and this would be for slum clearance and for old people. It was not until December 1964 that plans were approved for the demolition of pre-fabs on land fronting Willow Gardens, St. Leonards Road and Chetwode Road, and the erection on those sites of flats and houses. This was Stage 2 of the massive development of this area. Stage 3 was for 115 "dwelling units", consisting of blocks of flats ranging in size from one to four bedrooms. This was approved by the Council in March 1967, and the Government gave its consent the following month, stipulating, however, that this should constitute the entire Council building programme for 1967-8.

At times, during the programme of development, the Council had difficulty in deciding which course to follow in relation to land available to them, including the former pre-fab sites. The land could be developed by the

Council itself, either for Council housing or for sale to people on the "housing list". It could be sold to private developers, with stipulations that at least part of the development should be reserved for such people. On the other hand, it could simply be sold without conditions except any imposed by the planning authorities.

The difficulty of deciding the right course was clearly illustrated by the case of what was known as the "Rosebushes Estate". This was thirty acres of land between Yew Tree Bottom Road and the Reigate Road, which the Council had bought in 1952. In October 1957 the Council applied for planning permission for the layout of roads there and the erection of 175 buildings; but this was frustrated when, in December 1957, the Government imposed a 20 per cent cut on public building.

In June 1958 the Council resolved to sell the land off in individual plots, but this proposal eventually failed to take shape. In its place, in April 1960, the Council agreed to sell the whole property to a development company, Downs Estates Limited, on condition that they sold plots only to private individuals, and not to other developers. Then the Company ran into trouble. It was not until April 1963 that approval was sought and given for the full development for 179 dwellings. It seems that in the end these were not by any means all built by the Downs Estate Company.

A similar dilemma arose in November 1970 with regard to Fir Tree Close, an area of 2.75 acres adjoining Fir Tree Road, formerly a pre-fab site. It was proposed that the Council should build houses there for sale on 99-year leases. This scheme also failed. In July 1972 the Council decided to invite tenders for purchase of the land for private housing development. In October of that year a tender of £236,200 was accepted from a development company. Following this, planning permission was given for the erection of 12 pairs of semi-detached houses.

At the end of the 1960s and in the 1970s, further developments took place at the Tadworth end of the old Nork -Great Burgh Estate. The London Borough of Merton were in November 1971 given permission to build on seven acres of land at the rear of houses in Shelvers Way and Copley Way; and in January 1973 planning approval was given for the building by the Banstead U.D.C. of flats and terraced houses on a site of 4.334 acres on the Waterfield - Preston Hawe Estate.

The Cemetery Site and the Swimming Pool

The Waterfield development was something of a new departure. Extensive developments had taken place to the east of Merland Rise and at its southern end in the Preston Lane area; but a large area of land, between the buildings on the western side of Merland Rise and the Tadworth to Tattenham Corner railway line, had remained open land, occupied under grazing licences, apart from a disused wartime oilpipe line depot belonging to the Ministry of Works.

The land had been bought by the Council in 1938 for the purposes of a cemetery; but, in spite of a panicky moment in 1939, no steps had ever been taken towards the construction of a cemetery, though the land was always referred to as "the Cemetery Site".[3] In 1963, enquiries confirmed that there was no likelihood of the land being required for cemetery purposes in the foreseeable future. This was welcome news to the Council. Proposals were put forward in 1965 for about four acres of land at the Tadworth (Waterfield) end of the land to be turned into an Industrial Estate, whilst just under ten acres would be sold for housing.

The project took time to mature; but in November 1969 approval was given for an estate road for the proposed industrial estate and for a single-storey factory of 30,000 square feet. Grind All Limited were named as possible tenants of the factory.

The proposed sale of the former cemetery site for residential purposes was linked by the Council with proposals for a public swimming pool. Up to this time, the only swimming pools available to people in Banstead had been the privately owned pools at the two "road houses" at Burgh Heath, The Galleon and Il Pirata (formerly The Sugar Bowl). This was unsatisfactory, and inadequate for the much increased population. By October 1968, the idea of a public swimming pool had become positive enough for the Council's General Purposes Committee to recommend reservation of a triangular area for that purpose at the southern end of Nork Park, between Church Lane and the Reigate Road. The full Council, however, referred this recommendation back to the Committee. In December 1969 application for planning permission for a swimming pool on the Nork Park site was rejected by the Council; but in March 1970 they recommended that a swimming pool should be constructed at the Merland Rise Recreation Ground.

The proposal to sell land for residential development was activated in October 1972. It was then decreed, presumably to make the sale more attractive, that in future the description "Cemetery Site" should be dropped, and the property should be referred to as "Headley View". Planning

3   Strangely enough, part of the land is now known to have been the site of an Anglo-Saxon burial ground.
    (See Chapter 1).

Figure 41. Swimming Pool, Merland Rise

permission for residential development of Headley View was applied for. At the same time, an application was made to the Surrey County Council to permit re-appropriation of the Merland Rise Allotments site, adjoining the existing Recreation Ground, for recreational purposes. This was to clear the way for the swimming pool project.

By February 1973, both applications had been approved. A firm decision was then made by the Council that capital proceeds of the sale of the Headley View land were to be applied towards the cost of the Swimming Pool, for which consulting engineers were to be asked to prepare drawings. The Headley View land was put up for sale by tender, and sold to Ideal Homes Ltd. for £801,000. Planning permission for the swimming pool premises was given in July 1973. There remained much more to be done before the Swimming Pool could be constructed and brought into the service of the public in the district; but work was started in September 1975 with a view to completion a year later.

Traffic Problems and the Village School

Two other matters figured prominently in the minds of residents and the local Council over these years and indeed long afterwards. One was that of traffic problems in the High Street, coupled with the question of the provision of car parks. The other was the relocation and replacement of the Village School, which, though there had been alterations and extensions from time to time, had occupied a site at the corner of Avenue Road and High Street since it opened in 1858.

Traffic Problems

Relief from traffic passing through the High Street had been afforded by the by-pass road, Winkworth Road, built in the early 1930s. But this relief had largely been counter-acted by the ever increasing number of cars and commercial vehicles in use by the 1970s. Resistance from residents to proposals for a car park in the High Street had in 1955 caused the Council to withdraw the idea. But traffic continued to build up. Various measures were considered for "no parking" or "no waiting" restrictions in parts of the High Street, and some were tried out or even implemented. The need for something more positive in the shape of provision of car parks was all the time becoming increasingly obvious.

Curiously enough, as in the case of Chucks Meadow, action by the Council was in the end virtually forced upon them; this time by the owners of the land behind Woolworth's store, who were refused planning permission to build on it. They then compelled the Council to buy the land from them. Even after the purchase was completed in February 1962, the Council deferred a decision as to its use. However, in May of that year they finally agreed that the land should be used as a public car park. By November 1963 the project had sufficiently advanced for an order to be made to regulate use of the car park. In 1966 the car park was resurfaced. The idea of making charges was raised, but rejected, as it continued to be throughout this period.

By 1968 it was becoming clear that still more parking space was needed. The Council received a report which suggested that the Surrey County Council should be asked to agree to the use of land on the Walton Lodge Estate for the purpose. In February 1970 it was agreed to take a lease of the land. This car park was completed towards the end of 1970. Again, no parking charges were to be made.

The Village School

Building of a new school to replace the existing one had become a live issue as early as 1960, when the Village Ratepayers Association expressed concern about the site of the existing school. They had heard that a new school in Bolters Lane for children from five to eleven years of age was proposed, and that it would be erected "in some two years". The Association expressed the fear that the site of the existing school might be sold to a private developer who would build shops on it. There was no doubt about the need to improve the accommodation for the school, which was over-crowded. How this should be done, and what should happen to the old school buildings, was the subject of a heated debate which was to go on for the next thirty years.

The first positive moves were made in 1964, when the County Council wrote to the Banstead U.D.C., suggesting re-siting the school on the Walton Lodge Estate. The Ratepayers Association found several objections to this: amongst other things, it would be "almost on the boundary of the Village Ward, and could be inconvenient for parents". The proposal then seems to have lapsed for several years. In 1969, the County Council said that the existing School site was "unlikely to be vacated for five to ten years, and then would probably be used for a nursery school". By October 1971, the County Planning Officer had a quite different idea. He put forward to the Banstead U.D.C. tentative suggestions for shops and flats to be built on the site, when it became available. The Banstead U.D.C.'s response was that the site should continue to be used for educational purposes.

In July 1973, the Surrey County Council formally proposed building a new First School next to the Middle School which had already been built in The Horseshoe on the Walton Lodge Estate. The new building would be financed by the sale of the High Street premises. In October 1973, the Banstead U.D.C. made a counter-suggestion. This was that the old School site should be sold to them, so that the playground could be used as a temporary car park, and the buildings used "for other purposes to be determined at a later date". With the Banstead U.D.C. coming to the end of its days, this was not a very convincing proposal, nor was it ever to bear fruit. This was to prove a long-running saga, not reaching its climax until 1989.

Social and Recreational Activities

The steady increase in the population created increasing pressure on the available facilities for leisure activities; and this pressure was only partly met by extra provisions. During the long struggle to produce a Hall for the Banstead Community Association, all its various activities had to be carried on by its different sections in an assortment of places.

The Church Institute remained until 1975 the only large hall in the Village, though occasional use could be made of the Village School for meetings or exhibitions, in accordance with a reservation made when it was transferred to the School Board in 1874. A good deal of social activity was also carried on at the Civil Defence Centre behind the Council House in the Brighton Road, as this had a fair-sized hall. The Civil Defence unit had its ups and downs, but survived until 1968. It was then officially wound up; the premises were taken over by the Council; and the hall became available for public meetings. But this was no answer to the main problem, which would be solved only when the Community Hall was opened.

The Nork Community Association, a very lively organisation with numerous activities, made use of a converted barn at Warren Farm for dances and other activities, until their Community Centre was opened in 1966. Some of the more spectacular events, however, such as theatrical and musical performances, were put on at the Church Institute in Banstead, and so became part of the life of the whole community. The Tattenham and Merland Rise area, with a fast growing population, needed a Community Centre; and this was recognised in 1958, when the Council considered proposals for "a physical, cultural, and recreational centre" at what was already the Merland Rise Recreation Ground. As was to be expected, this took a few years to achieve. A Youth Centre on the Walton Lodge Estate was an important addition towards the end of the period.

Banstead never had a cinema of its own, though over the years several proposals actually did receive planning permission. In the post-war years, when a weekly visit to "The Pictures" was still quite a recognised custom, people went to Epsom or Sutton, which were well provided.

The spread of television eventually put paid to any idea of a cinema in Banstead; and even the Film Society's shows in the Institute came to an end. More positively, activities such as those of the Workers' Education Association (the W.E.A.) flourished in spite of the variety of venues, which included such places as the Lady Neville Recreation Ground Pavilion, school rooms and so on.

The Library Services, which had been carried on keenly, but with considerable difficulty, in a converted shop in the High Street, improved immensely with the completion of the Central Library in Bolters Lane and the Branch Library at Tattenham Crescent in 1961. The Travelling Library, instituted by the County Council in 1958, served more out-of-the-way parts of the district.

Outdoor sports of most kinds were pretty well provided for by the public recreation grounds and the open spaces which had been used traditionally or opened-up before the war, with various subsequent improvements. A paddling pool at the Lady Neville Recreation Ground was provided by the charitable efforts of the Banstead Round Table in about 1973; a new Pavilion and hard tennis courts were provided at the Tattenham Way Recreation Ground in 1959-60; and better play-grounds were provided for children. A large field in Nork Park was also leased to the County Council for school playing field purposes. The Banstead Athletic Football ground at Merland Rise was improved from time to time.

In 1964 the Banstead Cricket Club finally succeeded in obtaining a second ground adjoining The Green. This ground had formerly been part of the Rosehill School playing fields. The Cricket club had first tried to buy it during the war in 1942. In 1966, when the new pitch was ready for use, the Club gave up use of the Garton Recreation Ground in Garratts Lane for their two lower teams; this was later used by boys of The Priory School. The old pavilion at The Green, built back in 1892, was given a thorough repair, since a projected new Pavilion would have to wait for a while. In fact, a few years later, a new wooden Club Room was erected to supplement the Old Pavilion.

On the Tattenham Way Recreation Ground, the Burgh Heath Cricket Club ran two Saturday teams and a Sunday team.

Riding had always been a popular pastime in Banstead; not surprisingly, in view of the open nature of the district and the tradition of horse racing on the Downs. In spite of the building developments, there remained plenty of people interested in riding for pleasure.

In 1966, four Riding Establishments held licences in the immediate vicinity of Banstead. One was Mr. J.C. Henderson's Riding Stables in the old Garratts Hall stables, known by now as No. 2 Colcokes Road. A string of horses being led by Mr. Henderson up Garratts Lane was a regular feature of the neighbourhood, though not conducive to a smooth flow of traffic. Other establishments included the Santa Teresa School of Equitation at Warren Farm, a School at Hengist Farm in Woodmansterne Lane, and the Drift Bridge Riding and Hiring Stables in Ruden Way.

The churches of different denominations, which had by this time become well established in the area, were prominent promoters of social and recreational activities amongst their congregations, young and old.

For walkers and nature enthusiasts, a larger part of Banstead Woods became available in 1965. Perrotts Wood, and other parts of the Woods around the Queen Elizabeth Hospital, amounting to some 75 acres, were bought from the Minister of Health by the Banstead U.D.C.; and in 1967, in collaboration with the Surrey Naturalists' Trust, an Open Nature Reserve was created there.

Demise of the Banstead Urban District Council

The Banstead Urban District Council had survived a threat to its existence in 1962, when the creation of a Council for "Greater London" was being considered. It was suggested that Banstead should be included in this Greater London area. The Urban District Council at that time made a detailed submission, opposing the proposition, saying that local residents opposed the idea almost unanimously. Following this, the Ministry concerned rejected the proposition, stating specifically that the Banstead area was not part of the continuously built-up suburban districts which it would be right to include in "Greater London".

As a "fringe area", the Banstead District next received the attention of the Boundary Commission in relation to realignment of Parliamentary constituencies. For a good many years, the Banstead District had been in the Carshalton Division of Surrey. In 1965 it was proposed that the Banstead Urban District should be included, with the Borough of Reigate, in a new constituency of "Reigate". The Urban District Council agreed, and the change was made; but the Council's suggestion that the constituency should be named "Reigate and Banstead" was rejected.

In 1971 a new round of Local Government reorganisation started. New districts were to be areas with population between 75,000 and 100,000. The prospects for Banstead were described by its Urban District Council as "disturbing". This assessment was correct. By May 1972, detailed Government proposals had been published. These showed that the Banstead Urban District area was to be merged with that of the Borough of Reigate, with a population totalling 101,074. The Banstead U.D.C. decided at once to lodge objections, which were amply supported by Residents' Associations.

A petition against the merger with Reigate, signed by 12,000 people, was presented to the Boundary Commission. The Banstead District Federation of Ratepayers' and Residents' Associations wrote to the Boundary Commission stating why they considered the merger to be inappropriate. They pointed out that there was no natural affinity between Banstead and Reigate. Public transport between the two towns was poor; Reigate lay in the plain, and was more densely developed and industrialised than Banstead; and Reigate

Figure 42. Mint Cottages with 'The Mint' in the distance

traditionally looked south across the plain rather than northwards over the escarpment.

Many more efforts were made to oppose the merger, but all failed; and by the beginning of 1973 the merger had been approved by Parliament. A joint committee of the Banstead Urban District Council and the Reigate Borough Council was to be formed to implement the merger. Elections would be held on the 7th of June 1973, and the new District would come into being on the 1st of April 1974. There would be 22 councillors for the existing Banstead Urban District area, and 28 for the Borough of Reigate area.

Last Months of the Council

The Banstead Urban District Council in the meantime continued to carry on its various functions. In July 1973 confirmation was received of a Conservation Area Order relating to an area round Banstead Place, including Mint Farm and Mint Cottages. Planning approval was given for a new Vicarage in Court Road, on part of the grave-yard land. Outline permission

Figure 43. Mint Farm from the South

was given for the demolition of a private school, known as Beacon School, in Beacon Way, Nork, which had been run for many years by Miss E. B. Batts. It was to be replaced by flats.

A number of other developments were approved. These included the erection of seventeen five-bedroom houses in a new cul-de-sac off Bolters Lane, to be known as Ashley Drive. Ten houses were to be built in Holly Lane East; and others at the rear of houses in Picquets Way and the Brighton Road, to be known as The Brindles.

The London Borough of Wandsworth, which had become responsible for Beechholme, decided that the 200 children still resident there should be put into homes in its own area. Accordingly in 1974 the establishment closed. This made way for a new housing estate known as High Beeches.

It would have been pleasant if the last months of the Banstead Urban District Council could have passed in a relaxed atmosphere; but the early months of 1974 were far from relaxing. 1973 had seen a number of national strikes, giving rise to an acute fuel crisis. On the 13th of December 1973 the

Government announced that businesses must conserve fuel from the 31st of December by working on only three days each week wherever the use of electricity was involved.

These restrictions hit the private and public sectors alike. On the 2nd of January 1974, the General Purposes Committee of the Banstead Council discussed whether to alter the dates of meetings to ensure that they fell on days when heating and lighting would be available; but it was resolved to stick to the scheduled dates. Council and Committee meetings would be held with the use of emergency lighting, such as individual gas lamps and candles. These were conditions which would have been familiar to the old Banstead Vestry a hundred years before. Only after a General Election and the appointment of a new Government was there a general removal of the restrictions on the use of electricity. This was in March 1974.

The final meeting of the Banstead Urban District Council was held on the 26th of March 1974, when letters of appreciation from a number of Residents' Associations in the area were read. There had been some opposition to the formation of the Council in 1933, and no doubt differences between the Council and residents at times. But there was obviously a feeling that overall the Council had served the Banstead area well.

Its achievements in housing were recorded in 1973 in their last official Guide to the District. In 1933 they had taken over 220 houses and flats from the former Rural District Council. By 1939 they had built a further 91 dwellings. After the War, 300 pre-fabs were provided, though most of them, having served their purpose, were replaced by 1973. Since 1946, the Council had erected a further 2,056 houses, flats and elderly persons' dwellings.

The Council's housing estates at Yewlands, Horsecroft and Pound Road in 1973 comprised about 250 dwellings; in Nork there were 240 dwellings, with 54 flats at Eastgate; at Great Tattenhams and Shawley Crescent, 336 dwellings; at Preston Lane, Tadworth, 126; and at Chapel Way, more than 500. There were other smaller housing developments; and at Preston Hawe there was a massive estate of 700 dwellings, which had been developed for the over-spill of three neighbouring authorities, in a joint scheme. Other housing projects were in prospect. It was a formidable record of achievement.

There was clearly much regret that Banstead was to cease to be the centre of its own area of local administration, with the Council and its officers readily and locally available. It would become, as it had been before 1933, one place in a very large administrative area; and it would lie very much on the fringe of that area. A certain loss of local identity seemed to be the likely result.

Chapter 12

Modern Times (1975-2004)

Fortunately the life of a community goes on without too much disruption, whatever may be the latest notion as to the range and function of Local Authorities. So it was with Banstead after the transfer of local administration to the new Reigate and Banstead Borough Council with its headquarters in Reigate

The New Council

There was in fact no complete break with the past. A number of the Councillors who had represented Wards in the Banstead Urban District were elected to represent the same, or substantially the same, Wards in the new Borough. Some of the senior officers in the old Council retired, but others of the staff remained, and for some years the old Council Offices in the Brighton Road were retained to house Departments of the new Council.

One thing which can be said with some certainty of Local Government is that in time and often too soon, proposals will come up for reform of the structure or funding or both. In 1962 the proposal had been to merge the area into Greater London. In 1979 it consisted of abolishing the County Councils and passing their functions to the District Councils. A rather similar idea came up again in 1991. But none of the proposals succeeded.

Apart from some inconvenience and a certain feeling of being at the fringe of the new Council's attentions rather than at the centre, Banstead did not appear to suffer very much from the changes made in 1974. Change and development continued in the ordinary way.

Figure 44. Opening Day at the new First School, The Horseshoe, Sept 1990.
Miss Nicholson, Headmistress, (left) escorting three children

Housing Development in the Period

At first housing development was at a steady rate. In the late 1990s and the first years of the new century the pace notably accelerated, as economic developments brought an increased move of population into the area in and around Greater London. The available housing was quite inadequate to cope with this increase, and the result was the dual one of rising prices for existing houses and a boom in housing development.

Apart from the virtual completion of building in the Headley Drive area, most developments in Banstead made use of pieces of open land which could be found in built-up areas. This included parts of large gardens, which were a feature of many houses in Nork, and also some in Banstead village. These seemed to have lost their attraction for most people. Front gardens were largely replaced by hard standing car parks. "Infilling" might be of a plot with wide frontage to a road; but more often, where access could be made from the road, of garden spaces behind existing houses. If no such access was possible, a house or houses might be demolished to provide access. Prices were swollen for the land and for the new houses, making it difficult for people of modest income to buy - but there seemed to be no lack of purchasers at the higher prices.

Another feature of the development was a vastly increased number of flats, including "sheltered accommodation". Existing buildings could be used as a base for conversion into a number of flats. A good example would be the building in Park Road, originally Rooks Nest, then Rosehill and later Castle House, given a new wing and considerable alteration. What had been Wingfield House and then Waitrose Store and adjoining premises provided more flats ("Wingfield Court"); and when the old Council House in the Brighton Road and the buildings at its rear ceased to be used by the Borough, the House was replaced by flats ("Holmwood House") and the other buildings by houses ("The Fieldings"). In Bolters Lane a more drastic development consisted of the demolition of three houses to make way for a block of "sheltered accommodation" flats. These were just a few of the many developments.

Holly Hill House, a large house with pleasant grounds and a large fruit and vegetable garden, was also turned into flats and named "The Manor House", and houses were built in the garden. Other such developments are inevitable.

The Railway Stations

The search for housing sites also affected two local railway stations. Both the Epsom Downs and Tattenham Corner stations had a number of platforms to cope with the racecourse crowds who used to come there, but in modern times no longer did so. Both were severely reduced in size, and Epsom Downs Station was relocated down the line to make space for housing developments. This coincided with a very large drop in the number of commuters using the branches and an equally larger reduction in the train services, no doubt adding to the traffic problems on the roads.

Other Developments

There was at least one considerable commercial development. Great Burgh, originally a house built in 1912 for Mr Colman's son, but occupied for many years by Beechams, the Distillers and other companies, was taken over by the Toyota car making company. They constructed buildings in the grounds for their own use. The mansion was occupied by another company and houses were built on the rest of the site.

The Public Sector

In the public sector, the Horseshoe area became substantially more built up, now being the site not only of the Library, the Civic Centre, the Clinic, the Youth Centre, the First and Second Schools, the Surrey Ambulance Headquarters and the Social Services offices and Workshop, but also of new institutional blocks - the Ridgemount Residential Care Home, replacing a former home, and the Greenacres Residential Home.

The provision of houses for people who could not afford to buy had long been a matter for the Council; but in 2001, in accordance with what was becoming a common pattern, all the "Council Houses" were taken over by a separate agency, the Reigate and Banstead Housing Trust, with representation for the tenants on the managing committee.

Traffic

Along with the housing developments came an ever increasing number of cars. Traffic troubles became much more acute in the village, and there was practically no improvement in the road system to cope with the new demand. Car parking in the High Street, in Court Road, and in older roads leading off the High Street became a serious problem. The existing public car parks remained much as before, though they were now the subject of parking charges. A slightly larger park was provided behind the new Waitrose store; but that store attracted a great deal of customer traffic as well as very large trucks bringing in the goods. A mini-roundabout was installed at the eastern end of the High Street, making it necessary to reposition the War Memorial.

The Police

Another administrative change towards the end of the period occurred in 2001 when the slightly anomalous situation that Banstead was in the Metropolitan Police area though in the County of Surrey was ended, and the Surrey Police took over responsibility. This was the end of a very long standing arrangement which had started as early as 1839, probably because at that time Surrey had no police force. The Police Station remained, and the public would hardly have noticed any difference.

The Hurricane

The most dramatic event in the district for many years occurred in the early hours of the 16th of October 1987, when, contrary to all the forecasts, a gale of wind reaching over 100 miles an hour in places turned course from along the English Channel and travelled across Sussex and Surrey and onwards, causing severe damage in the swathe of country on its route. No such storm had been experienced since 1703; and it was estimated that 15 million trees were destroyed in all and 19 people killed.[1] Roads, railways and power lines were badly affected. The next day travelling was practically impossible until Council workers and residents who came out to help combined gradually to cut away the many tree trunks causing the obstructions and move the trunks to the side. It was the nearest thing to a wartime post-Blitz situation likely to be experienced in peacetime.

As an example, one resident in Garratts Lane looked out over his back garden to see at the end a complete barricade which turned out to be three trees felled across each other. Another tree was standing but at an angle which made it obvious that it would fall unless the top hamper was removed; and a large branch from a tall Wellingtonia tree next door lay on the lawn. One greenhouse had its glass shattered; another had been blown off its base against the fence. To walk down to the High Street meant a sort of steeplechase, jumping or climbing over fallen tree trunks. A few doors away, a Wellingtonia had fallen on Little Garratts, crushing the top floor. (Ultimately it had to be removed by a huge crane)

It has to be said that, comparatively speaking, Banstead and the Banstead Woods got off fairly lightly. A very large number of beech trees in Nork were felled. There were a considerable number of trees blown down in the Banstead Woods; but, probably because they lie mostly on a north-facing slope, the damage was very small compared with that at the Carshalton Oaks, where 15,000 trees were blown down.

Social Amenities

There were some welcome new amenities. The long-awaited Swimming Pool at Merland Rise, completed in 1976, and the other facilities of a Leisure Centre were much used both by schools and the public. The football ground was used by Banstead Athletic. The Tattenham Way Recreation ground was used for both football and cricket.

The Banstead Cricket Club continued to play both on The Green and the adjoining field, whilst on the Lady Neville ground (with a new Pavilion after a fire) Bowls and Tennis were played.

In 1983 a Day Centre for the elderly was built in the Horseshoe; and later this was enlarged and combined with a "Helpshop" providing information and easy access to Departments of the Borough Council - the whole being given the title of "the Civic Centre". It provided space for public meetings, in

1   "Surrey in the Hurricane" by Mark Davison and Ian Currie, Froglet Publications Ltd, 1988.

addition to that available at the Church Institute and the Community Hall in Chucks Meadow, which were both the venue for a great deal of activity.

For those interested in the Arts, the Arts Festival organisation provided concerts and other events. Study groups of many kinds were provided by the Council, by the Workers Educational Association, and by the Banstead branch of the new "University of the Third Age".

A Local History Centre was opened in the Library in 2004.

Supermarket and Shops

A new supermarket was built for ASDA on a site off the Reigate Road near Burgh Heath, with a large car park. In the time of the Colman family's ownership of the Nork Estate this had been the site of a Riding School, and then from 1950 it had been a "Cash and Carry" depot for Kinloch Ltd.

This, and the opening of other multiple shops would have its effect on trading in smaller shops in the Burgh Heath and Banstead areas. For this and other reasons by the end of the period, shop premises in Burgh Heath and in the Shrubland Road area had almost all closed as such, some being put to other commercial purposes. Even in Banstead High Street there was a proliferation of charities, building societies and estate agents occupying what had been ordinary shops.

Population and Schools

The population of Banstead - taking that to consist of the Banstead Village, Nork and Tattenham Wards - rose from 20642 in 1991 to 23135 in 2001, and the increase in children between 5 and 15 was from 2556 to 3123.[2] The statistics may be distorted to some extent by boundary changes or other factors; but the general conclusion must be that expansion of the population had resumed at a fair rate after a drop between 1971 and 1981 which had resulted in the closing of the de Burgh School in Marbles Way, and its merger with what had been known as the Picquets Way School and then as Nork Park School. The school was now renamed the Beacon School. The very obvious increase in development after 2001 will no doubt have led to an increase in the number of children, which must put a strain on the school accommodation, even though the modern First and Second Schools are now fairly established in the Horseshoe, and the Beacon School has been much enlarged, with facilities for Adult Evening Classes.

One of the unfortunate casualties of the period was the closure and demolition of the old Village School, even though it clearly needed to be replaced as such. For years it had been hoped and strongly contended that the

2   Reigate and Banstead Borough Council Census Area Profile 1991 and The Census Key
    Statistics Profile 2001

building should be retained and put to some other community purpose; but the County Council put it up for sale by tender on condition that the purchaser should at its own cost erect a new school in the Horseshoe.

The successful tenderer was Waitrose Ltd, who stated that their existing premises at the western end of the High Street were no longer sufficient. The new Waitrose store opened in December 1990, a few months after the new First School had opened in the Horseshoe.

Private schools such as Aberdour (now in the former Wood Lodge premises off the Brighton Road towards Burgh Heath), the Priory in Bolters Lane and Greenacre in Sutton Lane continued and flourished. So did St Anne's RC School, whose premises in the former Court Farm were extensively recast, with additional permanent buildings. Restoration work was done to some 18th century rooms at the back, though a 17th century room was lost.

Other Changes

Another contentious issue at this time was the use to be assigned to the former Banstead Hospital on the Downs between Banstead and Belmont. Originally known as the Middlesex County Asylum when it was opened in 1877, its grounds comprised what had been known as the Hundred Acres. The hospital was closed in 1986, and a great deal of argument arose as to an acceptable use of the premises and the land.

In the end this amounted to a choice between a large housing estate and a prison, and the authorities decided in fact to create two prisons on the site. In the first place a small prison was created, making use of existing buildings, for comparatively lesser offenders, whilst work was put in hand for the building of a larger prison which was to house more serious offenders in Category B. By 1992 both prisons were operative, being known respectively as Downview and High Down.

About ten years later, pressures on the Prison Service saw a change in their status, Downview being converted into a prison for women and High Down taking some of the most serious of criminals, in Category A.

In 2004, a further development robbed the High Street of one of its chief landmarks - the Victoria Inn at the western end, built in the 1860s. This was altered and extended to provide a licensed restaurant with flats over, leaving the village High Street with only one public house, the Woolpack. This and the closure of some of the smaller shops as such seemed to demonstrate a change in public habits as well as the character of the High Street.

At the eastern end of the High Street, the structure housing the Village Well, which was threatening to collapse, was restored.

The Banstead Woods

The Banstead Woods were for some years managed by the Council with the cooperation of the Surrey Wildlife Trust. They are protected by legislation so that they cannot be threatened as they were in the 1880s. In recent years the management has been taken over by the Downlanders. This was a body set up by several local authorities and relying mainly upon volunteers to carry out their work on the Downs, the Woods and other places such as the Wildlife Field created off Bolters Lane and Dunnymans Road in Banstead. They carry on in the Woods some of the traditional forestry crafts as well as pollarding and other necessary tasks.

The Queen Elizabeth Hospital was closed and put up for the sale in 1997 with its garden and grounds in the middle of the Woods, but it has laid empty for years and (as happened when it was last empty) suffered damage from a fire.

Summary

Residents will hope that adequate open spaces will remain in the Village, that the neighbourhood will be preserved; and that it will remain possible to reach open country by a short walk from any part of Banstead. These are distinguishing features of Banstead for which the efforts made by determined and far-seeing people in the past are largely responsible. Such efforts may need to be repeated.

However, to assess the social and practical future for Banstead and its residents is beyond the scope of this book, which is concerned with the story of the transformation of a small village on the Down, clustering round the Well, into the present semi-urban community.

Chapter 13

Notable Families and Individuals

The Parish Records show that some families lived in Banstead for many generations. Amongst them were the Buckles, Johnsons, Killicks, Lamberts, Mathews, Merlands, Moys, Pupletts, Richbelles and Wilmots, all of whom were included in a list compiled for taxation purposes in 1593.

Over the years, as has been seen, one or two of these families played a specially important part in the local affairs of Banstead, along with other families who arrived later on. Besides the members of these families, some individuals with Banstead connections are notable either as figures of national importance or for their special qualities or attainments. In this chapter brief accounts are given of some of these families and individuals.

In the past, power and wealth lay mostly in the hands of the large landowners, whose estates normally passed on to their heirs. (In the case of Banstead, it was the youngest son who had priority.) Consequently it was the landowning families who had the most lasting influence in the district.

The Lamberts and the Wilmots

The Lambert family's connection with Banstead began in 1515, when John Lambert bought Perrotts Manor and Well Farm. The family already owned properties in other parts of Surrey. One branch of the family settled in Woodmansterne, and another in Banstead. From an early date the family also owned land in Bletchingley. Between the two local branches of the family there was a great deal of inter-marriage. Likewise, between the Lamberts and the Wilmot (or Willimot) family there was much inter-marriage. The Wilmot property in the 17th century included Well House.

The Lambert-Wilmot family connections also extended into commerce. The first John Lambert was a sheep farmer who made the most of the

Figure 45. Sir Daniel Lambert

popularity of Banstead lamb and wool. By the end of the 17th century, however, the Lamberts and Wilmots were City merchants. In the 18th century, the two families, by now inextricably associated, were involved in trade with Spain as importers of wine and textiles. Gradually the Wilmot line seems to have died out, whereas the prolific and prosperous Lamberts, with much Wilmot blood in their veins, took over both business and properties.

That the Lamberts were prolific is shown by the example of the first John Lambert's son, Jeffery Lambert, of Garrards (or Garratts) Hall, Banstead. He married five times, and left nineteen children when he died in 1566. The family's prosperity is evident from their acquisition of more and more property.

Their standing reached a peak in the person of Sir Daniel Lambert, who lived at Well House, Banstead, which he acquired from the Killick family in

1739. Born in 1685, he had become a noted City merchant. He was elected co-Sheriff for London and Middlesex for the year 1733-34. In 1737 he was elected Alderman of Tower Ward; and, following the death of the current Lord Mayor in the course of his year of office, Daniel Lambert became Lord Mayor of London from March to October 1741. In May 1741, he was elected as one of the Members of Parliament for the City of London, and he retained this office until 1747. Because of the invasion of the country by Charles Stuart and his supporters, this was a period of great turmoil.

Daniel Lambert's loyal service was rewarded by a knighthood in 1744. He died in 1750, as a result of carrying out his duties as an Alderman by attending at the Old Bailey. In a crowded Court there, he and the three others with him on the Bench, as well as forty people in the Court, were all fatally infected with what was then known as gaol fever.

Many generations of Sir Daniel Lambert's descendants continued to own Well House and also the Manor of Perrotts, which roughly comprised what is now Perrotts Farm. This farm was ultimately sold to Mr. Garton in 1921 and Well House was sold in the 1950s, a few years before its demolition. Members of the family had lived at Well House and played a prominent part in the village at least until the latter years of the 19th century.

Other important landowners who influenced life in the village in that century included Henry Thomas Lambert and his successors at Buff House in the High Street, and John Lambert of Garratts Hall and his family. As has been seen, it was John Lambert who acquired a very large part of the land around the village.

There are now no members of the family resident in Banstead, and very little, if anything, left in the way of property owned by the Lambert family in Banstead. As an outward mark of their former presence, the Lambert coat-of-arms can be seen on the Lodges at the junctions of Holly Lane with Garratts Lane and Shrubland Road with Garratts Lane. It can also be seen on the Lodge of St. Ann's Roman Catholic School. In All Saints Church there are memorial tablets to many members of the family, as well as inscriptions indicating family gifts to the church.

The Buckle Family

This family, descended from Sir Cuthbert Buckle, Lord Mayor of London in 1593, came to the Banstead district in 1614, when they bought what was known as the Great Burgh Estate from the Merland family. It appears that this Estate was made up of the sub-manors of Great and Little Burgh, Preston and North Tadworth, all created out of the original main Manor of Banstead. The

Great Burgh Estate comprised a Manor House known at first as Burgh House but later as Great Burgh, near what is now the junction of the Reigate Road with Great Tattenhams, and about four hundred acres of land, which was bounded on the east by the Brighton Road; stretching out to the west as far as Tattenham Corner; and extending to the south as far as the edge of Tadworth. In addition, the Buckles held with the Estate of Great Burgh the right to appoint the Vicar of All Saints' Church in Banstead.

By the 18th century, the Buckles had also acquired the Nork Estate. This was land stretching northwards from the Great Burgh Estate as far as what is today Fir Tree Road. The name of the road probably arose from the planting of fir trees along it by the Buckles, to assert the boundaries of the land they claimed to be theirs.[1]

In 1740 Christopher Buckle built on the Nork Estate a house which became known as Nork House, with a main drive (now The Drive) leading to the Brighton Road opposite Garratts Lane, and other accesses to the Reigate Road and Fir Tree Road. This House was intended as the residence of Christopher's eldest son (also Chrisopher). From him it passed to Matthew Buckle.

Matthew joined the Royal Navy in 1731, at the age of thirteen; served off the West Coast of Africa and in the West Indies; and was promoted Lieutenant. His naval career continued with great success. He was engaged in many battles with the French and Spanish fleets in the Atlantic and the Mediterranean, including the Battle of Quiberon Bay in 1759.

He was on almost continual active service until 1762, when, on the conclusion of peace with France and Spain, he resigned as a Captain, and came to live at Nork House. Eight years later, in 1770, he rejoined the service as a Rear Admiral; became a Vice-Admiral by 1778; and Admiral of the Blue Squadron in 1779. He died at Nork in 1784. His eldest son, another Matthew Buckle, also rose to the rank of Admiral, and was himself the father and grandfather of Admirals.

In 1812, the Nork Estate was sold to Lord Arden, of the Perceval family. Lord Arden's son succeeded him and became Sixth Earl of Egmont. In 1847 he bought the remainder of the Buckle family estates, including the Manor and lands of Great Burgh, and the right to appoint the Vicar of All Saints' Church, Banstead.

---

1   There was a legal dispute as to their title to some of this land, but it seems to have petered out. - Henry Lambert, History of Banstead Vol 2 pp. 78-80.

Figure 46. Admiral Matthew Buckle

This was the end of the Buckles as large landowners in the district; but some of the family remained in the village, mainly through a succession of members of the family as Vicars of All Saints', Banstead. In 1823, the Reverend William Buckle, who was at the time Vicar of a parish in Oxfordshire, exercised his right to appoint the Vicar of All Saints', Banstead, by appointing himself to the living. On his death in 1832, his son, the Reverend William Lewis Buckle, appointed himself to the living. In 1865, the Earl of Egmont, by then owner of the Great Burgh Estate, appointed the Reverend Edward Valentine Buckle as Vicar of All Saints, and he remained as such until 1906. In this way, the influence of the Buckle family continued in Banstead, long after they had ceased to be large landowners in the district.

The Egmont - Arden - Perceval Family

After the death of Admiral Matthew Buckle in 1784, his widow and children, together with his unmarried sister, Martha, moved to the fashionable town of

Bath. His Banstead residence, Nork House, was let. In 1790, the lease was taken up by Charles George Perceval, a young man who had married three years earlier. Perceval, who was to have a large family, wanted to buy Nork House, but its new owner, the sixth Christopher Buckle, refused to sell it at that time. He did this out of deference to the wishes of his aunt, Martha, who had been born there and had lived there with her brother, Matthew, until his death.

Charles George Perceval, who was later to become a Lord of the Admiralty, made many improvements to the house. He bought it in 1812, together with 59 acres of land; and he then set about enlarging the house further. After his death in 1840, his widow made more additions. By 1844 the relatively small house had been transformed into a large mansion. Included among the additions were a private chapel, and a magistrate's room in the west wing.

In 1802 Charles George Perceval had been created Second Baron Arden, of Arden in Warwickshire. His brother, Spencer, four years his junior, in 1812 achieved the dubious distinction of becoming the first and only British Prime Minister to be assassinated whilst in office. It is likely that he visited his brother at Nork House a number of times between 1790 and 1812.

Charles' wife, Margaret, Lady Arden, was a generous benefactor of the Parish. She endowed a Church of England school at Burgh Heath in 1837. A keen amateur painter, she was a pupil of David Cox, a well-known artist in her day.

On Charles' death his eldest son, George James Perceval, succeeded to the barony of Arden; and in the following year he became also 6th Earl of Egmont on the death of a cousin. The new Earl had joined the Navy in 1805 at the age of 11 and had served at the Battle of Trafalgar. He had a successful naval career, and retired as an Admiral. In 1847 he bought the remainder of the Buckle family estates in the Banstead area; and he lived at Nork House until his death in 1874.

The earldom then devolved to his nephew, Charles George, who lived at Nork until 1890, when financial pressure caused him to sell the combined Nork and Great Burgh Estate, amounting to some 2,430 acres of land. On his death in 1897, the earldom devolved to his cousin, Augustus Arthur, who died in 1910 and is buried in Banstead churchyard.

The Garton and Colman Families

References have been made in earlier chapters to the importance of these families as landowners. In 1893, Mr. Charles H. Garton bought the large

Banstead Wood Estate, which he held and enlarged until his death in 1934. He and his wife played a significant part in Banstead village affairs.

The Reverend A.W. Hopkinson, Vicar of Banstead from 1918 to 1929, described the lifestyle of the Gartons in Banstead Wood House in his time.[2] Every morning, Mrs. Garton drove herself in her pony cart to the eight o'clock Eucharist at All Saints' Church, and then galloped back to take "family prayers", which involved the family and any guests, as well as the butler and footmen, the cook and nine housemaids. She then presided over family breakfast. Mrs. Garton was "super-eminently a great-hearted woman"; whilst Mr. Charles Garton "was never impulsive, never impatient, an amazingly shrewd judge of men". Their home was "a revelation of what hospitality can be, a power-house of refreshment and recreation".

The Vicar went on to say that for years the Gartons entertained the Oxford University crew for a weekend of relaxation before the Boat Race. Many other people, "tired workers of all types and ages", found a refuge there. There was fun, "sometimes uproarious, but healthy because it was Christian". It was a happy, contented household life, "feudal maybe, patriarchal certainly, but above all matriarchal".

For their part, the Vicar and his wife accepted from the Gartons daily gifts of flowers, fruit and game; trips to dinner or to the London theatres; and holidays in the Holy Land, in Algiers and on Dartmoor. It was a very close relationship which, as the Vicar admitted, did not escape some criticism in the village.

People who were children in the village at this time have given quite different accounts of the way in which the villagers regarded Mrs. Garton. One spoke of her as having taken the part of a great lady, who insisted that all the boys should doff their caps and all the girls curtsey when she passed by. Indeed, a story was current that the father of a boy who failed to doff his cap had been sacked by the Gartons. But other informants said how kind Mrs. Garton had been, and gave accounts of good works which she had done for the villagers. For instance, during the First World War she had distributed rabbits shot on the Estate to households throughout the village; she had arranged for the cowman to send milk to a village shop, so that any mother with a baby could buy a pint for two-pence each day, and she served the milk herself; she made gifts of pounds of sugar to villagers. All these things were invaluable helps in a time of great shortage.

2   In his book 'Pastor's Progress', The Faith Press, Revised Edition, 1958.

Figure 47. Frederick Edward Colman

After the war, the good works continued. Mrs. Garton provided pre-fabricated huts in Pound Road for ex-Servicemen; and she set up a laundry in Chipstead Road for housewives who had no proper facilities for laundering. She appears indeed to have been a "matriarchal" lady of an old-fashioned kind, to whom it was natural that the villagers had varied reactions.

If Mrs. Garton was assuming a matriarchal role towards the villagers, it seems that to some extent Mr. Charles Garton took on the patriarchal role which had in the past been played by the old-established families of landowners, such as the Buckles and the Lamberts. In about 1910 he became Chairman of the Parish Council, and he held that position for seventeen years. On more than one occasion he gave practical assistance to the villagers by lending tractors to help to remove heavy snowfalls; and during the First

World War he provided land for allotments. Later he gave land to the Parish for the recreation ground in Garratts Lane which is named after him.

Following his death, the Banstead Wood Estate was broken up; so that he was in effect the last of the large Estate owners in the district.

Turning to the Colman family, it was in 1890 that Mr. F. E. Colman, Managing Director of the family's Mustard Factory, bought the Nork and Great Burgh Estate. After his death in 1900, his wife and family retained the estate until it was sold off in 1923. Over the period from 1890 to 1923, the Colman family seem to have made comparatively little impact on Banstead village life, though they obviously had a great influence over those who lived or worked on their large estate.

Hubert de Burgh (1170-1243)

Hubert de Burgh is thought to have been born in the 1170s of a family of local gentry in Norfolk. He became attached to the court of King Richard I, probably through the influence of the family of his first wife, a daughter of the Earl Warrene.

Within two years of the death of King Richard in 1199, Hubert had carried out a perilous mission to Portugal for King John and had been named the King's Chamberlain. In 1201, he was sent to guard the Welsh Marches. He later campaigned with King John in France. In January 1203, Prince Arthur, Duke of Brittany, died in captivity. This prince had strong claims to what had been Richard I's French dominions; and Shakespeare's play, "King John", gives Hubert de Burgh an important and unpleasant role in this affair. The facts, however, are uncertain.

In his private, as in his public life, Hubert sought advancement in every possible way. On the death of his first wife in 1214 Hubert married Isabella, divorced wife of King John. In 1215, Hubert was one of King John's advisers in negotiations for the Magna Carta drawn up between the King and Barons at Runnymede, and he was a signatory to the Charter. At about this time, he was appointed Justiciar of England.

When King John died in 1216, Hubert was engaged as a soldier, holding Dover Castle against a siege by Prince Louis of France, who, with considerable support from some of the English barons, had seized London and most of the southern ports, as well as dominating most of the eastern part of the country.

The accession to the throne of Henry III, a boy nine years of age, created a change of feeling in the country. Hubert secured a truce at Dover in 1216, and joined the new King and his main supporters at a Great Council at Bristol, when the Earl Marshal was appointed Regent of the country. The fighting continued spasmodically in 1217, but the tide had turned against Prince Louis and his supporters, who suffered a disastrous defeat at Lincoln in May of that year. A treaty was concluded in September. Prince Louis agreed to withdraw after receiving a considerable payment. A general amnesty was announced, and forfeited estates were to be restored. It was, nevertheless, at this time that Hubert acquired the Manor of Banstead from William de Mowbray, one of the barons who had fought with Prince Louis and had been taken prisoner at Lincoln.

After peace was restored, the government was carried on by the Earl Marshal, William, Earl of Pembroke, with a council of noblemen, clergy and officials, including the papal legate, until the Earl's death in 1219. As a member of this council, Hubert exercised increasing influence, and became Constable of the Tower of London. After 1219, the council was dominated by Hubert, by Stephen Langton, Archbishop of Canterbury, and by the papal legate. Hubert was created Earl of Kent, and he acquired three castles in what is now Gwent, as well as a new castle at Montgomery. In 1220, Henry III, now aged thirteen, was officially crowned; but, the papal legate having been removed, Hubert and Stephen Langton virtually controlled the country.

Hubert's second wife had died in 1217. In 1221 he married Margaret, Princess of Scotland, who had been kept at the English Court as a hostage to ensure the good behaviour towards England of her father, King Alexander of Scotland.

In 1227, Henry III proclaimed himself to be of full age and authority. For five years after this, Hubert maintained a strong hold on the country, but he had made some powerful enemies. By continuing to build up his family's fortunes as well as advancing the King's personal authority, he increased his unpopularity.

In June 1232 Peter de Rivaux, was appointed treasurer of the royal household. This was a signal for Hubert's fall from power. In the following month, a new Justiciar of England was appointed. Hubert was ordered to hand over custody of the royal estates which he held, and, in August, to surrender to the King the castles which were his own property. Hubert was charged with treasonable activities; but, as an Earl, he was allowed to go to the Priory of Merton to prepare his defence for a formal trial.

There followed a series of dramatic events. After fleeing to take sanctuary in a chapel at Brentwood in Essex, Hubert was seized and finally imprisoned in the Tower of London for trial before the King's Court in November. He "threw himself on the King's mercy". It was agreed that he should be kept in custody in the castle at Devizes, retaining his noble rank and his private lands, but losing all his public offices, royal castles and wardships. Peter de Rivaux, with a small group of counsellors, took over the administration.

This small group of counsellors soon became even more unpopular with the current Earl Marshal, Richard, Earl of Pembroke, than Hubert de Burgh had been. The Lords of the Welsh Marches revolted. Hubert was eventually rescued by the Earl Marshal's men and taken to Chepstow Castle. A truce in England was agreed in 1234. De Rivaux was removed from office; des Roches left the country to serve the Vatican; and Hubert de Burgh was re-appointed to the King's council, although not to his former office.

Two years later, in 1236, some of the earlier charges were raised again against Hubert, and new charges introduced, including that of plotting to kill the King. Hubert's strenuous rejection of these charges met with some success. He was finally permitted to retain his title and to retire to his Manor of Banstead. Here he spent the next four years in what a mediaeval historian termed "melancholy retirement", until his death in Banstead on the 12th of May 1243. He was buried in a convent of the Black Friars in London.

Hubert de Burgh left two sons, the elder of whom, John de Burgh, was knighted and became Constable of the Tower of London. Hubert's wife, Princess Margaret of Scotland, survived him and succeeded, after some disputation, to the Manor of Banstead, which she held until her death in 1258. John de Burgh, who then inherited the Manor, parted with it to King Edward I in 1273, in exchange for land elsewhere. This ended the family's connection with Banstead.

Hubert de Burgh had owned the Manor for twenty-six years, apart from a period when it was held by the Knights Templar as security for debts owed by him. It is not known whether he lived in the Manor House at any time other than his last years. Nor is much known about the Manor House itself. It must have been a substantial building, situated somewhere between the old part of the churchyard and what is now Avenue Road.

[3]Although Hubert de Burgh may have been mainly an absentee landlord of the Manor of Banstead, his connection with the village is a notable one, for he held over a number of years one of the highest positions in the government of the country. He is a truly remarkable figure in English history.

---

3   Information about Hubert de Burgh from a number of sources, but particularly from Henry Lambert; The Oxford History of England; the Dictionary of National Biography; and "The Minority of Henry III" by D. A.Carpenter, Methuen & Co, 1990.

Thomas Henry Maudslay (1792-1864)

T. H. Maudslay was the eldest son of Henry Maudslay (1770-1831), an engineer who had set up on his own account at a works in Westminster Bridge Road, Lambeth. Henry Maudslay has been described as "the father of the modern machine-shop". The firm prospered chiefly as marine engineers. A close collaborator with them was Marc Brunel, whose son, Isambard Kingdom Brunel, owed much of his early knowledge of machinery to the time which he spent with the firm.

T. H. Maudslay became a partner in the firm, by then known as Maudslay Sons and Field; and for twenty-five years they constructed engines for the Royal Navy. His brother, Joseph, designed engines for H.M.S. Rattler, the Admiralty's first screw steamer.[4]

In the 1850s, T. H. Maudslay bought the house called Park Wood House or Banstead House, formerly the home of Mrs. Spencer, Lord of the Manor in the 1840s. This House adjoined what is now the Park Farm Depot in Holly Lane, Banstead, with about eight acres of grounds, some farming land and the Banstead Woods. By the time of his death in 1864, he had made considerable alterations to the House.

Sir Allen Sarle (1828-1903)

Allen Sarle was born in the Orkney Islands. He was educated at Selkirk Grammar School and at the High School at Edinburgh. In 1845, he came to London, where he found employment with the Shropshire Union Railways Company, whose offices were in Westminster. Three years later, he moved to the audit office of the London, Brighton and South Coast Railway Company; and in 1854 he became the Company's Accountant. In 1867, when the Company's Secretary resigned through ill-health, Sarle took his place. In 1885 he was made General Manager as well as Secretary. He carried on in both capacities until 1897. He was knighted in 1896.

Sarle superintended great changes in the Railway Company's operations during his time in office. Far better conditions were introduced for passengers; and there was an enormous increase in their numbers.[5]

Apart from his railway duties, Sarle took an active part in the local affairs of Banstead, where he lived for many years. In 1871 he, his wife and three servants were in residence at Bentley Lodge, a large residence with some

---

4   Information about T. H. Maudslay and his firm from the Dictionary of National Biography; and from "Isambard Kingdom Brunel", by L. T. C. Rolt, Pelican Books, 1970.
5   Dictionary of National Biography; and The Railway Magazine, January 1898.

three acres of ground standing back from Bolters Lane on the western side. By 1881 he had moved to Greenhayes, another large house with ample grounds, on the eastern side of Bolters Lane. He lived there until his death in 1903.

Sarle's influence was largely responsible for widening the career prospects of Banstead boys. The head boy of the Village School in 1874 was given a job in the offices of the London, Brighton and South Coast Railway Company. Over the years, a number of other boys from Banstead also found employment with the Railway Company.

Sarle was one of the founder members of the Banstead Cricket Club, when it was formally established in 1874. By 1881, he was in the Chair. By 1889, he had become a Patron of the Club.

He was a Justice of the Peace; and he attended the first Banstead Parish Council meeting on the 3rd of January 1895, when he was appointed Chairman of the Council. In the same year, he became one of the Trustees of the Parochial Charities. It was not until 1901 that Sir Allen Sarle retired both from the Chair of the Parish Council and from membership of the Council.

Marshal of the RAF, Lord Tedder (1890-1967)

Sir Maurice Dean, who was Head of the Air Staff Secretariat in World War II, summed up Lord Tedder in glowing terms as "a university graduate of great intelligence and with great powers of leadership". He was "an intellectual with military leanings".[6]

After serving as Director of Training and Director-General of Research and Development for the Royal Air Force before the war, Tedder was appointed to take charge of the Middle East Air Command, handling the complex problems of air forces in the Middle East, both before and after the entry of the United States into the war.

After the landing of American, British and other forces in French North Africa in 1942, Tedder quickly won the confidence of General Eisenhower, the Allied Forces Commander in that area. Soon Tedder was commanding all the Allied Air Forces in the Mediterranean; and, when Eisenhower became Supreme Commander for the invasion of Europe in 1944, he chose Tedder as his Deputy. The Americans regarded Tedder as a man on the British side with whom they could always work with confidence; and he played a major part in the success of the operations which culminated in the German surrender.

6   "The Royal Air Force and Two World Wars", Cassell, 1979.

INVASION of EUROPE

AND THE MEN WHO WILL LEAD THE ALLIED ARMIES

BATTLE HONOURS

El Alamein

Tobruk

Benghazi

Tripoli

Mareth

Cap Bon

Casablanca

Oran

Algiers

Sicily

Italy

Supreme Commander

General Dwight D. Eisenhower, 53, Supreme Commander of the British and American Expeditionary Forces organising in the United Kingdom.

And His Deputy

Air Chief Marshal Sir Arthur Tedder, 53, Deputy Supreme Commander, was formerly Air Officer C.-in-C. in the Middle East.

Figure 48. *General Eisenhower and Air Chief Marshal Sir Arthur Tedder, 1944*

In 1954 Lord Tedder bought Well Farm, a house of considerable antiquity, dating in part from the 15th century, in Woodmansterne Lane, Banstead. He lived there until his death in 1967.

Edward Willard (Died 1915)

Edward Willard was a well-known Actor-Manager. His first stage appearance was in 1869, and for twelve years he acted in the provinces. From 1881, he made a number of appearances in London plays. In 1889-90 he was co-manager of the Shaftesbury Theatre. In 1890 he appeared in New York, and altogether he made thirteen American tours. In June 1894 he appeared at the Comedy Theatre under his own management. In 1895 he was manager of the Garrick Theatre. In 1903 he produced The Cardinal at the St. James Theatre. In 1911 he appeared at the Coronation Gala Performance at Her Majesty's Theatre.[7]

Edward Willard lived at Buff House in Banstead High Street for some years. In 1904 he gave to All Saints' Church a copy of the King Edward VII prayer book, 1903, printed at Chipping Campden and bound in a carved wood and leather cover. He died on the 9th of November 1915.

---

7   "Who was Who", Volume 1 (Appendix).

Chapter 14

Churches in Banstead

For centuries, the only recognised church in Banstead was the Parish Church of All Saints. The 19th century meetings of Calvinistic Independents have been mentioned in Chapter 3. Other congregations were formed late in the 19th century and during the expansion of the Village in the 20th century.

In recent years, there has been much co-operation between the churches in Banstead, a good deal of it under the organisation known as the Banstead Five Churches.

All Saints Church, Banstead

A church at Banstead is recorded in the Domesday Book, but the present building was not erected until some time between 1190 and 1220. The site of the church and the oldest part of the church-yard were given to the Church by Nigel de Mowbray, Lord of the Manor, who died in 1192. This seems to have been confirmation of an earlier grant. The oldest parts of the Church are thought to be the arches of the nave arcade, and the west arch of the north chapel. Viewed from the north, the church reveals its flint facing and tiled roofs. The sturdy tower, with walls over six feet thick, supports a shingle-topped spire, crowned with a cross and a gilded cock.

Restoration of the interior of the tower in 1862 was paid for by John Lambert in memory of his brother, Thomas. This early 13th century tower is now the bell-ringing chamber. Above is the organ loft and the belfry, containing eight bells. The vestry was added to the north side of the tower in 1868.

The north doorway dates from the 15th century, but the north and south porches are modern. Inside the church, the nave leading to the chancel is arcaded with an aisle on each side. Each aisle leads to a chapel.

The stained glass west window was designed by Dante Gabriel Rossetti and William Morris in a pre-Raphaelite style. It was produced in 1862 in the studio of William Morris.

The three-lancet east window dates from 1861, when it replaced a 15th century window. The mural of Christ on the Cross, over the arch at the entrance to the chancel, is all that remains of the murals that once decorated the walls of the church. The bowl of the font is 14th century, with each side decorated in a different design. The pedestal and base are modern.

In 1837 the south chapel was built by the Lambert family. In 1861 they rebuilt the south aisle. There are mural monuments to various members of the family, notably Sir Daniel Lambert, Lord Mayor of London in 1741. The east chapel, at the end of the aisle, bears the family name. It was restored by the family in 1863, with windows added five years later. Further alterations were carried out a few years later. Over the years, there have been other works of restoration to the roof, steeple and floor, together with certain alterations including some works carried out in 2003.

The Lady Chapel had links with the Buckle family, who at one time held the right to appoint the Vicar of All Saints. Their family vault is indicated by a notice in the church-yard on the east wall, which states "The vault of the family Buckle of Burgh 1826. Members of this family were buried inside the church from 1642-1821".

The names of Banstead men who fell in World War I are recorded on panels beneath the windows of the Lady Chapel. A Book of Remembrance lists all local men who served overseas in that war. Another Book of Remembrance, in the lower case, lists those whose ashes are buried in the Garden of Remembrance in the church-yard.

The church-yard has twice been enlarged. In 1861, John Lambert made a gift of half an acre to the east. In 1904, the addition of land between the old church-yard and Court Road was made through the benefaction of a Committee of Parishioners. Also in 1904, The Orchard, between the Church and the High Street, was conveyed to the Church by the Earl of Egmont.[1]

---

1   Much of the information comes from The Story of All Saints Church, Banstead, by C. H. Falcon.

Banstead Methodist Church

In 1930, in spite of the rapid expansion of Banstead, no Wesleyan Chapel had been established there, and people who came to live in Nork walked across the meadows to the Wesleyan Chapel which had been set up much earlier near the pond at Burgh Heath. During the week, this Chapel served as a school. On Sundays, a removable pulpit took the place of the blackboard. A three-foot stove in the centre of the building, with a stove pipe through the roof, provided the heating. (The Chapel was closed in the early 1950s, when the congregation joined the new Methodist Church at Great Tattenhams).

The present church site in The Drive, Banstead, had been purchased in 1926 by the London Mission and Extension Committee of the Wesleyan Church. At the instigation of Mr. Frank Ashmole, then manager of Barclays Bank in Nork, Mr. and Mrs. G. S. Taylerson joined Mr. Ashmole and his wife in an effort to start a Chapel in Banstead.

The Ashmole and Taylerson families started by gathering a few people together to hold evening services at No. 28 Green Curve at the invitation of Mrs. Hayman. Later, they moved to the Hillcrest Tea Rooms in Eastgate. In 1934, it was decided to begin the building of a Methodist church. This was after the Wesleyan and other Methodist churches had united as such in 1932. After much fund-raising, a formal stone-laying Service was held on the 22nd of September 1934. The church was opened on the 8th of February 1935, and was placed in the charge of the Reverend A. E. Salmon, a retired Methodist minister who had moved to Belmont. At this time, much help was given by the Burgh Heath congregation.

Church membership gradually increased. In 1939 the Reverend F. Hudson was appointed to the church. During the 1939-45 war, the church provided a canteen for troops stationed in Nork Park. A Church Youth Council was set up to co-ordinate emerging youth organisations; and this Council flourished after the war.

In 1949, the Reverend Hubert Teare, who had followed Mr. Hudson, was himself succeeded by the Reverend A. H. Clulow. During the latter's eight years of office, church membership nearly doubled. There were by then 250 young folk associated with the church; and the Sports Club ran three football teams.

In 1960, a Church Hall, to be known as the Vallins Hall, was erected behind the church; and the church itself was replaced in 1971 by a new church built "in the Round" style.[2]

2 Much of the information supplied by Mr. G. S. Taylerson.

Banstead Baptist Church

This started just before the beginning of the 20th century as a Free Baptist Church in Banstead, and the first Pastor was appointed in 1907. The first church was a rented house called "Kylemore" in Court Road. For some years the church continued with a fairly small congregation.

In 1936, a former member of the Metropolitan Tabernacle, Mr. J. H. Wilson, took over.

Wartime damage to the wood and corrugated iron building, situated towards the eastern end of the High Street, which was in use at that time as the church, led to small services being held in a room at the rear of the church. Following post-war renovations, the church was publicly re-opened on Wednesday, the 6th of October 1948.

By 1950, membership had dwindled to ten, and Mr. Wilson appealed to Cheam Baptist Church for help. This appeal was answered by Cheam, and gradually local people in Banstead took an interest. From 1952-55, Student Pastors from the London Bible College offered their services. One of these young men, Mr. David Luce, was ordained in Banstead in November 1955. By 1959, membership had risen to over fifty.

In 1961, the Reverend Ben W. Peake became part-time pastor, and Banstead achieved financial independence from Cheam. Building extensions included a new entrance, with a vestibule and two rooms, in 1963; a hall at the rear in 1965; and the renovation of the main building in 1966. Purchases included a new organ.

Under the leadership of teachers from Cheam, much had been done for young people over the years: Children's Crusades were held in 1959 and 1963; a Bible class for girls was followed by a similar class for boys. In September 1968, the Reverend J. C. White became full-time pastor, and a manse was purchased to accommodate him. By 1970, the renovated "tin tabernacle" in the High Street was too small to accommodate the congregation, and the following year, a new building was erected. An upper-storey church lounge was added in 1976.

A full-time associate minister, Mr. Alan Turner, was appointed with special responsibility for outreach and youth work. Sadly, he was taken seriously ill and died while still in his forties. Mr. Roger Bishop was invited to succeed him as Associate Pastor. In 1979 his family moved into the manse, from which the Reverend J. C. White had moved to a house of his own in Banstead.

The entrance hall of the church was later re-structured to afford an additional entrance to the sanctuary. A church office was built, and the church itself was extended to provide more seating, a classroom, and a spacious foyer.

Reverend White retired in 1983 and the Reverend Roger Bishop became Pastor. The Church has a strong tradition of Missionary activities. It also has a long tradition of supporting youth work.[3]

St. Ann's Catholic Church

The need for a Catholic church in Banstead was being felt in the 1920s. There was a nucleus around the McDermott family, who had moved to 4 De Burgh Park in 1922. A few Catholics occasionally celebrated mass in the McDermotts' coach house. The need for a church in Banstead was obvious, but besides the problems of money and site, there was the snag that Banstead lay between the two established parishes of Epsom and Sutton. The village itself was in the parish of Sutton; the developing area of Nork and Drift Bridge was in that of Epsom.

With the approval of Bishop Amigo, Father Christall of Epsom finally arranged for the removal of an army hut from behind his Epsom church to a site acquired on the Brighton Road. By the autumn of 1930, the hut was erected and plans were being made to raise funds. The solemn opening by the Bishop took place in 1931. Father Christall then planned the erection of a presbytery.

In 1934 Father Dockery was appointed as resident priest. He was most anxious to get a school started. This was achieved in 1938, when St. Ann's School opened in the church itself. Its aim was to provide sound religious and general education for Catholic children between the ages of five and eleven. The first teacher was Mrs. Elsie Smith from Sutton.

In September 1940, the parish suffered the great misfortune of losing Father Dockery, who was killed by an enemy bomb.[4] Later in the war, Father Lawrence Ryan carried out two important developments. In 1944, he purchased Court House for the school; and he coped with the building of a permanent church, which was finally completed in 1950.

In 1951, Father Ryan was succeeded by Father Moriarty, who was in charge for seventeen years, during which time the parish population doubled from five hundred to one thousand. From 1954, Father Moriarty enlisted the

3   Information supplied by Mr. David Simmons.
4   See Chapter 9.

help of nuns of the Order of the Poor Servants of the Mother of God to run the school. Their convent quarters at Court House were established and paid for by their Order. The new Headmistress was Sister Ann Patricia. Known in later days as Sister Patricia Fitzgerald, she did much for the school and parish before she left in 1975.

1954 saw the formation of a Scout Troop by John Clifford, who carried on the good work for over a quarter of a century. In 1966 a Girl Guide Company was started by Pat Morrell. Brownies and Rangers followed in the next two years.

Father Moriarty was involved in seeking to have the school at Court House recognised as a Primary School with Voluntary Aided Status. (Up till this time, it had been a private school.) On his retirement in 1968, he was succeeded by Father James Kenny, who saw this objective achieved in 1969. The Order of the Poor Servants of the Mother of God had provided funds to build Josephvilla, the School's Assembly Hall block, and to buy an additional piece of land. To enable the Convent accommodation to be moved to the first floor, funds were raised with help from generous parents.

Then, in 1974, Father Kenny and the Managers raised further funds to build two new classrooms. This raised the status of the school to that of a combined First and Middle School, retaining pupils until the age of twelve, when they would proceed to the Senior School, St. Andrews, at Leatherhead.

The other major building event in Father Kenny's time was work on the front of the church. The present porch and portico, with the flanking steps, were designed by Mr. W. F. J. Nicholson, A.R.I.B.A. Father Kenny retired in 1977.

In 1981, a new St. Ann's Room development was completed, largely due to the care and energy of the architect, Mr. Denore.[5]

Banstead United Reformed Church

In view of the surge of house building in Banstead in the 1930s, a handful of Sutton Congregationalists, who had come to live in Banstead, decided to try to establish a church there.

On the 18th of February 1940, twenty-four worshippers attended a service in the Village School in the High Street. War-time congregations were understandably low and fluctuating, and some members were inclined to wait until the war was over, before persevering with a new church. Mrs. L. E.

---

5   Source: "St. Ann's, Banstead, 1936-1986", by Monsignor J. Macdonald.

Spencer, however, was an active enthusiast for carrying on. By 1942, the average attendance was up to twenty-one. By 1943, the Reverend S. J. Cowdy was taking an active part. In November 1943, the Banstead Congregational Church Council was set up, followed by the Church Fellowship, of which Ernest Tickner was secretary.

Although meetings continued to be held on the school premises, a move was made from the Junior School to the Infants' Hall. It was to be the meeting place for the next seven and a half years.

In 1944, a publicity campaign was undertaken, and a quarterly social and business meeting was established. Its original title was a Fellowship Meeting, but by 1946 this was changed to a Church Meeting. A Women's Guild was organised, with afternoon meetings in members' houses, and a Children's Club was formed.

In 1944, the Reverend Daniel Jenkins came as part-time minister. In April 1946, the Fellowship resolved to have itself constituted as a Congregational Church as soon as possible. On the 5th of October 1946, the Covenant Service took place, presided over by the Moderator, the Reverend Maxwell Janes. In addition to thirty members of Junior Church, about one hundred and sixty people were present in the Junior School Hall. Just before the service, the fifty-two original members had signed the Covenant. This document is displayed each October at the Covenant Service.

After this, church meetings took place in various premises, including the Lady Neville Pavilion as well as the Infants' School Hall. The need for a church building was increasingly felt. The present site had been reserved by the Congregational Union back in 1940, and during the war had served for allotments. In 1947, the Local Authority approved plans for a church which had been submitted by the local Church Council. On the 10th of June 1950, a Foundation Stone Ceremony took place. The new church building, in Woodmansterne Lane, consisted of what is now the main church hall. At that time, Well House stood next to it.

By the 14th of April 1951, the building was complete. A procession, led by the Moderator and the Reverend George Millar, made its way via Avenue Road and the High Street to the new church building, where there was a formal opening, followed by a Service attended by a congregation which packed the church.

The debt on the church was paid off by 1955, thanks to fund raising, to various donors, and to generous support from local churches. By this time, a

Church Extension Committee and a Manse Committee were making plans for future developments.

Number 3 Fiddicroft Avenue, immediately adjoining the church, was offered by the Goff family, and accepted as a manse, in 1955-6.

In 1957, a new church building was built, with a sanctuary accommodating 200 people. Later, a Fellowship Room was erected. It was dedicated on the 22nd of July 1962.

In 1953 the Reverend Caryl Micklem was appointed the first full-time Minister. He became a well-known hymn-writer (words and music).

The local congregation had supported the union at national level of the Congregational and Presbyterian Churches. This took place on the 5th of October 1972, accompanied by a Service of Thanksgiving at Westminster Abbey. As a result, the Banstead Congregational Church was reborn as the Banstead United Reformed Church. A large extension has been added to the original building.[6]

St. Paul's Church, Nork

From 1923, the old Nork Estate was the subject of rapid building development. Members of the Church of England felt that there should be a church in the area.

A small Sunday school was established in 1926 under the supervision of an established lay-reader, meeting in the house of Mr. W. H. Wheeler in Nork Way. In 1928, formal consent was given for a Church and a Church Hall to be built on land in Warren Road. In 1930, St. Paul's, Nork came into existence, first as a "daughter church" of All Saints Banstead, then in 1931 as an ecclesiastical district created by Order in Council.

The original design of the church, intended as a temporary building, was drawn by Mr. W. E. Bowden from a sketch made by the Reverend A.W. Hopkinson, Vicar of All Saints. The church was completed in 1930 and dedicated by the Bishop of Guildford on the 6th of March 1930.

For the first two years, the Reverend W. B. Wilson, a curate of All Saints, supervised the running of the church. Then, in April 1932, the Reverend Percy R. Lobb was inducted as the first minister. The vicarage was a house in The Drive.

In 1934 a large hut was built as a temporary Church Hall; and in 1935, a vicarage was constructed in Warren Road. From 1936, Mr. Lobb was assisted

6   Main sources: United Reformed Church, Banstead, Surrey, Jubilee Book, 1940-1990, by
    Ivan Brown; and Tidings, Issue No. 18, Easter 1988 - Report of a talk by Peggie Mason.

by a curate, the Reverend R. F. W. Durrant. In 1937, the electoral roll contained 174 names. Activities in the following year included the Sunday school, the Mothers' Union, the production of Passion and Nativity plays, a Cub Pack, a Scout Troop and a Guide Company.

In May 1939, Mr. Lobb left and Mr. Durrant took charge until the arrival of the Reverend Charles Dearnley in September. With the outbreak of war, the choir lost most of its men, but Mr. and Mrs. Malvern and Mrs. Bird did their best to keep a choir going. The Sunday school was held in the Malverns' house, and the Mothers' Union met in Mrs. Jacobs' house in Roundwood Way.

In April 1941, the vicarage and the hall were damaged by a bomb; and in 1944, minor damage was done to the church and the hall on two occasions. No curate was available in wartime, but a deaconess was appointed in 1943. Her successor the following year stayed until 1948. By March 1945, membership of the Mothers' Union had risen to fifty, and Sunday school attendances were increasing. After the war, the Nork branch of the Church of England Men's Society was formed. Attention was given to church music and the choir flourished.

The Reverend Charles Dearnley left in 1956 and his place was taken by the Reverend L. Allan Carey.

Since finances did not run to the building of a new church, the Parochial Church Council decided to extend the existing church and to construct a new church hall. The hall was approved and erected during 1957; but it was not until May 1958 that work on the church extension was finally undertaken. The scheme was to build permanent brick walls eight feet out from the existing north and south walls, thus creating two aisles. The west wall, the walls of the Lady Chapel, the sanctuary and the vestry were replaced with permanent materials, and the horizontal beams were removed in the roof space above the nave. In January 1959, the enlarged church was consecrated by the Lord Bishop of Guildford.

In 1962, the Young Wives' drama section was extended to undertake mixed-cast plays. This led to the formation of St. Paul's Drama Group, which was to enjoy conspicuous success over a wide field, followed by the setting up of its own Youth Group.

In 1963, a new organ was purchased. Two stained glass windows were donated by relatives and friends living in Nork in memory of Marie Lloyd, the former Music Hall star. The choir became affiliated to the Royal School of Church Music. The Scouts, Venture Scouts, Guides and Brownies all flourished, and a Ranger Unit was started in 1973. In June 1977, after twenty-one years as Vicar, the Reverend Allan Carey retired. He was succeeded by the Reverend P. E. Naylor, who remained until 1991, when his successor was Father Peter Brooks.

In the 1970s, reconstruction was found to be necessary on the roofs over the two side aisles. Heating in the church hall was considered inadequate, and the old "hut" used by the Scouts and Guides needed replacing. Improved car-parking facilities were also due. To meet these needs, a Special Development Fund was set up.[7]

Other Local Churches

Other Church of England Churches in the vicinity of Banstead include St. Mary's, Burgh Heath, dedicated in 1909 and now in the hands of St. Paul's, Howell Hill; and what is now The United Church of Saint Mark in Great Tattenhams, Tattenham Corner. This comprises the Church of England St. Mark's, founded in 1951 and moved to a new building in 1967, and a Methodist Church founded in Great Tattenhams in 1953 and moved to a new building in 1960. That building has been left for redevelopment.

There is an Evangelical Free Church in Merland Rise. This was founded with the proceeds of the sale of a building at Tadworth which was formerly used as the Tadworth Free Church.[8]

---

7   Main source: A History of the Parish of Saint Paul, Nork, Banstead, Surrey, by Renee Willcox, 1985.

8   It appears that the original church at Tadworth was a metal hut this was replaced by a more substantial building. (Facts confirmed by the late Kenneth Clews)..

Chapter 15

Bus and Coach Services to Banstead

As early as 1845, a horse-drawn coach, which left the Woolpack Inn every weekday morning for London, returning in the evening, was described as "an omnibus". By 1855, it ran only as far as Sutton, to the Station on the new railway line. But it was when motor buses replaced the horse-drawn variety that Banstead began to enjoy effective bus services.

In 1913, a Sunday-tripper bus route was begun from Charing Cross via Banstead Downs to Kingswood. It could well have been one of those B-type "Old Bill" solid-tyred, open-top, double-decker motor buses which later spent the Great War moving troops around Flanders. A year later, in the summer of 1914, a further Sunday route was put on from Putney Bridge to Walton-on-the-Hill.

In the 1930s Frederick Greatley, who had what was then the Highfield Garage in the Brighton Road, ran coaches under the name of "Greatley Transport" from there and the yard of number 18a Ferndale Road but he did not run any regular services.[1]

The Beginning of Regular Bus Services

In the early 1920s, rural motor bus services really took off; and within a few years of the end of the Great War, Banstead had gained its own bus route. This was the 113, which started at the Victoria Inn, proceeded along the High Street, and then made its way down Sutton Lane and over Banstead Downs to Sutton's Cock Hotel, where a sharp left turn set the bus on its way to Cheam, Worcester Park and its terminus at Kingston. The total journey time was seventy minutes, and the through fare 10d. Early in the 1930s, this route was

---

1 Information from John Clifford and Geoff Pushman.

Bus	Route
77	(Sundays, every 10 minutes), King's Cross, Charing Cross, Clapham, Earlsfield, Sutton, Banstead Downs, Burgh Heath.
80	(Weekdays, hourly), Charing Cross, Clapham, Tooting, Sutton, Banstead Village, Burgh Heath, Lower Kingswood.
80A	(Daily: hourly Monday-Friday, half-hourly Week-ends), Charing Cross, same as the 80 to Banstead Village, then Tadworth, Walton-on-the-Hill.
80B	(Saturdays/Sundays, half-hourly), Charing Cross, same as the 80 to Banstead Village, then Drift Bridge, Epsom.
113	(Daily, half-hourly), Kingston, Worcester Park, Cheam, Sutton, Belmont, Banstead Village. .
128	(Sundays, every 10 minutes), Camberwell Green, Clapham, Tooting, Sutton, Banstead Downs,Burgh Heath, Lower Kingswood

Table 4. Bus routes to and from Banstead in the summer of 1924

diverted to Belmont via Carshalton and Banstead Road South. By 1935, it had been re-numbered 213.

The London General Omnibus Company, which had been established in 1829 with horse buses, was by the 1920s keen to open up new territories. Advantage was taken of the public's wish to get out into the countryside on Sundays, to places like Burgh Heath, Belmont, Box Hill, Kingswood and Walton-on-the-Hill, all of which in the 1920s were well provided with tea rooms. Burgh Heath, for example, had Uncle Tom's Cabin, where the Reigate Road garage later stood, and the Willow Tea Gardens, beside the pond.

Throughout the 1920s and early 1930s, there were frequent changes of route, but it is interesting to pick out just one of those early years, to give an idea of the remarkable length and frequency of some of the routes. Table 4 lists the bus routes to and from Banstead in the summer of 1924.

The Services Extend

At the same time that London General were expanding out of London, other rural parts of Surrey were served by the East Surrey Traction Company, based at Reigate. This ambitious company, started by Arthur Hawkins in 1911 with a horse-bus route between Reigate and Redhill, had by the summer of 1924 a considerable network of routes extending to Sevenoaks, Uckfield, Horsham and Guildford.

By 1931, building was well under way in the Banstead area, and although the 77 and 128 routes still came from London, the other routes to Banstead were by then running from Morden Station on the London Underground's Northern Line (or the Morden - Edgware line as it was then called).

There were three new bus routes early in the 1930s. The first of these was the 164, circular from Morden, to Sutton, Banstead Village, Drift Bridge, Reigate Road to Ewell, and then back to Morden. The second route was the 165, from Morden through Banstead Village to Burgh Heath, where the Surrey Yeoman was always the bus terminus. The third route was the 235, which ran from the Victoria Inn, Banstead, down Bolters Lane, and past Banstead Station to Cheam. The 164 was later diverted to Epsom. The 165 became the 164A and was diverted along the new Tattenham Way to Tattenham Corner. The 235 quietly disappeared.

By 1937, the pioneering routes of the previous fifteen years had settled down to a more established pattern, geared and related to a variety of changes. Firstly, in January 1924, the London General Omnibus Company had opened a new central bus garage in Bushey Road, Sutton. Secondly, with so much suburban housing going on all over the Banstead, Cheam and Worcester Park areas, bus routes were increasingly serving shoppers and workers travelling on to London by the Underground's Northern Line and the frequent electric trains of the Southern Railway. Sunday services still catered mainly for the needs of country-going ramblers. Thirdly, as from the first of July 1933, a new statutory body was set up under the name of the London Passenger Transport Board. London Transport, as it soon became known, controlled all public transport, except for the four main line railway companies, over a 700 square mile area stretching from Hertford to Horsham, and from Guildford to Tunbridge Wells.

London Transport took over the London General Omnibus Company; many other bus and coach operators; the vast London County Council tramway system; a dozen other tram and trolley-bus systems; and all the underground railways and deep-level tubes.

As far as road services were concerned, three separate divisions were set up: first, the existing red bus network, known as London Transport Central buses; second, a new division, called London Transport Country Services, which absorbed all the country bus operators, north and south of the Thames, including the East Surrey Traction Company; and third, all trams and trolley-buses.

Bus	Route
80	Morden, Banstead Downs, Lower Kingswood
80A	Morden, Banstead Downs, Walton-on-the-Hill.
164	Morden, Banstead Village, Epsom.
164A	Morden, Banstead Village, Tattenham Corner.

Table 5. Bus routes immediately preceding World War II

In the years immediately preceding World War II, a pattern of bus routes in the Banstead area was set up. This lasted almost into the 1980s. Table 5 lists the routes.

The Green Line Coaches in the Years Before World War II

A Green Line Coach, route J, ran from Reigate, over Banstead Downs, to Central London and on to Watford. At that time, the fare was two shillings return, as compared with the return fare of one shilling and seven pence from Banstead to Victoria Station on the Southern Railway.

Most Green Line routes closed down during the war, when the vehicles were used as ambulances. When they resumed after the war, Banstead's local route became number 711, running from Reigate, over Banstead Downs, and on to London and High Wycombe. This was one of a network of Green Line coach routes which conveyed passengers speedily, comfortably and cheaply to and beyond London from almost every country town within thirty miles of the capital. Like the old coach route J, the 711 Green Line took passengers from Banstead to the heart of London, stopping at Trafalgar Square, Oxford Street and Baker Street. After an evening out in the West End, it was especially convenient to take the last coach from Trafalgar Square, around 11.15 p.m., back to Banstead.

Peak and Decline of the Services

All the normal London Transport bus routes continued during the war. Afterwards, the 1950s proved to be the peak years in terms of the number of passengers carried, by both bus and coach. There were frequent services on all the local bus routes. The first bus in the morning from Banstead to Sutton was the 6.41 a.m., and the last at night the 12.16 a.m. The routes numbers 80 and 80A ran to Mitcham and Tooting, instead of to Morden. The Green Line Coach needed double-decker relief vehicles to and from London in peak hours.

Due to increasing car ownership, the 1960s and 1970s saw a slow decline in regular bus and coach services throughout the country. In particular, the Green Line Coach routes, all of which passed through central London, became steadily less used because of delays resulting from traffic congestion. One by one, nearly all these routes ceased operation.

Route 711 became one-man operated in the 1970s, and was diverted through Banstead village, instead of running straight over the Downs. It ceased in 1978, to be replaced by a limited-stop country bus route, the number 422, running between Sutton, Banstead, Kingswood, Reigate and Redhill, on weekdays only.

Bus	Route
80	Morden, Banstead, Kingswood (Sundays).
80A	Morden, Banstead, Tattenham Corner, Walton-on-the-Hill (Sundays).
164	Morden, Banstead, Epsom (daily).
280	Tooting, Banstead, Kingswood (weekdays).
280A	Tooting, Banstead, Tattenham Corner, Walton-on-the-Hill (weekdays).
422	Sutton, Banstead, Kingswood, Redhill (weekdays).

Table 6. Bus routes to and from Banstead from 1979

In 1968, London Transport's country bus operations were transferred to the newly-created National Bus Company, which was an umbrella group for all the old United Kingdom companies, such as Southdown, Eastern National and so on. All the old colour schemes disappeared, leaving each company with the choice of either dull green or brick red. The new Outer London company became London Country Bus Services Limited. It operated green buses in a belt all round outer London, with its headquarters at the old home of the East Surrey Traction Company in Reigate.

In March 1979, there was a re-organisation of Banstead's bus routes which finally put paid to the pattern set up in the late 1930s. All buses became one-man operated, and route 164A disappeared. The routes running through Banstead now were as listed in Table 6.

In April 1982, the Surrey County Council decided that it would be more economical for local routes beyond Banstead to be operated by London Country Bus Services. So, after nearly seventy years, red London Transport buses were no longer to be seen at Kingswood, Burgh Heath or Walton-on-the-Hill.

In 1984, the 422 route was extended to Gatwick and Crawley. In the same year, London Country Bus Services also started Green Line 'Seaside Specials' on various days, running from Sutton through Banstead to Brighton and Eastbourne.

Independent Operators
In the late 1950s, Banstead Coaches, a local company which had been established in 1950, started a regular bus service from Banstead Station, through the village to Woodmansterne, and on to The Midday Sun Public House in the Chipstead Valley. The Midday Sun had been used as a bus terminus for many years by London Transport buses from the Croydon area. Initially the route ran every 40 minutes from 7 a.m. to 11.30 p.m., seven days a week. Later, it ceased to serve Banstead Station and was withdrawn on Sundays, but on weekdays it still ran every 40 minutes until about 6.30 p.m.

Figure 49. The "Candy Floss" Bus

Figure 50. A London General Omnibus number 113 outside the Victoria Inn.

This friendly and helpful service continued for over a quarter of a century. From the first, Banstead Coaches adopted a colour scheme of pink and white, and their first distinctive single-decker bus soon gained the nickname of "Candyfloss". The principal driver, Vic Smith, would stop anywhere safe, once he was outside the village area. Sometimes he would drop off bundles of heavy groceries for people who lived on the route.

The route ceased at the end of September 1986, as the company was finding it difficult to break even on the operation, despite a subsidy from the Surrey County Council. The final day was a nostalgic one, with the last pink and white bus cheerfully decorated with streamers and balloons inside, as well as a display of historic photographs.

Deregulation

A further considerable shake-up in the pattern of bus operations in the Banstead area occurred on the first of October 1986, when Bus Deregulation came into force. There followed a series of changes. Services were provided by Epsom Coaches as well as by London Transport and the London Country Bus Service. There have continued to be further changes over the years, both in the routes served and the operators. The general picture is one of marked reduction of provision.

Some Special Reminiscences of Bus Services in Earlier Days

Race day on Epsom Downs

People recall that, before World War II, race days on Epsom Downs provided an amazing spectacle, as red buses of all types and ages, culled from bus garages all over London, made their way in a continuous stream from Morden and over Banstead Downs to Tattenham Corner. Boys at Aberdour School, then in the Brighton Road near the Banstead cross-roads, used to enjoy watching the seemingly unending flow of buses passing by every thirty seconds or so.

Steaming radiators

On more ordinary days, for older buses, it was quite a stiff climb from Sutton up to Banstead village. A steaming radiator was a common sight, even in the 1930s, upon arrival at the Woolpack Inn in Banstead High Street. An old watering can was kept stationed by the pub, and it was filled with water to top up the overheated radiators. There was a time-clock by the bus stop outside the old smithy at the same end of the High Street, where conductors had to time-stamp their route cards as an aid to punctual running.

Bus tickets

Bus tickets were more interesting than those of today. Each route had its own pre-printed Bell Punch tickets, with all fare stages printed on them. Tickets of each value were printed in a distinct colour. Bus fares were cheaper where they ran in competition with trams; but in outer areas like Banstead, the fares were for many years one penny a mile (with children under fourteen charged half-price). The journey from Sutton Station to the Victoria Inn at Banstead comprised six half-mile fare stages, so passengers on that journey were given a blue three-penny ticket. From the Woolpack Inn at Banstead to Epsom was a four-mile four-penny journey, for which passengers received a green ticket. The first increase in the long-standing one penny a mile fare system came in July 1940, when the one-penny fare shot up to one and a half pence[2]. Residents at the time must have been outraged! [3]

---

2   The amounts mentioned are of the pre-decimalisation coinage. For more information, refer to The History of Banstead Volume 1, Appendix B - The system of old money.

3   This chapter has been drawn from a comprehensive memoir "125 Years of Public Transport in a Surrey Village", by John H. Clifford, with his kind permission.

Chapter 16

Postal Services to Banstead

Delivery of mail began to be recognised as a Crown service in the 16th century; but it was an Ordinance of Oliver Cromwell as Protector in 1657 which firmly established the Post Office, under the control of a Postmaster-General. This Ordinance was replaced by an Act of Parliament after the Restoration; so that the service could then aptly be called the Royal Mail. The mail was first carried on horseback and later by mail coach along certain main routes, all radiating from London, with staging posts, where the horses were changed. Receiving Offices for mail were set up at the staging posts. Later some cross-routes were started between places on the different main routes. Yet a great many places were still not served directly.

Generally speaking, letters were not delivered to individual houses or premises: they had to be taken to or collected from the Receiving Offices. Some of the local postmasters at the Receiving Offices did unofficially deliver letters to houses, and they made their own charges for doing so. In time, Penny Posts were organised by private enterprise in London, Edinburgh and some other large towns. Delivery within the town limits was made for a fixed fee of a penny, paid in advance, but this was exceptional.

Mail to Epsom and Banstead

By 1678, mail was being carried between London and Epsom on three days each week. This soon became a daily service during the 'season of drinking the waters' at what was then the well-favoured Epsom Spa. Letters addressed to Banstead were delivered to the Epsom Receiving Office. They could then be collected by the addressee, or his servant or private messenger, at the Office. Or again he could pay a charge for delivery by a messenger employed privately by "the Deputy", who would be the local postmaster. This situation lasted for some one hundred and twenty years.

In 1801 an Act of Parliament was passed to authorise the first official scheme for delivery of mail to villages and towns off the main and the cross routes. It was the fifth clause of this Act which authorised the Postmaster-General to make these services available, and the service came to be known as the Fifth Clause Posts. Fees for the service, usually one penny or one half-penny, according to the distance involved, had to be agreed between the Postmaster-General and the villagers. The latter had to provide a guarantee to make good any loss incurred by the Post Office. The scheme was not in general very popular; but a Fifth Clause Post was established between Epsom, Ewell, Cheam, Sutton and Banstead in 1802.

A single messenger was employed by the Post Office to deal with the delivery of letters to and from the villages. His duty was to carry the letters on foot from the Receiving Office at Epsom, in the morning, to Receiving Houses at Ewell, Cheam, Sutton and Banstead. In the evening, he made the return journey. Each walk would be about ten miles on a direct route.

Under the Fifth Clause of the 1801 Act, the Postmaster-General could authorise delivery of letters within specified areas in the villages. It is likely that the Fifth Clause messenger delivered letters to some houses in Banstead, even as early as 1802; but no proof of that has as yet been found, though an official minute seen by Leslie Bond appeared to indicate that such was the case at least after 1828. Delivery to houses in most country districts became common in the 1850s and 1860s; and delivery to all houses in the country as a statutory right was introduced in 1897. The messenger to Banstead continued on foot until the 1880s; but by 1895 he was replaced by a "horse messenger".

The Post Office in Banstead

It is believed that the original Receiving Houses on the walk were all set up in public-houses: The Bull's Head in Ewell, The Harrow in Cheam, The Greyhound in Sutton, and The Woolpack in Banstead. Certainly by the 1820s, John Ingrimes, landlord of The Woolpack at Banstead, was also Receiver of Mail; and on his death in 1826, he was succeeded, both as landlord of The Woolpack and Receiver of Mail, by Thomas Jeal. Jeal did not retain the post of Receiver until his death, which occurred in 1841. At some time between 1834 and 1838 he handed over the post of Receiver to John Cooper. Cooper was described at the time as a bricklayer, and later as a builder; but he owned a grocery business at Ivy Cottage in the High Street. The shop was probably run for the most part by his wife, formerly Mary Selsby, an Epsom girl whom he had married in 1830.

Figure 51. Tonge's Shop and Post Office

Early in Cooper's time as Receiver, the Post Office took an enormous step forward by accepting proposals for a postal service to be provided to every part of the United Kingdom for a uniform basic rate of one penny for a letter of not more than one half of an ounce in weight. This would be payable in advance by a new method - adhesive postage stamps stuck on the letter. The alternative was a charge of two pence, to be paid at the Receiving Office to which the letter was delivered. The new system came into force in 1840, and soon led to a much greater flow of letters and the creation of a large number of new post offices. In addition, the use of railways in place of mail coaches speeded up the service on the main routes.

In 1851, John Cooper was succeeded as Receiver (or sub-postmaster) at Banstead by James Selsby, who was probably a nephew of Mrs. Cooper. The Receiving House was moved to a grocer's shop run by Selsby in a cottage between Ivy Cottage and The Woolpack Inn. Selsby held the office for some thirty years. He was married, but it appears that he had no children. From 1851 onwards, James Tonge, a nephew of Mrs. Selsby, lived with the Selsby family and worked as assistant in the shop. He dealt with both groceries and the mail. By 1881, he was established as a Civil Servant in the capacity of Postal Clerk and Telegraphist. He had married in 1875, and his wife, Betsy Ann, no doubt soon became familiar with the business.[1]

When James Selsby retired, James Tonge took over the shop and the office of sub-postmaster; but after about ten years, he handed over the office of sub-postmaster to his wife. This was between 1891 and 1895, when he and his wife were both in their late forties. He died in 1908; but Betsy Ann Tonge carried on both the grocery and the sub-post office until her death in 1924.

Even then the family connection with the post office did not come to an end, for the Tonges' son, William Charles Tonge, became sub-postmaster. The shop was run jointly by him and his sister, Sophia Eve Tonge, as W.C. and S.E. Tonge. In about 1926, Sophia married Leslie Cadle; in 1928, she took over the sub-post office; and in 1932, she passed it on to her husband.

It was not until 1934, after almost one hundred years, that the family connection with the post office came to an end. The new sub-postmaster was Robert Edward Turner, a grocer in the new parade of shops on the opposite side of the High Street; but he held the job for only a few months, as in December 1934 a new purpose-built Post Office was opened at the western end of the High street. This has now closed, and as in the 19th century, the Post Office is now in a shop in the High street.

Sub-Post Offices

Apart from the High Street office, a sub-post office had been opened in 1912 at No. 2 Ferndale Road, with Edgar Pushman as sub-postmaster, followed in the early 1920s by Mrs. C. Pushman. Between 1928 and 1930, this sub-post office was transferred to No. 20 Ferndale Road, where Francis William Ford had a drapery shop. This sub-post office was ultimately closed in the 1980s.

In Nork, a sub-post office was opened in about 1930 at No. 4 Nork Way. It was moved later, first to No. 13, and then to No. 31 Nork Way. Other sub-post offices were set up at Tattenham Corner and at The Parade in Tattenham Way, though these were not in the Banstead Postal District. Another was at No. 10 Drift Bridge Parade.[2]

---

1   A summary of available information about postal collections and deliveries, and letter-boxes in Banstead in the nineteenth century is contained in Appendix B. The number of each increased considerably in the early part of the twentieth century.

2   Much of the information in this chapter was provided by Leslie K. Bond, and by the late Peter Hodson. Other local sources were Pigot & Company's Directory, and Post Office and Kelly's Directories. One source of general information was Royal Mail, by F. George Kay (Rockliffe, London, 1951)

Appendix A

The Fight to Save the Banstead Commons

The Banstead Commons comprise Banstead Downs, Park Downs, Burgh Heath and Banstead Heath. They contain in all about 1,300 acres. By the middle of the 19th century, they were not in fact used to any extent by the inhabitants of the old Manor of Banstead for the purposes for which as owners of land they had "commoners' rights". The most important of these had been the grazing of sheep for wool and for mutton, but by that time the local trade in this respect had practically disappeared. The value of the commons to the inhabitants as open spaces for recreation and exercise was recognised, but not by the law, which authorised only the former uses under the custom of the Manor.

Even in the early 1870s, there were people looking out for areas of land reasonably near to London with a view to building development. One such person was Sir John Hartopp who bought the Lordship of the Manor in 1873. He was particularly interested in Banstead Downs, which might provide a large and reasonably flat area for a building estate, with easy access to the Brighton Road and also to the Sutton to Epsom Downs branch of the railway.

Construction of this branch, completed in 1865, had itself been the subject of an enabling Act of Parliament, and of statutory procedures to establish commoners' rights to compensation which included a Public Inquiry and a Commissioners' Award.

Sir John Hartopp's advisers saw that, whilst the grazing rights over the Commons were probably in practice hardly used, they could legally be used to thwart his plans. So they set to work to buy in from as many commoners as possible the rights of common which they had. The idea was that, when a sufficient number of these rights had been brought to an end, Hartopp would announce that he intended to enclose most of Banstead Downs, but that he

Figure 52. Horse-drawn cart on Sutton Lane over the Banstead Downs, early 1900s

would leave open enough land to satisfy the theoretical rights of grazing still outstanding.

Twenty-seven people, owning between them more than 1,400 acres of land to which the rights were attached, gave those rights up to Hartopp. This cost him about £18,000; and he had also to make some bargains with landowners to release to them some of his own rights over their land.

By 1876, Hartopp thought that he had reached the point at which he could start enclosing the Commons, and he showed his hand by actually erecting a row of houses on Banstead Downs, in what is now Downs Road, Belmont, and by enclosing a piece of Banstead Heath.

This put the fat in the fire with a vengeance. Local residents got in touch with an organisation called The Commons Preservation Society, which had been formed in 1865 to fight enclosures of commons, particularly those around London which were under great pressure at that time.[1] As a result, a

1   The Society is now known as the Open Spaces Society. It operates nationwide.

local committee was set up in Banstead to fight Hartopp's proposals. This was called the Banstead Commons Protection Society. The Committee included a number of landowners who had retained their commoners' rights. One of them was Mr. James Nisbet Robertson, who was at the time lessee of a large house called Yewlands, in Park Road, and of the twenty-three acres of land held with it. He, with two other commoners, was chosen to challenge Hartopp's plans in the Courts, on behalf of the commoners in general. Proceedings were started in January 1877, claiming the rights and asking that Hartopp be restrained from making his enclosure.

The Committee were supported financially by local contributions. They had promises of help from the Corporation of London, and advice from The Commons Preservation Society. Eventually they also gained support from the largest landowner in the area of the old Manor. This was the seventh Earl of Egmont, who in 1874 had succeeded to the title and to the Nork and Great Burgh Estate, which included some 2,000 acres of land to which commoners' rights were attached. His predecessor had been about to come to an arrangement to surrender these rights to Hartopp; but the new Earl took a different view and decided not to proceed with the arrangement.

This was a big boost to the Committee's chances of success; but the legal proceedings, which were very costly, took a number of twists and turns, and raised a number of difficult and doubtful legal points. By 1884 Hartopp suggested a compromise under which he would give up one half of the Commons and make that open to the public, whilst he would be allowed to enclose the other half. Even Lord Eversley, the redoubtable Chairman of The Commons Preservation Society, was almost convinced that this compromise would have to be accepted.

But suddenly the whole picture changed. Hartopp had mortgaged his property, including the Commons, to two ladies for a total of about £31,000, and he was also involved in various dealings being carried out by his solicitors. The solicitors became insolvent, and absconded; and Hartopp himself became bankrupt. The case was far from being closed, because the mortgagees took it over with Hartopp's property, but the Committee's position was greatly strengthened. By this time, they had the support, not only of Lord Egmont, but also of Francis Baring, who owned the Banstead Wood Estate, and of Sir Charles Russell, M.P., Q.C., (later Lord Russell of Killowen) of Tadworth Court. Compromise was no longer on the cards.

The fact that the mortgagees had to be brought into the proceedings unfortunately caused further legal complications. The case came before the Court in 1886, and the Judge then ruled against enclosure of the Commons.

He declined to rule out claims made by the mortgagees to cut turf and dig gravel from the Commons, and ordered an inquiry to be conducted by a Referee to establish who exactly were the persons entitled to commoners' rights and how much land was required to satisfy these rights. In doing so, the Judge gave a very significant direction for the Referee, which was that he should assume that the right of grazing sheep on the Commons was at the rate of two sheep per acre of the land to which the rights were attached.

The Inquiry involved forty days of hearings before the Referee, who then needed time to prepare his report. When this was made, in March 1888, it was wholly favourable to the commoners. But even then, further legal arguments were raised. In April 1889, Mr. Justice Sterling gave judgment for the commoners; but the mortgagees appealed. It was not until 21st of December 1889, nearly thirteen years after the action had started, that their appeal was rejected, and the Court proceedings were brought to an end.

Despite this very costly success in the courts, the commoners realised that the position for the future was far from secure. They applied to the Board of Agriculture for a statutory scheme to regulate the Commons. The Board had been given power to make such schemes by two Metropolitan Commons Acts, sponsored by the supporters of The Commons Preservation Society. The Board put forward a scheme for the Banstead Commons. This had to be confirmed by a Confirmation Bill. So there was another bitter confrontation, this time before the Select Committees in both Houses of Parliament.

In the end, Parliament approved the scheme, with some modifications, and it was embodied in the Metropolitan Commons (Banstead) Supplemental Act 1893. In brief, this provided for the appointment of a Board of Conservators of the Commons, some appointed by the local authority and some by the owners of the soil of the Commons. The Board were given powers of management of the Commons, regulation of their use, including the making of byelaws, and a duty to protect them from interference. That remains the position to this day, though in fact the Council of the Borough of Reigate and Banstead now appoint all the Conservators, since the Lordship of the Manor, carrying with it ownership of the Commons, was bought by the Banstead Urban District Council in 1959.

Appendix B

Deliveries and Collections of Mail in the 19th Century

Year	Delivery time to Banstead Receiving Office (Sub-Post Office)	Time of despatch from the Office	Method and Route
1832	11.30 am.	4.30 pm.	By foot messenger from / to Epsom.
1839	12 noon	4.30 pm.	....
1845	12 noon	5.00 pm.	....
1855	9 am.	6.00 pm.	....
1867	?	6.10 pm.	....
1871	8.00 am, 11.30 am.	2.00 pm, 6.20 pm.	....
1882	7.40 am., 11.30 am.	1.35 pm, 6.25 pm	....
1895	7.10 am., 10.40 am, 4.25 pm. (Sundays: 8.10 am.)	7.50 am, 2.20 pm 4.25 pm, 6.25 pm (Sundays: 11.25 am.)	By horse messenger from / to Epsom.

Mail Letter Boxes in 1895

Location of Box	Times of Collection from Box
Brighton Road near 'Wheatsheaf.	8.10 am., 2.40 pm.and 6.40 pm. (Sundays: 11.45 am.)
Railway Station	8.20 am., 2.50 pm and 6.55 pm.
Kensington & Chelsea Schools, Fir Tree Road (later Beechholme)	8.30 am., 3.00 pmand 7.00 pm. (Sundays: 11.50 am.)

Appendix C

Main Sources

Authors	Books
Aubrey, John	Antiquities of Surrey
Carpenter D.A.	The Minority of Henry III, Methuen & Co. Ltd., 1990
Chamberlain E.R	Life in Wartime Britain, Batsford, 1972
Croft-Cooke, Rupert	The Gardens of Camelot, Putnam, 1958
Cross, Rupert	The Bombers, Bantam Press, 1987
Davison, Mark Davison and Currie, Ian	Surrey in the Hurricane, Froglet Publications Ltd, 1988.
Dean, Sir Maurice	The Royal Air Force and Two World Wars, Cassell, 1979
Defoe, Daniel	Tour of the Whole Island of Great Britain, 1724
Eversley, Lord	Commons, Forests and Footpaths, Cassell, 1910 Revised Edn
Fiennes, Celia	.Through England on a Sidesaddle in the time of William and Mary
Hopkinson, Revd A.W.	Pastor's Progress, The Faith Press, 1958 Revised Edn.
HowarthT.E.B	Prospect and Reality, Collins 1985
Hunn, David	Epsom Racecourse, Davis-Poynter, 1972
Jackson, Alan A.	Semi-detached London, Wild Swan Publications Ltd, 2nd Edn., 1991
Kay, F. George	Royal Mail, Rockliffe, 1951

Authors	Books
Lambert, Sir Henry	History of Banstead in Surrey, O.U.P., Vol.1, 1912 and Vol. II, 1931 Banstead, Three Lectures on its History, (London: Simpkin, Marshall, Hamilton, Kent & Co. Ltd. Sutton: William Pile Ltd), 1923
Lewis, Peter	A People's War, Methuen, 1986
Maxwell, Gordon S.	Just Beyond London, Methuen, 1927
Monk, L.A.	Britain, 1945 - 1970, Bell & Sons Ltd, 1976
Pepys, Samuel	Diary (1663)
Robinson, David	Surrey Through the Century, 1889 - 1989, Surrey County Council, 1989
Rolt, L.T.C	Isambard Kingdom Brunel, Pelican Books, 1970
Tames, Richard	Radicals, Reforms and Railways, Batsford, 1986
Weston, G. Neville	W.G. Grace, The Great Cricketer, 1973

Booklets and articles etc.

Authors	Booklets and Articles
Brown, Ivan B	United Reformed Church, Banstead, Jubilee Book, 1940 - 1990
Clifford, John H	125 Years of Public Transport in a Surrey Village, 1992
Macdonald, Monsignor J.	Saint Ann's, Banstead, 1936 - 1986
O'Shea, Irene	The Picquets Way Schools, 1936 - 1986
Randall, Val	Focus on Banstead, 1971
Robinson, Geoffrey A	Nork in the 1920s, Nork Quarterly Magazine, 1976/7
Shivas, J.D	The History of the Banstead Community Association, 1981
Totman, SJ	History of the Manor and Parish of Burgh, 1970
Willcox, Renee	A History of the Parish of Saint Paul, Nork, Banstead, 1985

Banstead History Research Group (BHRG) Publications referred to

Village School, Banstead, 1981
World War II - The Banstead Wood Camp, 1995
Beechholme, 1998
A History of Poor Law and Charity Relief in Banstead, 2004

Books of reference

The Victoria County History, Vol. 3 (1911)
The Dictionary of National Biography
The Oxford History of England, Vols. Ill and IV
Who was Who, Vol. 1
Banstead Then and Now - Banstead History Research Group

Directories etc.

Pigot & Company's Directory, 1839
Kelly's (Post Office) Directories, 1845 - 1938
Banstead U.D.C. Official Guides

Local Authority Proceedings

Banstead Vestry Book, 1830 to 1894
Minutes of:Banstead Parish Meeting, 1894 to 1932
Banstead Parish Council, 1895 to 1932
Epsom Rural District Council, 1928 to 1933
Banstead Urban District Council, 1933 to 1974

Census Returns From 1841 To 1891

Maps

Poor Law Assessment Map, 1841
Tithe Apportionment Map, 1843
25" Ordnance Survey Maps from 1868 onwards

Deeds and Documents held by

Surrey History Centre, Woking, Surrey
The Borough of Reigate & Banstead
The Church Commissioners for England, and many others

Interviews, correspondence, magazines, newspapers etc.

Index